LUCERNA

LUCERNA

STUDIES
OF SOME PROBLEMS
IN THE EARLY HISTORY
OF ENGLAND

by

H. P. R. FINBERG
M.A., D.LITT., F.S.A., F.R.HIST.S.

*Professor of English Local History
in the University of Leicester*

LONDON
MACMILLAN & CO LTD
NEW YORK · ST MARTIN'S PRESS
1964

MACMILLAN AND COMPANY LIMITED
St Martin's Street London WC2
also Bombay Calcutta Madras Melbourne

THE MACMILLAN COMPANY OF CANADA LIMITED
70 Bond Street Toronto 2

ST MARTIN'S PRESS INC
175 Fifth Avenue New York 10 NY

PRINTED IN GREAT BRITAIN

PREFACE

FACED with certain situations, Madame de Sévigné, that quintessence of civilized European womanhood, used to quote with relish an ironical couplet from Ariosto. The lines occur at the close of a passage in which the heroine, Angelica, relates her adventures to a knight she has just encountered in a wood. She tells him how she has wandered with Orlando from China to the Pyrenees, constantly protected by the hero from all hazards; and she assures him that at the end of it all she is still as intact a maiden as on the day she left her father's house. At this point the poet interjects a comment of his own. "It may have been true," he says, "but no man in his senses would believe it."

> Forse era ver, ma non però credibile
> A chi del senso suo fosse signore.

Much the same thought occurs to some of us as we turn the pages of historical textbooks. The authors are not romancing; their statements of fact are well founded, and their arguments are not obviously fallacious; yet an inner voice irrepressibly assures us that that is just not the way things happen. And never, perhaps, is the sceptical murmur more insistent than when our teachers undertake to depict the end of Roman Britain and the beginnings of Anglo-Saxon England. Those well-appointed, centrally heated villas — were so many of them burnt to the ground by Picts and Scots? The Roman towns — Canterbury, London, Dorchester, and the rest — in which the missionaries who came from Rome to convert the English hastened to establish their episcopal sees: were they indeed half-derelict at the time? And what of those Germanic warrior-peasants who, when not debating in public assemblies or fighting the Britons, are supposed to have introduced a wholly new system of rural economy? More than a century ago the founding father of modern Anglo-Saxon studies, J. M. Kemble, declared the traditional account of the Anglo-Saxon settlement in Britain to be "devoid of historical truth in every detail." Notwithstanding all that has been written since 1849, early English history still confronts us with a series of unanswered questions.

The problems are not only fascinating in their complexity; they are also of immediate contemporary interest. For we too see the great houses being abandoned one by one and either demolished or converted to less lordly uses. In the minds of our children as in those of the sixth-century Britons the imperial thoughts of yesterday will soon be only faded memories. We too are living in a period of dissolution which may yet prove to have been the seed-time of a new order.

The studies brought together in this book have been written in the intervals of other work during the last twelve years. They deal with only a few of the more challenging problems, but the nature of the enquiry has made it necessary to marshal a wide variety of documentary and topographical evidence. The evidence has its own value, and will, it is hoped, be of interest even to those readers who find the author's conclusions unacceptable. It should be understood that on few, if any, topics does he claim to offer final conclusions. The Roman *lucerna* was an oil-lamp which cast only a flickering light of no great candle-power. So here. Much brighter illumination is required before we can feel our way at all confidently through the darkest period of English history, but even a faint new glimmer may serve to reinforce the beams from lamps already lighted by other explorers.

H.P.R.F.

CONTENTS

MAPS

BIBLIOGRAPHICAL NOTE

'Roman and Saxon Withington' was first published in 1955 as No. 8 in the series of Occasional Papers issued by the Department of English Local History in the University of Leicester; and 'Hyple's Old Land' is extracted from No. 2 (1953) in the same series. They are reprinted by permission of the Leicester University Press. 'Sherborne, Glastonbury, and the Expansion of Wessex' is a revised version of a paper originally published in the *Transactions of the Royal Historical Society*, 5th ser., III, 1953, pp. 101–24. 'The Domesday Plough-Team' is reprinted from the *English Historical Review*, LXV, 1951, pp. 67–71, by courtesy of Messrs Longmans, Green and Co. 'The Making of a Boundary', 'Childe's Tomb', and 'Uffculme' were originally published in *Devonshire Studies*, by W. G. Hoskins and H. P. R. Finberg, 1952, a book now out of print and very scarce. The other studies are printed here for the first time.

LIST OF ABBREVIATIONS

AD = *Adami de Domerham Historia de Rebus Gestis Glastoniensibus*, ed. T. Hearne. Oxford, 1727.

BGAS = Bristol and Gloucestershire Archaeological Society (*Transactions*).

BM = British Museum.

CS = *Cartularium Saxonicum*, ed. W. de G. Birch. 3 vols. London, 1885–93.

DA = Devonshire Association (*Transactions*).

DB = Domesday Book.

DS = W. G. Hoskins and H. P. R. Finberg, *Devonshire Studies*. London, 1952.

EHD = *English Historical Documents*, ed. D. C. Douglas. (*In progress*).

EHR = *English Historical Review*.

Ha = Harmer, F. E. (ed.), *Select English Historical Documents*. Cambridge, 1914.

K = Kemble, J. M. (ed.), *Codex Diplomaticus Aevi Saxonici*. 6 vols. London, 1839–48.

R = Robertson, A. J. (ed.), *Anglo-Saxon Charters* (2nd ed.). Cambridge, 1956.

VCH = (followed by the name of a county) Victoria County History.

Wills = Whitelock, D. (ed.), *Anglo-Saxon Wills*. Cambridge, 1930.

CONTINUITY OR CATACLYSM?[1]

IN THE first volume of the Oxford History of England Dr J. N. L. Myres depicts the Anglo-Saxon conquest of Britain as a cataclysm in which the old social order was completely, or almost completely, overwhelmed. On the chalk hills of Wessex and Sussex "the conquest involved a complete break with the agricultural past." In other districts the invaders may not always have found it necessary to occupy new land at once; and for a number of reasons it is "unwise to argue without misgivings that the open-field villages of Saxon England have inherited no legacy whatever from Roman Britain." Still, when every allowance has been made, it remains true that "the whole structure of rural society was shattered and reformed" by the English conquest, and that "the towns and manors of late Saxon England can claim no demonstrable connection with the Roman past."[2]

The conclusion thus authoritatively expressed sums up a debate begun as far back as 1883, when Frederic Seebohm published his *English Village Community*. In that admirable work Seebohm marshalled a wealth of British and continental evidence. Basing his argument on laws, charters, field-systems, and place-names, he concluded that "the manorial system grew up in Britain ... as the compound product of barbarian and Roman institutions" mixing together at first under Roman rule and later under the impact of Teutonic conquest.[3] Seebohm's critics, headed by F. W. Maitland and Paul Vinogradoff, disputed this doctrine with a variety of arguments which need not be recapitulated here. Maitland's *Domesday Book and Beyond* was indeed largely written by way of rejoinder to Seebohm, whom he represented, more concisely than accurately, as "tracing the

[1] This study is a revised and enlarged version of my unpublished O'Donnell Lecture delivered at Edinburgh in May 1957.

[2] R. G. Collingwood and J. N. L. Myres, *Roman Britain and the English Settlements*, 2nd ed., Oxford, 1945, pp. 440–4.

[3] F. Seebohm, *The English Village Community*, 4th ed., 1890, p. 422.

English manor back to the Roman villa."[1] In this controversy the views of Maitland and Vinogradoff have on the whole prevailed. Nevertheless Vinogradoff was prepared to allow a place for Roman elements in the evolution of the English manor;[2] and Maitland did not deny that "from the time of the Teutonic conquest of England onwards, there may have been servile villages, Roman villas with slaves and *coloni* cultivating the owner's demesne, which had passed bodily to a new master."[3] When such notable qualifications have to be made, it cannot be said that one side in this battle of giants has completely routed the other.

After allowing the possibility that in some areas the social order of Roman Britain might have survived the English conquest, Maitland qualified his admission by adding: "We have no evidence that is capable of disproving or of proving this." More recently Dr W. G. Hoskins, no fanatic on this subject, has remarked: "It yet remains to be proved that any English village has had a continuous existence since Romano-British times."[4] And it is true that nobody will ever be able to demonstrate it as certainly as we can prove that King John, for example, formally accepted the Great Charter at Runnymede on a June day in 1215. But it is pertinent to ask how anybody would "prove" the continuous existence of an English village which appears for the first time in a Saxon charter of the eighth century, reappears in Domesday Book three hundred years later, and is then again lost to view until the thirteenth century. The truth is that early English history is not a study in which legal or mathematical certainty can fairly be expected, nor, as a rule, is strict proof demanded except in reaction against new

[1] *Domesday Book and Beyond*, Cambridge, 1907, pp. 221, 327. Cf. F. M. Stenton: "The discussion of manorial origins by Maitland and Vinogradoff was largely directed against Seebohm's argument for continuity between the Roman *villa* and the Anglo-Saxon village."—*Trans. R. Hist. Soc.*, 4th series, XXVIII, 1946, p. 9.

[2] "The tradition of Roman estates could not be entirely swept away. . . . It would be preposterous to suppose that Roman landmarks and arrangements were wilfully destroyed and no advantage taken of the existing stock and labour arrangements."—*The Growth of the Manor*, London, 1905, p. 221.

[3] *Domesday Book and Beyond*, p. 321.

[4] *Medieval England*, ed. A. L. Poole, Oxford, 1958, I, p. 3.

ideas or controversial opinions. The best we can hope to do is to establish a weight of probability sufficient to persuade any one who approaches the subject with an open mind.

THE ARCHAEOLOGICAL EVIDENCE

Among archaeologists the cataclysmic version of the Anglo-Saxon conquest seems to find decreasing support as knowledge grows. It will suffice here to quote briefly from the volume of studies produced not long ago in memory of E. T. Leeds. Reviewing the numismatic evidence, Mr C. H. V. Sutherland opines that small coins of the Theodosian epoch remained current down to 450 or even later; then the Britons drew upon old hoards to pay the Saxons they had hired as mercenary troops; after which the Anglo-Saxons struck imitations of Roman-British coins until, by the seventh century, they were able to produce mature issues in a style of their own. Dr Myres finds that post-Roman pottery "reflects in varying degrees the survival of the native population in different communities," and he concludes: "It may be necessary to envisage a wider degree of cultural overlap in eastern England than has been usually reckoned to be probable." If this is true of eastern England, exposed as it was to the first and fullest impact of Teutonic immigration, it is presumably truer still of the west; and indeed Mr H. N. Savory detects a similar "interpenetration of Celtic and Germanic culture" in the west midlands. Finally, Mr T. C. Lethbridge remarks that "the Anglo-Saxon culture in England is really a mixture of two cultures in which much inspiration was drawn from provincial Roman sources. It cannot even be proved that the people we find in graves and call Anglo-Saxons are not half-breeds, octoroons, or whatever 'blood' we choose, of Teuton and Romano-Briton." This mixed people was "more Teutonic in the east, more Romano-British in the west and south." And he concludes: "A picture of Anglo-Saxon England begins to form which is quite unlike that which was given to us a generation ago, but is, I venture to think, a much more reasonable one." It is not the evidence which is changing, but our interpretation of the evidence.[1]

For the historian the idea that the Britons in the fifth and

---

[1] *Dark-Age Britain*, ed. D. B. Harden, 1956, pp. 7-10, 34, 38, 58, 119, 121.

sixth centuries were either slaughtered to a man or driven clean out of their homes, leaving the Anglo-Saxons to start building up an entirely new social order in an almost empty land, has had great and obvious attractions. Every narrative is the better for having a well-marked, as it were natural, beginning; and better still if the ending is equally well-marked. The span of time from the Anglo-Saxon 'invasions' to the Norman Conquest has presented itself as just such a clear-cut theme. Further, by postulating a cataclysm at the start, we save ourselves all the trouble of investigating in detail what may well turn out to have been a highly complex evolutionary process. Terms like the 'Dark Age' and the 'Lost Centuries' invite criticism on several counts, but they do at least testify to the difficulty of assembling and interpreting evidence which is itself both scanty and obscure.

ROMAN AND SAXON RELIGION

Take for example the religious history of the period. It is never an entirely simple matter to correlate written records with archaeological findings. Written records inform us that Christianity, the official faith of the empire, was securely established in Britain under Roman rule, but archaeological evidence — admittedly scattered and incomplete — suggests that its adherents were mainly landowners, townspeople, and servants of the state. Outside the towns, forts, and country mansions, heathen cults persisted.[1] The progress of excavation may bring discoveries that will modify this picture, but it is clear that an immense work of evangelization remained to be carried out, and was in fact undertaken during the fifth and sixth centuries, so that by the time Gildas took it upon himself to rebuke the failings of his compatriots, they were all — so he implies — Christians, however unworthy of the name. During that interval the Roman-British Church, with its urban episcopate, transformed itself by stages invisible to us into a monastically centred Church combining ascetic fervour with missionary zeal.

[1] J. M. C. Toynbee, 'Christianity in Roman Britain', *Journal of the British Archaeological Association*, XVI, 1953, pp. 1–24; W. H. C. Frend, 'Religion in Roman Britain in the Fourth Century', *ibid.*, XVIII, 1955, pp. 1–18.

By contrast, the Anglo-Saxon immigrants were not missionaries. Although they continued for some generations to worship their own gods, there is not the slightest indication that they ever tried to impose the cult of Thor and Woden on the Britons. Doubtless they looted churches, and in a general massacre like that at Pevensey in 491 the clergy would not escape, but the conduct of King Æthelfrith at the battle of Chester, in refusing to recognize the monks of Bangor-is-Coed as non-combatants and putting most of them to the sword, is related as something portentous, one might almost say ungentlemanly, and it is noticeable that the nickname bestowed on Æthelfrith by the Britons of the north was not 'Butcher' or the like, but 'Flesaur', that is, 'Artful Dodger'. Even so, the massacre made a sufficiently painful and lasting impression on the northern clergy to make them flee whenever they saw an Anglo-Saxon war-band coming.

The normally tolerant attitude of the Anglo-Saxon rulers towards the indigenous faith is illustrated by the conduct of Rædwald, king of East Anglia, who set up a Christian altar in his chapel but retained the old one for continued sacrifices to his ancestral gods. In the midlands Penda, though himself a pagan to the last, never obstructed the propagation of Christianity among his fellow Anglians.[1] In the valley of the lower Severn the principality of the Hwicce was ruled under him by a family of whose conversion we hear nothing: indeed, Bede implies that they shared the creed of their subjects from the start.[2]

Altogether, when we survey the conversion of the Anglo-Saxon dynasties through eyes less other-worldly than the Venerable Bede's; when we note the diplomatic exchanges with the papacy and with the Frankish court which paved the way for it, and the skilful stage-management implied in such famous scenes as King Ethelbert's first interview with Augustine and the discussion in King Edwin's council, we can

[1] ". . . in sua, hoc est Merciorum, natione."—Bede, *Historia Ecclesiastica*, III, 21. The British population, who did not need to be converted, make only incidental appearances in Bede's pages; his subject is the ecclesiastical history of the English.

[2] *Hist. Eccl.*, IV, 13; H. P. R. Finberg, *The Early Charters of the West Midlands*, Leicester, 1961, p. 171.

scarcely help suspecting that there were kings in seventh-century England who would have found themselves in perfect accord, much later on, with Henry of Navarre, and for the same reason: namely, that Paris, or in their case Britain, was well worth a mass. However that may have been, their conversion involved a deliberate acceptance of things Roman. The language of the Church they entered was the language of the empire; the head of that Church was the bishop of Rome, upon whom something of the imperial majesty had devolved. To provide the Church with permanent endowments, they introduced a *jus ecclesiasticum* based on the *jus perpetuum* of the late empire.[1] Thus, in becoming Christians, they also became, and meant to become, in more than one sense, Romans.

It is one of the ironies of history that once they had made their formal entry into the Roman world they quickly became more Roman than the Britons. At first there was no dissidence. If the 'responses' of Pope Gregory to Augustine are genuine, the pope seems to have anticipated no difficulty in placing the British bishops under Augustine's authority. In the event the Britons repudiated Augustine, not as the pope's representative, but on personal grounds. In the Anglo-Celtic kingdom of Wessex British monasteries at Sherborne, Shaftesbury, and perhaps Glastonbury maintained their corporate existence undisturbed, sometimes under abbots with British names.[2] St Chad received episcopal consecration from a Saxon bishop of Winchester and two British bishops. There is no need to suppose that his two co-consecrators came from Wales or Cornwall. A confused tradition which makes Congresbury in Somerset the seat of an ancient bishopric may well be founded on fact, for the place certainly takes its name from Congar, a Celtic saint.[3] Up in the north we find St Wilfrid taking over the churches and endowments vacated by fugitive British clergy.[4] But in 664 the fateful synod of Whitby

[1] Cf. E. John, *Land Tenure in Early England*, Leicester, 1960, pp. 1–23.

[2] For Glastonbury and Sherborne, see pp. 85, 98 below. CS 107, 186 deal with a monastery in Dorset under an abbot with a British name, Catwali. Both texts come from the cartulary of Shaftesbury, and may be taken as referring to a monastery there: cf. VCH *Wilts.*, II, p. 25.

[3] *Ecclesiastical Documents*, ed. J. Hunter, Camden Soc., 1840, p. 10.

[4] EHD I, p. 693.

made friendly relations between the British and Saxon Churches impossible, the principal bone of contention being that the former, set in its old-fashioned ways, had not kept pace with Roman reforms.[1]

Now it is clearly a great simplification of the historian's task if he can bring himself to believe that Christianity, after the collapse of Roman rule, was driven into the far west and re-quired missionaries from Iona and Rome to re-create it in a mainly heathen land. This assumption absolves him from the necessity of filling in as best he can the blank spaces in Bede's narrative. The alternative course is very far from simple. It requires him to unravel two historic processes: first, the pro-pagation of Christianity from its unrecorded beginnings under the empire through the age of the Celtic saints to that of the Roman emissaries, Augustine, Birinus, and finally Theodore; then, secondly, the introduction of Teutonic heathenism at an equally indeterminate date, its wide extension under Anglo-Saxon political dominance, its formal extinction after the baptism of the Anglo-Saxon dynasties, and its underground survival in popular tradition.

Apart from Bede and a handful of other writings, what have we to guide us through this labyrinth? There are inscriptions, crosses, wall-paintings, and other tangible remains, forming a picture which has to be modified almost yearly in accordance with the often fortuitous character of archaeological discovery. There are place-names, the evidence from which is gradually being assembled,[2] but remains incomplete: we still need, for example, a full topographical and lexicographical investigation of names like Eccles, based on the Roman-British word for 'church'. There are the dedications of early churches, which, besides revealing fashions in devotion, sometimes provide a clue to origins. Dedications, however, are a class of evidence which requires particularly cautious handling.[3] The Lives of

[1] On the date and character of the meeting at Whitby see P. Grosjean in *Analecta Bollandiana*, LXXXVIII, 1960, pp. 233–74.

[2] See, in particular, Margaret Gelling, 'Place-Names and Anglo-Saxon Paganism', *University of Birmingham Historical Journal*, VIII, 1961, pp. 7–25.

[3] Cf. O. Chadwick, 'The Evidence of Dedications in the Early History of the Welsh Church', in *Studies in Early British History*, ed. N. K. Chadwick, Cambridge, 1954, pp. 173–88.

B

7

saints are another such class. Written commonly for edification and entertainment rather than as history, they demand the critical acumen of a Doble or a Grosjean to make the tedious mass of rubbish yield up the occasional precious grain of fact.

Yes, it will be an arduous business to unwind the threads of continuity here; but there are grounds for believing that historians of the rising generation will not decline the challenge.

TRIBUTE AND TAXATION

From a very early date the Anglo-Saxon kings recognized one of their number as *Bretwalda*, 'ruler of Britain'. Whatever else this title implied, it certainly gave its holder some authority over English kingdoms other than his own, and a right to exact tribute from them.[1] But tribute implies assessment, and some regular mode of assessment, however rough and ready, also lay behind the tax on landed property from which the ordinary expenses of government were defrayed. There is room for a fresh historical and semantic investigation of the word 'hide' and the related *hiwisc* which the English employed to denote the unit of assessment. Both words are certainly Germanic, but it would be rash to infer from this that the Anglo-Saxons had imposed a new cadastral system of their own. When the men of Wessex followed up the defeat of three British kings by capturing Gloucester, Cirencester, and Bath; and when Edwin of Northumbria annexed the British kingdom of Elmet, they took over states which must have kept up more than the rudiments of political and fiscal organization, else they could never have put armies into the field and countered the Saxon peril, as they did, with a resistance more obstinate than was seen anywhere else in the empire. If it is true that an army marches on its stomach, the forces Ambrosius Aurelianus led to victory must have been nourished on something better than grass and acorns.

The local chieftains who took up the reins of government in Britain during the fifth century, styling themselves kings, must have been as familiar as were the Frankish conquerors of Gaul with the *tributum*, the land-tax of the later empire. Under imperial rule the unit of assessment to this tax had been termed a *caput* or *jugum*, but the language of the provinces employed a

[1] F. M. Stenton, *Anglo-Saxon England*, Oxford, 1943, p. 36.

variety of equivalent terms. In Gaul the unit became known as a *mansus* and its occupants as *manentes*. There the tax was still being collected under its Roman name at the close of the seventh century.[1] Is there any reason to suppose that the British princes would have abandoned so familiar and convenient a levy? And if not, what of the English who stepped into their shoes?

From the reign of Diocletian onwards the *tributum* had been paid partly in money, partly in produce. Since the Britons struck no coinage of their own, it may well be that payments in cash were altogether superseded by the system of food-rents we encounter in later Welsh custom. Food-rents, which the English called *feorm*, outlived both the Saxon and the Norman conquests, and, as Vinogradoff says, there is hardly any room for doubt that this ancient form of tribute ran in an uninterrupted sequence from the period of British rule.[2] There is here more than a hint of administrative continuity. As for the unit of assessment, the Anglo-Saxons admittedly had their own word for it, but when an Anglo-Saxon king made a grant of land and the grant came to be put in writing, the hide clothed itself in the terminology of the imperial successor-states. Its occupants were called *manentes, cassati,* or — still more significantly — *tributarii*.

A PROBLEM OF AGRARIAN HISTORY

In 1770 Arthur Young estimated that nearly half the population of England still made their livelihood directly from agriculture.[3] In earlier centuries the proportion was certainly much higher. This consideration is one which historians and archaeologists must be urged to bear constantly in mind, living as they do for the most part, like the great majority of their fellow-countrymen today, in cities, and hardly knowing or caring where or how their food is grown. To bring the urban outlook characteristic of the present time into the study of any period before the Industrial Revolution is a serious mistake, for it leads the historian to dismiss as of only minor significance the pursuit of husbandry in all its forms and the whole way of life associated with this cardinal element of the economy.

---

[1] Fustel de Coulanges, *La Monarchie Franque*, Paris, 1888, pp. 265, 266.
[2] *The Growth of the Manor*, p. 223.   [3] EHD x, pp. 413, 426.

The presidential address which Dr Myres delivered in 1961 to the Council for British Archaeology exemplifies the pitfalls of this anachronism. In a most instructive discourse Dr Myres epitomized a mass of archaeological evidence from Dorchester-on-Thames, York, Malton, Ancaster, Cambridge, Leicester, Caistor-by-Norwich, Canterbury, and elsewhere, evidence which, as he said, "points unmistakably to the conclusion that until about the middle of the fifth century a good deal of the Anglo-Saxon *settlement*, as distinct from raiding, that had taken place in Britain had been the result of more or less official arrangement with the British authorities. Whether these authorities were deliberately establishing the settlers to act as a protective screen for themselves, or whether they were being reluctantly forced to admit a flood of immigrants whom in the last resort they were powerless to exclude, they probably contrived to retain some degree of legal initiative in dealing with the newcomers, and to conclude with them bargains of the kind to which the term *foederatio* had long been applied in the frontier provinces of the Roman Empire."[1] After reading this passage, we might expect to find the author modifying to some extent the belief in discontinuity expressed so resolutely in his earlier work.[2] But no. Gildas (that lucid and accurate historian!) has much to say concerning the destruction of the Roman cities. The result of that destruction was that "a blanket of illiteracy and heathenism suffocated the last embers of urban life. . . . And so, if Britons survived, as they must have done, to bequeath some Celtic blood, however diluted, to the existing population of England, they survived not as a coherent community but as isolated bits of wreckage, mostly enslaved and to a large extent cultureless."[3] To recover our sense of proportion at this point, we need to remind ourselves that the second largest town in Roman Britain contained within its walls no more than 240 acres, and that many of the other towns covered only 30 or 40 acres.

The problem of continuity, then, between Roman Britain and Saxon England, rightly stated, poses itself as before all else a problem of agrarian history. Once this is grasped, the terms

---

[1] Council for British Archaeology, Report No. 11, 1961, p. 42.
[2] Cf. p. 1 *supra.*   [3] CBA Report No. 11, pp. 43, 45.

of the problem can be stated with some precision. We have to ask ourselves what forms and degrees of continuity may reasonably be expected not so much in the towns as in the villages and hamlets. To what extent did people of the same blood and speech continue to till the same fields by the same methods as before? What alteration was there of boundaries, and how much occupation of new sites?

A POPULATION OF MINGLED STOCK

It is probably futile to ask what proportion of pre-English blood flows in the veins of the English people today. In a population which has been exposed to wave upon wave of immigration — Celtic, Roman, Saxon, Scandinavian, Norman, Welsh, Scottish, French, Irish, and Central European — the data of physical anthropology will be more confusing than instructive. Nor do personal names give any sure indication of ancestry; they merely testify to prevailing fashions in nomenclature. Mr R. H. C. Davis has quoted the records of Bury St Edmunds as showing that at the end of the eleventh century St Edmund's freemen and sokemen bore either Scandinavian or English names, but by the end of the twelfth century something between one-half and three-quarters of their descendants bore names that had been introduced by the Normans: William, Robert, Henry, and the like.[1] In 967 King Edgar granted some land in Cornwall to his "faithful vassal Wulfnoth Rumuncant," and two years later another Cornishman, Ælfheah Gerent or Geraint, received a grant from the same king.[2] Here the recipients have coupled their indigenous names with names borrowed from the dominant English; it is always the dominant people who set the fashion. A generation or two later the Celtic descent of these Cornish families will in all probability be completely masked under English names.

Amid such ambiguities, and in the absence of statistics, all that can be said with certainty is that the intermingling of Celtic and Teutonic stocks began long before the middle of the fifth century, the traditional date for the "coming of the Saxons." Towards the end of the third century Burgundians and Vandals from northern Germany were planted in Britain

---

[1] *Trans. Royal Hist. Soc.*, 5th ser., v, 1955, p. 29.   [2] CS 1197, 1231.

by the Emperor Probus. Ammianus Marcellinus states that in 372 a numerous troop of Alamanni in Britain were placed by Valentinian I under the command of one Fraomar, who had formerly governed a tribe dwelling opposite Mainz.[1] Without entering into the question whether the coast from the eastern side of the Wash to the Solent was called the Saxon Shore because it was manned by Saxon *foederati*, or because it was fortified against Saxon raiders, we can be tolerably sure that by the time the Anglo-Saxons began to assert themselves as a political force, the island contained a strong hybrid element of Romano-Saxon population.

It would be interesting to know whether some groups of Teutonic origin were brought in for other than military purposes: for example, to provide agricultural labour. There are indications that an acute shortage of man-power was one of the many troubles which beset the province in the last years of imperial rule and for some time afterwards. The withdrawal of the Roman army by Constantine III; the massive emigration from the south-west to Brittany which began in the middle of the fifth and continued into the seventh century; the drowning of the Fenland, which between the first and fourth centuries had supported a considerable population;[2] a succession of bad harvests, bringing famine — Gildas, for what he is worth, speaks of a time when all food was lacking except such as could be got from hunting; epidemics, including the *mortalitas magna* recorded in the *Annales Cambriae* as having ravaged the country in 547: here were reasons enough for land to go out of cultivation and country mansions to be deserted. Reason too for employing Teutonic immigrants as ploughmen, weavers, and potters. The wretched hovels which E. T. Leeds excavated at Sutton Courtenay do not sound like the dwellings of victorious invaders.[3]

[1] Ammianus Marcellinus, xxix, 4. The passage has been misquoted by Collingwood and others. It does not state that Fraomar's former subjects were transplanted to Britain, but that he was appointed commander of German troops who were already here.

[2] H. E. Hallam, *The New Lands of Elloe*, Leicester, 1954, p. 3.

[3] R. H. Hodgkin, *History of the Anglo-Saxons*, Oxford, 2nd ed., 1939, pp. 221-5.

THE LINGUISTIC EVIDENCE

That the English language ousted the native speech over the greater part of Britain is indisputable, but not all the inferences drawn from the fact will bear close examination. As J. C. Wedgwood pointed out, "the isolated coloured race that inhabits St Helena, and the almost equally isolated Cape Boys of Cape Colony, speak English or Dutch and have forgotten their original tongue in less than two centuries."[1] How long did it take the Britons to forget theirs? The great Hilda of Whitby, whose father, incidentally, had spent his last days at the court of a British king, employed a neatherd with an obviously British name, Cædmon,[2] yet Cædmon spoke English, and indeed is accounted the earliest English poet.[3]

In this connection the evidence of place-names has often been misinterpreted. It is well known that many British words and names, especially those denoting hills, rivers, and other natural features, passed into the English language, and this is rightly taken as evidence that Welsh-speaking people survived into the Anglo-Saxon period; but some scholars have argued that compounds like Pen Hill, in which the Welsh word for hill is coupled with an explanatory English word, show that the Anglo-Saxons did not understand Welsh.[4] No doubt they ceased to understand it after a while, but the question we ought to ask is how soon they did so. As late as the tenth century Hackpen Hill in Wiltshire is still *Hacan pen* and Pen Hill in the same county is *Ættan Pen*.[5] In the one case the prefix is the Old English word for 'hook', in the other it is an Old English personal name, Ætta; but 'hill' is not added until later. Again, there are scholars who believe that the element -chester, from Latin *castra*, normally applied to Roman towns, cities, and fortified places in general, would not have been attached to a

---

[1] *Collections for a History of Staffordshire*, William Salt Arch. Soc., 1916, p. 146.

[2] This was emphatically the opinion both of Henry Bradley and of York Powell: cf. J. C. Atkinson, *Memorials of Old Whitby*, 1894, p. 33.

[3] Bede, *Hist. Eccl.*, IV, 23, 24: "ita ut ... verbis poeticis maxima suavitate et compunctione compositis, in sua, id est, Anglorum lingua proferret."

[4] F. T. Wainwright in *Trans. Hist. Soc. Lancs. and Cheshire*, XCIII, 1941, p. 22.

[5] CS 734, 1093.

villa-site like Woodchester in Gloucestershire if the Anglo-Saxons had understood what a Roman villa really was; but to reason thus is to overlook the analogous development of the Welsh *caer*, which, at first signifying fortified places, usually Roman as at Carlisle and Caerleon, presently developed the secondary meaning of a hamlet or manor-house and farm protected by some form of defensive stockade.[1]

Before we can estimate the duration of the bilingual phase in which English and Welsh were both understood, the evidence of place-names will have to be sifted chronologically: no easy task, since early name-forms are rarely plentiful. But this is not all. The logic of such evidence needs to be discussed critically in the light of toponymic developments not in this country alone but all over the world. The study of place-names is comparatively new, and the principles of its historical application have not yet been fully worked out. Until this is done, it will remain exposed to faulty reasoning and erroneous conclusions.

FIELD SYSTEMS

Turning from the names of places to the actual fields, villages, and hamlets, we are told that "one of the basic and still unsolved problems of the whole period lies in deciding if the open-field system of agriculture was brought, virtually lock, stock, and barrel, from the Continent by the invading Germanic peoples."[2] Modern German scholars, however, are generally agreed that the fully fledged common-field system, with its intermixture of arable strip-holdings and its common rights of pasturage, is the product in their country of a lengthy evolutionary process which had scarcely begun at the time of the Teutonic migration to Britain.[3] As for technique, "there is no

[1] Kenneth Jackson, in *Angles and Britons*, Cardiff, 1963, p. 80.

[2] H. R. Loyn, *Anglo-Saxon England and the Norman Conquest*, 1962, p. 148. Cf. Stenton, *Anglo-Saxon England*, p. 277: the system "may well go back, there [i.e. in eastern Yorkshire, Lincolnshire, and the eastern midlands] and in Wessex, to the beginning of permanent English settlement, for it agrees in general type with the system prevailing in north-western Germany."

[3] I am indebted to my colleague Dr Joan Thirsk for allowing me to see her forthcoming article, 'The Common Fields', in which this subject is discussed at length.

evidence whatsoever that the Anglo-Saxons came to Britain already possessed of better agricultural equipment than they found here. The [improved] plough assigned to them in modern writings is a product of modern imagination."[1]

Dr S. Applebaum has shown that the two common fields at Great Wymondley in Hertfordshire, which survived until 1821, were laid out on a Roman road and surrounded a Roman villa site. Their pattern showed clear traces of a Roman grid-division into 200-jugera squares. In a number of cases the strips could be demonstrated to be subdivisions of the Roman *centuriae*, averaging some 750 by 230 feet. Similar 200-jugera squares subdivided into strips have been detected at Cliffe in north Kent.[2] Only further investigation will show whether these are isolated examples.

CONTINUITY OF SITE

How many English settlements overlie Roman-British or even older sites? The archaeologists who have been excavating Wharram Percy recently found Roman sherds and Iron-Age pottery under the manor-house at the north end of the village, as well as under houses in the village itself: unexpected pointers to continuity of settlement at this spot high on the Yorkshire wolds.[3] But Wharram Percy has been for centuries a deserted village; it is not feasible to apply the more drastic techniques of exploration in places which are still inhabited.

Continuity of settlement does not necessarily imply an exact coincidence between an earlier and a later site. The early Saxon village at Sutton Courtenay lay to the west of the present village. There is abundant evidence of continued settlement in the loop of the Thames opposite Dorchester, including a cemetery containing Roman, pagan Saxon, and Christian Saxon burials, and about two miles away a village site covering at least 250 acres,[4] but both are remote from the present village of Long Wittenham, which presents the typical appearance of a nucleated English settlement lying between its common arable

[1] F. G. Payne, 'The Plough in Ancient Britain', *Archaeological Journal*, CIV, 1948, p. 109.

[2] *Agricultural History Review*, VI, 1958, pp. 72, 73.

[3] Wharram Percy 1961, Interim Report.

[4] VCH *Berkshire*, I, pp. 220–2, 229–32.

fields: indeed, the older village site adjoins a farm situated in the middle of the now enclosed North Field, and named after it. The migration of rural communities from an original site to a new one at a little distance is another topic awaiting systematic investigation.

TOPOGRAPHICAL EVIDENCE

Far too little use has been made hitherto of topographical evidence. It is instructive to note how topography was regarded by the protagonists in the great debate. Seebohm illustrated his book with eleven beautifully drawn and coloured maps. Maitland's book contains two maps, and Vinogradoff's none. This physical detail betokens a significant difference of method and approach. Seebohm used topography as a vital part of the evidence; his critics contented themselves with citing written records and analysing legal concepts. Not that they ignored the value of topography. Maitland described the Ordnance map as "that marvellous palimpsest," and looked forward to the time when we should have learnt to construe the testimony of our fields and walls and hedges.[1] Vinogradoff, in the preface to his first book, declared that one most fruitful way to approach the study of early English society would be "to restrict oneself to a definite provincial territory, to get intimately acquainted with all details of its geography, local history, peculiarities of custom, and to trace the social evolution of this tract of land as far back as possible." He went on to explain that "being a foreigner," he felt unable to take this course. "I could not trust myself to become sufficiently familiar with local life, even if I had the time and opportunity to study it closely." But he added: "I hope such investigations may be taken up by scholars in every part of England and may prosper in their hands; the gain to general history would be simply invaluable."[2]

THE CASE OF BLOCKLEY

A single illustration may be given here to show how topographical analysis can open unexpected vistas for the historian. In the third quarter of the eighth century King Ethelbald of

[1] *Domesday Book and Beyond*, pp. 15, 16.
[2] Vinogradoff, *Villainage in England*, Oxford, 1892, p. viii.

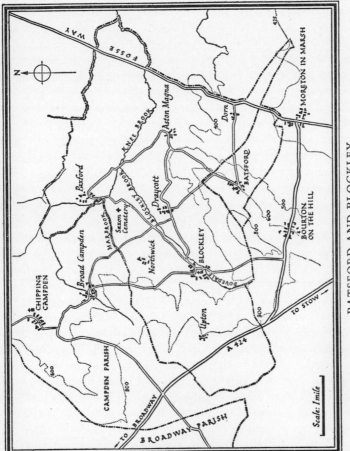

BATSFORD AND BLOCKLEY

Scale: 1 mile

17

Mercia granted to the bishop of Worcester an estate at "Bæcceshora," the modern Batsford.[1] This parish extends from the 400-ft contour line on the level ground near Moreton-in-Marsh up the slope of a hill which rises to 800 feet, commanding, at the summit, a fine view over Blockley and the country to the north. In the last 200 feet the ground rises steeply, and it falls away just as abruptly on the northern side. The ridge thus formed is part of the watershed between the Thames and Severn. It is the *ora* (= brink of a hill) which forms the second element in the name Bæcceshora.

King Ethelbald's grant names no habitation-site, but the bounds were drawn in such a way as to include at the south-east corner, on the Roman Fosse Way, a hamlet named Dorn. This has long been known as a Roman site. Haverfield saw nearly two hundred Roman coins at the present farm. In a large arable field lying between the farm and the Fosse Way traces of stone foundations have been observed, with many fragments of Roman pottery. West of this, in the railway cutting, two sculptured stones were found.[2] Dorn now figures on the Ordnance Survey map of Roman Britain as a "major settlement." According to Ekwall, the name is probably derived from the British *duro-*, signifying a gate, or a town with gateways, a walled town. Some years ago the late Philip Corder pointed out that at least seven places that were not even marked as villages in the 1928 edition of the map of Roman Britain are now known to have been walled towns. He suggested that these and similar rural strongholds formed self-supporting units on which the continued prosperity of the province depended at a time when the larger towns like Verulamium were falling into decline.[3] But since no town is strictly self-supporting, we must suppose that each of these places formed the market centre for an agricultural or pastoral hinterland. And if so, there can be no doubt that the hinterland of Dorn lay not on the marshy, waterlogged ground east of the Fosse Way, but on the *ora* of the Saxon place-name, the high ground between Dorn and Blockley, and beyond it, the valley of the Blockley Brook, which forms the western boundary of Ethelbald's grant.

[1] CS 163. [2] VCH *Worcestershire*, I, p. 221.
[3] *Archaeological Journal*, CXII, 1955, p. 42.

In the course of the following century the bishop of Worcester laid successful claim to an estate on the other side of the valley, named Upton because it lay high up on the wold.[1] This too was in all probability a Roman site. Coins from the reign of Constantine were being found there a hundred years ago, and other Roman objects have come to light in the course of recent excavation.[2] Before its acquisition by the bishop, Upton belonged to the Mercian royal house.

To meet the spiritual needs of his now extensive manor, the bishop built a church down in the central valley at a *leah* or woodland clearing named after one Blocca. This church became the mother-church of the whole district. The bishop's manor-house too was built here, and the estate as a whole was henceforth known as *Bloccan-leah*, or Blockley.[3] Now if we looked only at Blockley itself, its purely Anglo-Saxon name, and its history from the ninth century onwards, we might be excused for taking it as just another instance of the "unanswered protest" with which the names of our English villages, according to Maitland, refute any notion of a link between their inhabitants and the Roman past.[4] In reality, as we have seen, Blockley comes into existence to serve the needs of two earlier settlements, one probably, the other certainly, Roman. At Dorn, a market centre of some importance on the Fosse Way which had retained its pre-English name in living use at a time when the neighbouring settlements, Bourton, Daylesford, and Evenlode, had already received English names, the survival of a Welsh-speaking community under Saxon lordship seems clearly indicated.

ROMAN AND SAXON WITHINGTON

In the following study an attempt is made to elucidate the early history of another Gloucestershire village. An examination of its written records, its boundaries, land-use, geology,

---

[1] H. P. R. Finberg, *The Early Charters of the West Midlands*, Nos. 63, 78, 86.

[2] A. J. Soden, *History of Blockley*, Coventry, 1875, p. 103; information kindly supplied by Professor R. H. Hilton.

[3] The name is first recorded in 855 as "the minster called Bloccanleeh."— CS 489.

[4] *Domesday Book and Beyond*, p. 222.

and manorial custom, will show that the life of this Cotswold settlement has kept through many centuries a remarkably even tenor. It has not however been a static life. If we strip away the accretions which have gathered round it in the last twelve hundred years, it will be possible to form some idea of what Withington was like when it first came into Anglo-Saxon hands. Then, approaching it as it were from the other end of the tunnel, and enquiring what archaeology can tell us about pre-Saxon Withington, we may be able to break down a little of the dark barrier that separates, in this parish and in others round about, the Roman from the Saxon period.

The method of local investigation on which Vinogradoff so resolutely and — it could be argued — so unfortunately turned his back is applied here on a small scale. It need hardly be said that no study of a single parish will resolve the problem of continuity between Roman Britain and Saxon England. The attempt will however serve a useful purpose if it points the way to similar researches elsewhere by the method which perhaps offers the best hope of advance in this difficult field. It must again be emphasized that neither by this nor by any other method will strict proof be attained. But for the last three quarters of a century historians have proceeded on the assumption that every feature in the life of rural England for which a higher antiquity cannot be proved must be of Anglo-Saxon or later origin. It was never a realistic assumption, and the time has come for it to be discarded. A growing mass of evidence encourages us to believe that the strands of continuity are not the less real for being so elusive. A willingness to look for them accords better with the nature of historical processes in general, and opens up exciting possibilities of new research.

ROMAN AND SAXON WITHINGTON

§1

THE EARLIEST document bearing on the history of Withington takes us back to the time when Gloucestershire, Worcestershire, and the western half of Warwickshire formed a more or less autonomous division of the Mercian realm, administered by the Anglo-Saxon princes of the Hwicce. At some time in the reign of Ethelred of Mercia — that is, between 674 and 704 — Oshere, under-king of the Hwicce, persuaded Ethelred to establish a minster at Withington and to endow it with a tract of land in the valley of the Coln. This foundation may well have been inspired by the great Wilfrid of York, who after his expulsion from Northumbria in 691 spent eleven years with Ethelred of Mercia and is known to have founded a number of monasteries.[1] In the middle years of the seventh century many Anglo-Saxon families had sent their daughters to be educated in Gaul, especially at Brie, Chelles, and Andelys. These were monasteries for both sexes, ruled by abbesses. Before long similar institutions were being founded on this side of the Channel, and it is probable that all the houses for women were double monasteries, for wherever detailed evidence is forthcoming this character appears.[2] Of the one at Withington we are told that it was first established for the benefit of a lady named Dunne and her daughter Bucge. Ethelred's charter included a *descriptio* of its territory: that is, it defined the boundaries of the land beside the Coln; but this document is unfortunately lost.

In 736 or the following year a synod presided over by Nothhelm, archbishop of Canterbury, had to adjudicate upon the succession to the minster and its property. Dunne had bequeathed it to her granddaughter Hrothwaru, then a minor

---

[1] F. M. Stenton, *Anglo-Saxon England*, Oxford, 1943, p. 143.
[2] Mary Bateson, 'Origin and Early History of Double Monasteries' *Trans. Royal Historical Soc.*, N.S. XIII, 1899, p. 182.

under the tutelage of her mother, but when the heiress came of age her mother refused to surrender the title-deed. The synod decreed that Hrothwaru should take possession, and that after her lifetime the minster, with its endowments and charter, should revert to the bishop of Worcester, "as it was settled before by her ancestors."[1]

This arrangement left the bishop firmly in control of what would otherwise have become a hereditary private estate. In 774, Hrothwaru having died or resigned, the bishop appointed a new abbess, Æthelburg, again with the proviso that after her death the church of Worcester should re-enter into possession.[2]

Some years later the property was enlarged by a new gift. A certain abbot named Headda had inherited an estate at "Dogodeswella and Tyreltune," and in 759 he had acquired, by gift from the princes of the Hwicce, another property at "Onnanforda." He left the whole of this land, both inherited and acquired, to his descendants in priestly orders, with reversion to the bishop of Worcester.[3] The identification of the places named is not free from difficulty, but it seems that the estate devised to Headda in 759 consisted of Upper Dowdeswell with Pegglesworth and Andoversford.[4] His inheritance adjoined this on the north. *Dogodeswell* is (Lower) Dowdeswell, and I believe

---

[1] CS 156; EHD I, p. 454.   [2] CS 217; EHD I, p. 464.   [3] CS 187 and 283.

[4] According to the charter of 759, the land at Onnanforda was bounded on the south by *Wisleag*, on the west by *Rindburna*, on the north by *Meosgelegeo*, and on the east by *Onnanduun*. In attempting to elucidate these bounds, G. B. Grundy proposed to shift the compass points (*Saxon Charters and Field Names of Gloucestershire*, 1935–6, p. 114). But there is no need to fall back on so desperate an expedient. The first name, *Wisleag*, figures on the map as Wistley Hill. It is now confined to the western portion of the upland tract crossed by A436, the highway from Stow to Gloucester. If, however, as seems probable, the first element is *wisc*, 'damp meadow', and the name really signifies a marshy glade, we must suppose that it referred originally to a spot near the source of the Hilcot Brook, where Pegglesworth stands to-day. This is about half a mile east of the present Wistley Hill. *Rindburna* is obviously a stream-name; it probably refers to the brook along which the western boundary of Dowdeswell runs, near Lineover Wood. *Onnanduun* must be the expanse of down on the east side of the Upper Coln near Andoversford, which is the *Onnanforda* of the charter (E. Ekwall, *Concise Oxford Dictionary of English Place Names*, 1960, p. 10). The name of the northern boundary, *Meosgelegeo*, means a mossy tract of land; it may be located somewhere east of Rossley, in the valley of the Chelt.

the now lost name *Tyreltune* refers to the neighbouring village, which has been known since the eleventh century as Whittington.[1]

At some date after 774 the conventual establishment at Withington ceased to exist. It may well be that Æthelburg was the last representative of the family for whose behoof it had been founded.[2] Thenceforth Withington bears no other character in the records than that of a rural manor and parish belonging to the see of Worcester. It is possible that one of the later Anglo-Saxon kings permitted a charter to be drawn up, vesting the lordship of Withington permanently in the bishop and his successors. If so, the document has not survived. There does however exist an Old English description of the boundaries which may have been copied from this or an older charter. It is preserved in the manuscript commonly known as Hemming's Cartulary.[3] Dr Neil R. Ker has demonstrated that the portion of the manuscript in which the Withington boundary is given dates from the first half, and in all probability from the earliest decade, of the eleventh century.[4] In this perambulation the manor is described at its fullest extension, including the whole of Withington and Dowdeswell, and also the greater part of Whittington: in all, an area of not much less than fifteen square miles.[5]

[1] It will be shown presently that the Withington boundary at its fullest extent took in the greater part if not the whole of Whittington.

[2] She held two other minsters on the same terms as Withington: one, at Twyning, given her by her father Alfred, the other, at Fladbury, given by Ealdred, under-king of the Hwicce, who refers to her as his kinswoman. Ealdred was the last known member of this local dynasty.—H. P. R. Finberg, *The Early Charters of the West Midlands*, Leicester, 1961, pp. 38, 94.

[3] British Museum, Cotton MS. Tiberius A. xiii; printed in CS 299.

[4] *Studies in Medieval History presented to F. M. Powicke*, Oxford, 1948, pp. 49–75.

[5] For a detailed elucidation of the boundary, see Grundy, *op. cit.*, pp. 262–71, and H. P. R. Finberg, *op. cit.*, p. 84. It will be observed that Grundy is not entirely happy over some of the northern landmarks. He has missed a clue to the whereabouts of the "alder spring" (*alre wyllan*) in landmark 33 through failing to notice that its name survives in Arle Grove, a couple of furlongs east of the spring. I venture to propose the following revision of the last few boundary points, beginning at 31, the "green way" which forms the western boundary of Whittington, 1½ furlongs east of Colgate. The per-

By 1066 Whittington had passed out of the bishop's hands. Withington remained in his immediate lordship, but Dowdeswell appears in Domesday Book as held under the bishop by one of his knights. Like other estates in feudal tenure, it gradually acquired the status of a distinct manor and parish. In 1413 the parishioners of Dowdeswell stated that by ancient observance their church was deemed to be subject as a daughter church to the parish church of Withington, and that although their own rector administered the sacraments, they carried their dead to Withington for burial. In response to their petition the pope granted them a cemetery of their own.[1] But down to 1858 the rector of Withington exercised a peculiar jurisdiction over the two parishes and held a court in which the wills of deceased parishioners were proved.[2] For secular purposes Withington was combined with Dowdeswell and several other Cotswold manors, including Notgrove and Aston Blank, into a judicial and administrative unit known as the hundred of Wacrescumbe.[3] Henry I upheld the bishop's rights over this hun-

---

ambulation follows this track, crossing the road that leads past Wood Farm to Whalley: this is the *Weallehes wege* of 32. It continues along the Whittington boundary until it comes to the road north of Arle Grove, which is the "stony way" of 33 (note the old quarry and earthwork shown on the Ordnance map at this point). Here it turns eastward, either along the stony way or following the present parish boundary. The "old dyke" of 34 was probably on the line of the road that leads past Whalley. The Honeybourne of 35 is the brook flowing down from Puckham towards Whittington, and the "other old dyke" was probably by the roadside on the way to Syreford. This brings us to the mill-pool of 36, at Syreford, and thence to the Portway, or main road from Stow to Gloucester, which is reached at a point six furlongs east of Andoversford. The boundary then turns westward along the main road, leaves it at the thorn-tree of 38, some 3½ furlongs east of Andoversford, passes a quarry or patch of covert, the *crundel* of 39, and rejoins the main road at Andoversford.

[1] *Calendar of Papal Letters*, VI (1404–15), p. 388. Rossley continued to form a detached portion of Withington until 1883, when it was transferred to Dowdeswell.

[2] BGAS XL, 1917, pp. 89–113.

[3] The hundred comprised Withington, Dowdeswell, Notgrove, and Aston Blank, assessed collectively at 30 hides; Shipton, 13 hides; Whittington, 3 hides; and Hampen, 6 hides. To these should perhaps be added the 20 hides of Sevenhampton, of which Domesday Book says only that they lay outside the hundred of Cheltenham. C. S. Taylor, in his *Analysis of the Domesday Survey of Gloucestershire*, Bristol, 1889, p. 270, exaggerates the

dred,[1] but by the thirteenth century it had been absorbed into the neighbouring hundred of Bradley. The bishop, however, retained full seignorial jurisdiction over the manors in his immediate lordship; and a relic of the ancient hundredal link between them appears as late as 1750, when thirty-five inhabitants of Notgrove and eighteen inhabitants of Aston Blank were named in the court roll as owing attendance at the manor court of Withington.

With only brief interruptions under the Tudors and the Commonwealth, the bishops of Worcester retained the lordship of Withington down to 1860. They then handed the estate over to the Ecclesiastical Commissioners, in whose hands it remained until 1926. Thanks to this long continuity of ownership the records have been well preserved. The archives of the Commissioners include a survey of the manor taken by order of parliament in 1647, a list of copyholds drawn up *circa* 1760, a rental of *circa* 1802, and the presentments of the manor court from 1707 to 1751.[2] A fine set of court rolls, running from 1497 to 1682, is now in the Public Record Office.[3] Three surveys of the episcopal manors transcribed in the volume known as the Red Book of Worcester take the evidence back to the twelfth and thirteenth centuries, and Hemming's cartulary of Worcester supplies the text of five Anglo-Saxon documents the gist of which has been given above. Lastly, a terrier of the rector's glebe, drawn up in 1680, throws much light on the agrarian organization of the parish before it was remodelled by enclosure.[4]

total hidage, because, as Maitland pointed out (*Domesday Book and Beyond*, p. 457), he has counted the subtenants' hides twice over. Maitland's criticism is amply borne out by the manorial surveys; cf. *Hemingi Chartularium*, ed. T. Hearne, Oxford, 1723, p. 83, and *The Red Book of Worcester*, ed. M. Hollings, Worcs. Historical Soc., 1934–50, p. 367.

[1] *Herefordshire Domesday*, ed. V. H. Galbraith and J. Tait, Pipe Roll Soc., LXIII (N.S. XXV), 1947–8, p. xxvi.

[2] The reference numbers of these documents in the Commissioners' deed registry are 44069a, 44043, 325122, and 44031. Other relevant documents which I have examined are numbered 44030, 44031a, 44034, 44035, 44038, 44040, and 47948–55.

[3] Eccl. 1, Bundles 188 and 194–200.

[4] Gloucestershire Records Office (Shire Hall, Gloucester), D 182.

§2

The pattern of fields, roads, and hedges visible at Withington today is a thing of modern creation. It dates from 1819, when Frederick Phelps, Daniel Trinder, and Joseph Large, commissioners under an Enclosure Act which had received the royal

assent in 1813, signed and sealed their award.[1] I have not been fortunate enough to find any map or plan of earlier date; but by comparing the enclosure map and award with the documents named above, and interpreting them in the light of explorations carried out for the most part on foot, it is possible

---

[1] The fruits of their handiwork elicited a characteristic burst of invective from William Cobbett when he passed through the village some years later. —*Rural Rides*, ed. G. D. H. and M. Cole, London, 1930, p. 449.

to reconstruct the thousand-year-old pattern which the commissioners blotted out.[1]

The backbone of Withington is a ridge of land rising from eight to nine hundred feet above sea level and running due north and south. On its western side a rivulet known today as the Hilcot Brook rises at Pegglesworth and flows down to meet another stream which the Saxons called *Col's burn* or Colesborne, a name now given to the adjacent parish. The united waters mingle here to form the river Churn. On the eastern side the ground slopes rather more gently down to the valley of the Coln. The core of Withington, including the church, rectory, and manor house, is situated on a level platform at the foot of the ridge, but well above the valley bottom. From this platform a further descent leads down to the river, which is here about eight feet wide.

For more than three thousand years the ridge formed the chief local artery of communication. A trackway called the White Way climbed out of the valley of the Churn at Cirencester and ran northward along the high ground east of the river, passing through what are now the parishes of Baunton, North Cerney, Rendcomb, Chedworth, and Withington, a distance of about ten miles. At the northern end of the Withington ridge it met, at right angles, the main Cotswold ridgeway. This is part of the great prehistoric track which modern archaeologists have christened the Jurassic Way, a thoroughfare from the Bristol Avon to the Humber. Ascending the Cotswold scarp at Lansdown, the Jurassic Way runs past Old Sodbury and the Duntisbournes to Birdlip, crosses the Coln at Andoversford and the Windrush at Naunton, and continues through Stow-on-the-Wold and Banbury to Northampton, Stamford, and Lincoln.[2] Withington lay some two and a half miles distant from this main thoroughfare, but connected with it by its own minor ridgeway. Two flint axes and an arrow-head found just on the Chedworth side of the parish boundary, and the fragment of a stone axe dug up at Foxcote, prove that neolithic

[1] The enclosure award and map are deposited in the Shire Hall at Gloucester.

[2] W. F. Grimes (ed.), *Aspects of Archaeology in Britain and Beyond*, London, 1951, pp. 151, 152; O. G. S. Crawford, *Archaeology in the Field*, London, 1953, pp. 81–5.

man came and went along the Withington ridge.[1] It is indeed more than probable that a neolithic community settled permanently somewhere in the district, for one of their long barrows remains nearly intact on the wooded hill between Withington and Chedworth.[2]

There are traces of fortification three-quarters of a mile south-west of the village, in the shape of a linear earthwork starting on the edge of a steep re-entrant valley and running across the ridge. It has a ditch on the south side, and looks as if designed to bar access from that direction; but it is much worn down, and without excavation we have no means of knowing whether it was intended as a barrier against the Roman or the Saxon.[3] Near its eastern end is a round barrow, of equally uncertain date.

When the valleys of the Coln and upper Isbourne came to be developed as Roman villa-estates, a new track was laid out to connect them with Cirencester. This road branched from the White Way in Chedworth and crossed the Coln at Cassey Compton, heading for Compton Abdale and the northern wolds. It left Withington even more secluded than before. The original line of track along the ridge figures, as "the old stone way," in the Anglo-Saxon boundary, and as "the Ridgeway" in the survey of 1299. In 1635 it was described as "the market way from Withington to Cheltenham."[4] It continued in use as the ordinary line of communication between the village and the outside world until 1819, when the enclosure commissioners decreed the construction of a new "public way" along the foot of the ridge. The visitor today who turns off the main Stow-Gloucester highway and enters the village by this modern road might easily mistake its rigid directness for a sign of Roman origin.

---

[1] The Chedworth finds are recorded on the Ordnance map; the Foxcote axe in BGAS LVIII, 1936, p. 284, and *Proceedings of the Prehistoric Society*, N.S. VII, 1941, p. 58, where it is shown that the axe was a product of the factory at Pike of Stickle, near Langdale, Westmorland.

[2] O. G. S. Crawford, *Long Barrows of the Cotswolds*, Gloucester, 1925, p. 145.

[3] I am indebted to Mrs H. E. O'Neil for this description of the cross-ridge dyke.

[4] Gloucestershire Records Office, D 444, T 79.

§3

Before the enclosure of the common fields the agricultural freeholds and copyholds of Withington were regularly described as fractions or multiples of a yardland. The term signified a unit of assessment laid upon holdings which in fact consisted of a number of strips in the arable fields, with appurtenant rights in the common pastures and woods. At Withington the acre was only two-thirds of the statute acre; and as a rule, the yardland seems to have comprised from forty to forty-eight acres of arable, measured by this customary standard.[1] But there was no uniformity. The best way to illustrate the varying and — as it would seem — arbitrary relationship between the assessment and the real acres in the fields will be to tabulate the particulars of the rector's glebe, as furnished to Henry VIII's commissioners in 1535, side by side with the more detailed account drawn up in 1680.[2] There is no reason to suppose that the glebe was appreciably or at all enlarged between these dates.

1535	1680
4 yardlands adjoining the rectory	46¼ acres in North Field
	34 a. in Upcote Field
	1 a. in Butts Field
	34 a. in Wood Field
	———
	115½ a.
1 yardland at Oldswell	25¼ a. in South Field
	13¾ a. in North Field
	15 a. in Upper Field
	———
	54 a.

[1] Thus in 1795 a holding of one and a half yardlands comprised "36 customary acres of arable land in the North Brookwell End Field containing about 24 statute acres, and 36 customary acres of arable in the South Brookwell End Field containing about 24 statute acres, with five acres of meadow and pasture ground."

[2] *Valor Ecclesiasticus*, London, 1810–34, II, p. 444; Gloucestershire Records Office, D 182.

1 yardland at Foxcote	22¾ a. in the Upper Field
	25 a. in the Lower Field
	————
	47¾ a.
1 yardland at Little Colesborne	10½ a. in South Field
	18 a. in North Field
	————
	28½ a.
1 yardland at Bowood	1 yardland called Bouwood Hitching
1 yardland in Brockhole End	18 a. in South Field
	21 a. in North Field
	————
	39 a.
1 yardland (Giles Chalff's)	1 yardland in the Staple Slade.

The 18 acres in the south field of Brockhole End consisted of twenty-five dispersed acre and half-acre strips, and the 21 acres in the north field of thirty-four similarly scattered parcels. Altogether the 284¾ acres enumerated above lay in 196 distinct parcels. We recognize here the familiar pattern of the open fields, a complex of strip-cultivation upon which the policy of a bygone age has imposed an assessment that perhaps never corresponded very exactly with the realities of agrarian life.

The yardland makes its last appearance in the enclosure award. Down to 1819 the records of the manor are full of it. Its Latin equivalent, *virgata*, appears constantly in the twelfth- and thirteenth-century surveys, and earlier still in Domesday Book, where it is reckoned as the fourth part of a hide. There is good reason to believe that the hides of Domesday represent the *cassati* of our earliest charters.[1] On the meaning of this term it will be necessary to say more presently. Here we need only note that successive additions to the "land of twenty *cassati*" which Ethelred of Mercia settled on the minster beside the Coln brought the Domesday assessment of Withington and its associated manors up to thirty hides, or 120 yardlands. The

[1] DB I, p. 164b. On the equivalence of hides and *cassati*, see C. S. Taylor, 'The Pre-Domesday Hide of Gloucestershire', BGAS XVIII, 1894, pp. 288–319.

incidence, as well as the amount, of the assessment was doubt-less changed from time to time,[1] but it is remarkable that the yardlands should have persisted as units of public and private obligation for well over a thousand years. We must be careful, of course, not to exaggerate the tenacity of local usage. When the jury of the manor court declared, as they did in 1665, that the custom of the manor was for tenants to hold by copy of court roll for one lifetime in possession and three lives in reversion, they were describing a system markedly different from the villeinage of the thirteenth-century surveys. But the transition from villein tenure to copyhold is a commonplace of manorial history, and here we are concerned with a remoter past. It is however important to note that down to 1819 social and economic change at Withington took place by gradual and almost imperceptible stages within a framework of tradition inherited from the time of the Mercian kings.

§4

In the survey of 1299 we read that "the bishop has in demesne 380 acres of arable [really 392, as the following figures show]. And it is divided into two fields, namely South Field and North Field. The South Field contains 191 acres of arable land, and the North Field contains 201 acres. Each acre is worth upon an average 6d. every other year, or 3d. per annum."[2]

There is no difficulty in locating the larger of these fields: its position is indicated by the present Northfield Farm. For the south field we turn to the enclosure award. There we find, south and east of the village, a field called Brockland. It covers the whole area of approximately 775 acres east of the Coln, with the exception of some enclosures in the south-east corner which have obviously been taken out of it to form the freehold of Cassey Compton. The county historians Atkyns (1712) and Rudder (1779), followed by the 1828 edition of the Ordnance map, give the name erroneously as Broadwell End, but this corrupt form has since been removed from the map. Earlier variants, Brookwell End (1798, 1707), Brookehole End (1600),

---

[1] The Domesday assessment may be compared with that drawn up about a century later (*Red Book of Worcester*, p. 367) and with the undated one in Hemming's cartulary (ed. Hearne, p. 83).

[2] *Red Book*, p. 354.

and Brokehall Ende (1530), make it clear that the name refers not to a well but to a badger-hole. The manorial records frequently refer to Brockhole End as the Lower End, thus distinguishing it from the Upper End of Withington, where the church, rectory, and manor house are situated, and to which the North Field, with its satellites, belonged.

On the face of it, the passage quoted from the survey of 1299 suggests a two-field system of the simplest and most orthodox type. Closer acquaintance with the documents, however, shows that the simplicity of the statement is deceptive. In the first place, the yardlands are not made up of strips in both fields. Whenever their composition is set forth in detail, they are found to lie wholly in the Upper or the Lower End. We have already seen that the four yardlands of glebe "adjoining the rectory" are enumerated separately from the yardland in Brockhole End. Moreover, it appears that each of the main fields was physically divided into two. In 1707 the manor court ordered "the Mound betwixt the two Fields in Brookwell End Field" to be kept in good order. In 1703 the court imposed a fine of sixpence for every sheep turned into the stubble "in the lower field of the Upper end" before Stow fair, that great red-letter day of the Cotswold year. The bailiff's account of 1798 describes one holding as lying partly dispersed in "North Upper End Field;" and of another it says: "This Estate [of three yardlands] is all uninclosed in the North and South Brookwell End Fields, and contains sixty customary Field acres in each Field, and twenty-two Statute acres of meadow and pasture land."

Now it would be natural to suppose that at some time between the thirteenth and the eighteenth centuries an original two-field system at Withington had been reorganized. H. L. Gray found a number of parishes in north Oxfordshire where the two ancient fields were divided into four and subjected to a four-course rotation of crops. The evidence he examined led him to believe that the change took place in the seventeenth century.[1] At Withington it would obviously make for convenience to group the strips of each yardlander on one side of the Coln or the other, instead of leaving them scattered over both sides of the valley, with perhaps a mile or more between

[1] H. L. Gray, *English Field Systems*, Cambridge (Mass.), 1915, pp. 125, 126, 135.

them. But were the yardlands originally composed of strips on both sides of the river? I have found no evidence that they were. Moreover the presentments of the manor court show the tenants of Brockhole End and those of the Upper End constantly speaking and acting as two distinct groups. United under the bishop's lordship, and meeting regularly to transact business in his court, they are nevertheless conscious of separate identities.

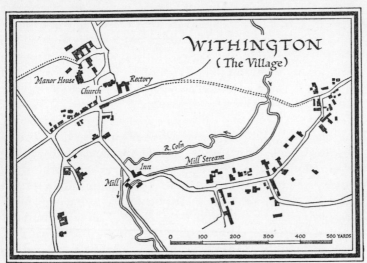

In 1672 "it is agreed between the farmers and tenants of the upper part of Withington that none of them shall depasture the ox, horse, or mare of any stranger." Item, "the inhabitants in Brookewell End have no pasture in the field called Upper End Field." In 1720 "we agree in the Upper End to abate and depasture two sheep out of a score, and so proporcionable . . . till Lammas Day." "We order and agree in the Brookwell End to make up the hedge from Townsend to Compton Grove." In 1636 a suit is brought in the Court of Common Pleas touching rights of pasture between Withington Down and Hilcot, the plaintiffs, John Howe and others, pleading "as well for themselves as for all the rest of the parishioners and inhabitants of the upper end," but not, be it noted, for their neighbours in Brockhole End.[1]

The truth is that the present village represents not one original

[1] Gloucestershire Records Office, D 444, T 79.

settlement but two. To any one who approaches it with these records in mind, or who examines a large-scale map, its duality is plainly visible. The upper end is a compact, rectangular nucleus of buildings and lanes, with a street leading westward out of it and up towards the old trackway along the top of the ridge. Skirting this nucleus, the road leads downhill and across the river, passing a mill which probably occupies the site of one mentioned in Domesday Book. There is then an appreciable interval before it winds round to the first cottages and farm-steads of the lower end. The buildings here are not clustered in a rectangular group, but strung out for more than a quarter of a mile along the road to Compton Abdale. It becomes apparent that two settlements have grown up here in close proximity, each with a two-field system of its own.

Withington is not the only dual village on the Cotswolds. The "east end" and "west end" of Sherborne, so described in 1355, are a mile apart, with the manor house and church between them. Similarly Westcote, where open-field strips have survived to the present day, stands half a mile distant from Nether Westcote. How are these phenomena to be explained? One possible explanation is that the Anglo-Saxon immigrants, instead of quartering themselves in the existing British hamlets, may have preferred to keep themselves apart from the natives and to establish new settlements of their own. In that case they would think and speak of the older hamlet as a Walton: that is, a *Wealatun* or Welshmen's *tun*, and the name would not bear the construction sometimes put upon it by modern scholars, namely that such hamlets were exceptional;[1] it would merely serve to distinguish the Welsh *tun* from its English neighbour. But before accepting this hypothesis, we must ask how far back in time the dual settlement at Withington can really be traced.

The question had better be framed in these terms: how old is Brockhole End? It is older than 1086, for Domesday Book in-forms us that already by that date a distinct settlement had grown up on the left bank of the Coln. And because this is the same side of the river as Cassey Compton and Compton Abdale, the settlement is said to lie "in Compton." The great record states, in the usual form, that the bishop of Worcester

[1] E. Ekwall, in *Introduction to the Survey of English Place-Names*, Part I, Cambridge, 1924, p. 18.

has two ploughs on his demesne at Withington, with six slaves to drive them; that sixteen *villani*, or yardlanders, and eight *bordarii*, or smallholders, all dependent on the bishop, have seven plough-teams between them; and that the bishop has ten acres of meadow, besides a good deal of woodland. It then begins afresh, and states that "in Contone" the bishop has one plough-team and two slaves as well as two *villani* and two *bordarii* with one team between them. There is also a mill, probably on the same site as the one that continued to grind corn down to the close of the nineteenth century.

Two documents in Hemming's Cartulary may help us to push the record a stage further back. In 962 a deacon named Ealhferth obtained from Bishop Oswald a lease for three lives of one *mansa* at "Cumtun;" and in 989, the former term having presumably expired, the same bishop gave a similar lease of one *mansa* at "Cumtun" to a layman named Eadwig.[1] An element of uncertainty arises here from the fact that the bishop owned another Compton near the mouth of the Severn, the village known today as Compton Greenfield. But the scribe who copied out these leases evidently took them to mean our Compton, for he transcribed them between a lease of Pegglesworth and the Anglo-Saxon perambulation of Withington. From another document in Hearne's edition of the cartulary we glean a fact which Domesday Book passes over in silence, namely that our "Compton" was assessed at one hide: a figure which corresponds nicely with the "one *mansa*" of the leases.[2]

At the present day the parish boundary on this side follows undeviatingly the line of the Anglo-Saxon perambulation. Starting from Andoversford, it comes down the Coln for nearly two miles, then leaves the river abruptly at a right angle, curves round the 775 acres of Brockhole End, and finally returns to the Coln at Cassey Compton. When we observe this behaviour, we cannot but suspect that the Coln formed the original boundary all along this side of the estate. We shall find additional reason for believing so when we move back into the Roman period. And finally, comparing the two earliest Withington charters, we observe that Dunne's minster was endowed

[1] CS 1089, from Hearne's edition of Hemming, p. 239; K 669, from *ibid.*, p. 236.
[2] *Hemingi Chartularium*, p. 83; cf. *Red Book*, p. 367.

at first with an estate of twenty hides, or *cassati*, but that in 774 the bishop states the number of hides as twenty-one. It is true that he also describes the land as being situated west of the river, but it seems reasonable to conclude that he is speaking elliptically: what he means to say is that it consists of twenty hides on the west bank, with one hide on the other bank which has been added at some date between the foundation of the minster and 774.

§5

After completing its account of "Contone," Domesday Book goes on to state that "in the same manor" of Withington is a priest who keeps twelve oxen — that is, a plough-team and a half — at work on his glebe. There are also four *radchenistri*, with a couple of teams between them. These *radchenistri*, whose lands are assessed altogether at 2¾ hides, belong to a superior class of tenants who emerge in the late Saxon period as charged with the duty of riding on their lord's errands, providing him with an escort when he travels, and generally serving him in the capacity of mounted retainers.

Then the record passes on to the foreign knights whom the bishop has settled in the manor since the Norman conquest, not in Withington itself but in the outlying hamlets. Some of these hamlets, we are told, contain meadow and wood, "but not much." They also contain arable land enough to employ sixteen ploughs on the knights' home-farms and twenty-eight ploughs on the land tilled by their subtenants.[1] Later documents, such as the terrier epitomized on an earlier page, reveal that several of the hamlets possessed field-systems of their own, reproducing on a smaller scale the agrarian pattern of Withington itself.[2]

From the time of Domesday onwards the hamlets have played a prominent part in the life of the parish. It behoves us, therefore, to ascertain, if we can, how much farther back their history can be traced.

[1] Unfortunately Domesday gives only aggregate figures, which include Notgrove and Aston Blank.

[2] Above, p. 31. In 1648 a deed of sale refers to the North Field of Pegglesworth. This suggests that originally there had been two arable fields or more, though by 1648 the north field had been converted into a sheepwalk. — BGAS LXVII, 1946-8, p. 130.

The antiquity of Pegglesworth has been obscured by a mis-reading of the earliest document in which its name appears. This is a lease which, as printed by Hearne and Kemble, refers to a place called Wæcgleswyrthe. In the manuscript, however, the initial P is unmistakable.[1] From this document we learn that Bishop Coenweald (929–57) gave a lease of three *cassati* at Pæccleswyrthe to a certain thegn, and the son of the thegn obtained a renewal from Bishop Oswald in 981. If the construc-tion we have put upon the Onnanford charter is correct, namely that in 759 the spot where Pegglesworth stands was part of a tract then known as Wistley,[2] we may probably conclude that Pæccel first made his *worth* or homestead at some date between 759 and 950.

Owdeswell makes its first recorded appearance in a survey of *c.* 1182 which merely records its liability for church-scot.[3] In the course of the next hundred years a certain Peter de Asrugge gave it to Studley Priory, an Augustinian house in Warwick-shire.[4] The prior thenceforth held Owdeswell in free tenure under the bishop, subject to the obligation of making sum-monses and levying distraints in the outlying portions of the hundred, and representing Withington in the shire-court.[5]

Upcote appears in the same documents as Owdeswell. Geographically it shows every sign of having been enclosed from the north field of Withington. It was probably one of the unnamed holdings of the Domesday *radchenistri*, for until 1288 its occupant was bound to carry the bishop's letters, when required, to any place in the diocese of Worcester.[6]

In 1086 two hides at "Colesburne" and "Willecot" were united in a single knightly tenure. "Colesburne" is not the parish of Colesborne, but Little Colesborne on the Withington side of the boundary. By "Willecot" the scribe meant Hilcot: that is, the portion of Withington lying west of the Hilcot

---

[1] *Hemingi Chartularium*, p. 235; K 681; Cotton MS. Tiberius A. xiii, fo. 111. The erroneous spelling occurs in the rubric of the manuscript; in the text, the name is spelt Pæccleswyrthe.

[2] Above, p. 22.

[3] *Red Book*, p. 367. The undated geld-list in *Hemingi Chartularium*, p. 83, gives "Aldeswell" an assessment of two hides.

[4] Dugdale, *Monasticon*, VI, p. 187.   [5] *Red Book*, p. 356.

[6] *Ibid.*, pp. 364, 365.

Brook. The parish boundary leaves the brook at Mercombe Wood and returns to it at the source below Pegglesworth, after taking in approximately 666 acres of hilly and thickly wooded land. This is just such a deviation as we have already noticed on the other side of the parish, and it suggests that Hilcot, like Brockhole End, is an addition to the original estate. If so, it was added before the Anglo-Saxon perambulation was put into writing, but that document seems to point back to a time when the brook had formed a natural boundary, for it identifies it with the river Churn and treats the Col's-burn as a tributary water.

So far, the hamlets appear chiefly in the light of holdings on which the bishop, towards the close of the Anglo-Saxon period, thought fit to settle his riding-men and other manorial retainers. Nowhere have we found any indication of pre-Saxon antiquity. At Pegglesworth, indeed, we discovered grounds for believing that the hamlet was of Saxon creation. It is always possible that the spade or the plough will bring new evidence to light, but hitherto no archaeological discoveries have been reported from any of these places. In this respect they stand in marked contrast with Foxcote. Besides the neolithic fragment already mentioned, Foxcote has yielded numerous relics of the Iron Age. Pottery dating from the first century B.C. has been found, with animal bones, near Foxcote Manor in a pit which appears to have been used as a cooking-hole.[1] A little to the south, on Foxcote Hill, a round tumulus measuring 78 feet across from north to south and 69 feet from east to west was found in 1863 to contain the remains of a female skeleton in a burial chamber near the centre. The tumulus also contained a flint chisel, animal bones, and a large hoard of Roman coins dating from the third and fourth centuries of the present era.[2]

[1] Helen E. Donovan and G. C. Dunning, 'Iron Age Pottery and Saxon Burials at Foxcote', BGAS LVIII, 1936, pp. 157–70.

[2] *Proceedings of the Cotteswold Naturalists' Field Club*, III, 1865, p. 198, and VI, 1877, p. 335; *Anthropological Review*, III, 1865, p. lxix. G. B. Witts, in BGAS IV, 1879–80, p. 201, and in his *Archaeological Handbook of Gloucestershire*, 1883, p. 98, mistakes this tumulus for a mound three-quarters of a mile away to the north-west, called St Paul's Epistle. It was perhaps in consequence of this mistake that a note "Roman coins found" was attached to St Paul's Epistle in the six-inch Ordnance map of 1924. This mound, however, is square, not circular, about four feet high and 36 feet long on each side.

Finally, at a still later date three pits were dug, one of them on the site of the Iron Age cooking-hole, the others a few yards away, and used as graves. Three female skeletons have been found there, lying in a crouched position, with the legs drawn up to the body, and with them fragments of combs, of a type occasionally found on late Roman sites but much more frequently in the sixth and seventh centuries. In the light of these discoveries, it is hardly rash to conclude that Foxcote has been occupied continuously for the best part of two thousand years.

§6

After this tour of the hamlets, we must return to the central village. Our exploration of Saxon and post-Saxon Withington is nearly at an end, but before leaving it we must note two characteristics that stand out very clearly from the records. One is the persistence with which Old English usages were maintained during and after the Norman conquest. A hundred years after Domesday one free tenant at Withington was still described as a "riding-man," and his name, Alfred, surely betokens Anglo-Saxon descent.[1] At that late date the bishop of Worcester was still trying, not very successfully, to deal with his knights on the Anglo-Saxon principle that every five hides of land ought to furnish one man to the national host.[2]

It is against this background of continuous tradition that we must set the evidence of change and expansion which also confronts us in the documents. In the first place, we can see the population slowly increasing. Towards the close of the twelfth century the manor counted in the lowest rank of its tenants nine "cotmen" and seven "Monday-men." A century later we find seven *coterelli*, fourteen Monday-men, and five *enches* or tenants performing specialized services and holding sixteen acres apiece.[3] We also hear of assarts, land newly brought under

[1] *Red Book*, p. 367.
[2] *Ibid.*, pp. xx–xxxviii; M. Hollings, 'The Survival of the Five Hide Unit in the Western Midlands', EHR LXIII, 1948, pp. 453–87.
[3] *Red Book*, pp. 360–4, 367. On the Monday-men and *enches*, see M. M. Postan, *The Famulus* (supplement to the *Economic History Review*), N.D. [1954], pp. 10, 31, 32. Professor Postan shows that the Monday-men paid for their holdings by working one day a week for the lord without wages, but drew wages for the remainder of the week.

cultivation to feed the growing number of mouths. Thus, one tenant is said to hold an assart "by grant of Bishop Simon" (1125–50).[1] Another, William Grenesty, left his name attached to a holding on Shill Hill, created in the same period.[2] A third assart is described as being held by grant of Bishop William of Blois (1218–36).[3] Less than half of the bishop's own arable was ploughed for him by the permanent staff of the demesne; for the rest he relied on the labour due from his serfs, and it is instructive to see how this was organized. Each yardlander owed the bishop one day's ploughing a week, and in the survey of 1299 the obligation is expressed as follows. "He ought to plough *on the Ridgeway* and elsewhere with the other customary tenants, once a week, or pay a penny if he does not."[4] In these entries we can almost watch the process by which cultivation, from its original nucleus down by the village, was gradually pushed farther up the sloping flank and over the crest of the ridge. It is probable that the survey of 1299 displays the agricultural economy of Withington at the fullest extension it attained before the Black Death brought its cruel relief to a hungry and over-populated countryside.

At that time the bishop had almost as many acres under plough in Brockhole End as in the North Field of Withington proper. But if we look back to Domesday, we shall find that he had then only one team at work here, as against two on the other side of the Coln, and the disparity between the tenants' ploughs was even greater: one "in Compton" to seven in Withington. This will not appear surprising to any one who walks over the ground and talks with those who farm it today. The soil of Brockhole End does not invite tillage, and parts of it are so steep that they can never have been under plough. Hence, while the addition of this tract on the east bank of the Coln stands out historically as the first move in a long process of manorial expansion, we should almost certainly misunderstand it if we supposed that the men who annexed this land were looking for more acres to plough. Throughout recent centuries the main emphasis of Cotswold husbandry has alternately

[1] *Red Book*, p.413.
[2] *Ibid.*, p. 356, where the name is misspelt Grevesty.
[3] *Ibid.*, p. 355.
[4] *Ibid.*, p. 356.

veered from corn to sheep and from sheep back to corn again.[1] But the early records have shown us the corn-growing area being gradually enlarged, and the further back we look, the more room we shall find for sheep. It is significant that just when the abbess of Withington was taking in a portion of "Compton," we find the abbess of Gloucester acquiring Pinswell, between the Hilcot Brook and the Churn, expressly for a sheep-walk.[2] One detail in the Saxon perambulation of Withington is eloquent of pastoral husbandry. When the boundary leaves the Coln, it turns up a little valley called Wacel's combe, destined to give its name to the Domesday hundred. At the top of this combe it reaches "the common lea." If we feel any doubt concerning the use to which this common was put, the name of the adjoining parish will resolve it for us, for what is "Shipton" but a sheep-farm?

The economic history of Saxon England is a subject on which we cannot hope to be fully informed. One relevant fact, however, does emerge from the correspondence of Offa and Charlemagne.[3] It appears that in the eighth century some kind of woollen garment was regularly exported from Mercia to the Frankish realm. The trade was important enough to figure in diplomatic exchanges between two leading European potentates. It would be idle to ask where these cloths were manufactured; but that part of the raw material was furnished by royal and episcopal sheep-flocks is not an extravagant surmise; and what better source of wool has Mercia ever possessed than the pastures of these Cotswold hills?[4]

We have now reached a point at which we can attempt an answer to the question: what was Withington like at the close of the seventh century, when Ethelred and Oshere chose it for the site of their new minster? In the first place, the territory they dealt with was smaller than it is today. From the present

[1] L. Richardson, *Memoirs of the Geological Survey: The Country around Cirencester*, London, 1933, p. 94.

[2] *Historia et Cartularium Monasterii S. Petri Gloucestriae*, ed. W. H. Hart, Rolls ser., 33, I, pp. lxxii, 4, 70.   [3] EHD I, p. 782.

[4] Dr W. G. Hoskins has pointed out that the place-names of the Oxfordshire Cotswolds bear witness to the prevalence of sheep-farming in the Anglo-Saxon period. — *The Oxford Region*, ed. A. F. Martin and R. W. Steel, Oxford, 1954, p. 107. See also H. P. R. Finberg, *Gloucestershire Studies*, Leicester, 1957, pp. 11-14.

5,830 acres we must subtract the 775 acres of Brockhole End, and probably also the 666 acres west of the Hilcot Brook. And as we look back, the arable shrinks and the pasture expands. We may reasonably locate the minster in the Upper End, and the plough-land just outside the village, in what the thirteenth and later centuries will call the North Field. Above it, on the side and crest of the ridge, the sheep-flock grazes, a flock assuredly not smaller than the one, six hundred strong, the bishop will keep there in the thirteenth century. For one fact stands out with a clarity luminous enough to dispel at least some of the darkness that precedes and surrounds the coming of the Saxons. It is, that in the judgement of those responsible for the conduct of public affairs in the principality of the Hwicce, Withington at this time was no derelict property, but an estate in working order, an economic unit capable of supporting not only the husbandmen it already fed and housed, but also a monastic institution with its church and refectory, an establishment formed to provide a home for royal and noble ladies and a place of education for their children. To account for this prosperity, we have postulated a flourishing traffic in wool. Whatever its basis, it was solid enough to make Withington a covetable possession, for less than fifty years later the ecclesiastical authorities had to settle a disputed claim to the ownership.

Behind the shadowy form of the abbess Dunne there lurks one figure even more inscrutably remote. When Ethelred and Oshere founded their minster, Withington already had its Anglo-Saxon occupants, and they had given it an Anglo-Saxon name. They called it Widiandun: that is, Widia's *dun*.[1] We shall never know when or how Widia became associated with the place, or who he was, but the second element of the name does tell us one thing. It proves that in the eyes of Widia and his contemporaries the most significant feature of the local scene was not the village nor the level ground on which it stood, but the ridge that loomed above it. And if we ask why this was so, modern scholarship is ready with its answer: it tells us that "an important special sense of *dun* is 'hill pasture'."[2] Thus every line of enquiry leads us ultimately back to the Cotswold sheep.

[1] Ekwall, *op. cit.*, p. 528.　　　　[2] *Ibid.*, p. 153.

§7

IT IS now time to consider such data as we possess concerning Roman Withington.

In the autumn of 1810 some farm-hands ploughing "in the common field on a piece of land belonging to Henry Charles Brooke, Esq., and Mrs Nicholls," accidentally unearthed some Roman tesserae. The site lay in Wood Field, an extension or appendage of the North Field, and the tesserae were found in a part known significantly as *The Old Town*. Thereupon Mr Brooke wrote to the well-known antiquary Samuel Lysons, inviting him to come and excavate. Beginning his investigation in the October of 1811 and continuing it in the following spring, Lysons uncovered the remains of a large Roman villa. In groundplan the villa appears to have been a variant of the tripartite corridor type, extending to a total length of about 160 feet, with two apsidal chambers at the east end built over a hypocaust. Eight of the other rooms had tessellated pavements. One of these, depicting Orpheus in a style now known to date from the early fourth century, was taken up in the course of excavation and deposited in the British Museum. At the western end the walls, built of local stone and plastered on the inside, were still some four feet high.[1]

Lysons was a careful observer, but any one who compares his report and plan with a modern example, such as Mrs O'Neil's account of her excavation at Whittington, will see at a glance what progress archaeology has made since 1811.[2] Lysons did not concern himself with the successive stages in the structural history of the villa, or with the post-Roman history of the site. Only a systematic re-excavation would enable us to

[1] *Archaeologia,* XVIII, 1817, pp. 118–21. For the date of the Orpheus mosaic, cf. BGAS LXX, 1951, p. 53. The authorities of the British Museum inform me that the statement in their *Guide to the Antiquities of Roman Britain,* 1951, p. 58, dating the mosaic as late third-century, stands in need of correction.

[2] BGAS LXXI, 1952, pp. 13–87. The correspondence between Lysons and H. C. Brooke betrays an almost exclusive preoccupation with mosaic pavements; see the letters printed in Lindsay Fleming's *Memoir and Select Letters of Samuel Lysons,* Oxford, 1934, pp. 36, 37. These letters make it clear that the Withington pavement was discovered, not in 1811, the date given by Lysons, but in the previous year, and that it lay some two feet below the surface of the field.

43

answer some of the questions it did not occur to him to ask.

The site is a quarter of a mile south of Upper Withington, and approximately on the same contour-line. Two considerations evidently guided the choice of this position. Behind and above it rises the Withington ridge, with its trackway leading directly to Corinium, the Roman predecessor of Cirencester. The ridge also sheltered the house from the prevailing westerly wind. Between the site and the river Coln a spring of water emerges. The occupants of the villa probably tapped this source by means of a well. The spring is called Walwell, a name which may refer either to the remains of walls, as Lysons thought, or to the surviving 'Welsh' inhabitants. Philologically speaking, either interpretation is possible.

We may safely assume that the Withington villa, like other Roman houses of the same type, was the headquarters of an estate laid out and managed as an economic unit. Seldom indeed have we any means of estimating the acreage of such an estate in Roman Britain, but at Withington we are not entirely in the dark. Southward the site is closed in by a ridge of thickly wooded ground, on the other side of which lies the much better-known and more thoroughly excavated Chedworth villa. The boundary between Chedworth and Withington must therefore have followed much the same line under Roman rule as it did in the Anglo-Saxon perambulation and as it still does today. No Roman remains have yet come to light in the area west of the Hilcot Brook, but a large villa discovered in 1779 at Combend, a mile and a half south-west of Colesborne, may well have included in its territory the whole valley of the upper Churn.[1] On the east we have found reason to believe that Saxon Withington was originally bounded by the river Coln, and the probability that this is true also of Roman Withington is reinforced by the discovery of a villa-site in Compton Grove, between Withington and Compton Abdale.[2] Then, if we follow the Coln up to a point about three furlongs beyond the parish boundary at Andoversford, we come to Wycomb, the site of a considerable Roman market-centre or military station.[3] Three-

[1] *Archaeologia*, XVIII, 1817, p. 112.
[2] *Journal of Roman Studies*, XXII, 1932, p. 214.
[3] *The Gentleman's Magazine*, N.S. XVI, 1864, pt i, pp. 86–8, and XVII, pt ii, pp. 85–7.

quarters of a mile north-west of Wycomb stood the fine villa at Whittington, lately excavated by Mrs O'Neil. Since the Withington villa-estate was thus surrounded by a constellation of other Roman settlements, we shall hardly be far out if we assign to it the area of the modern parish, minus the portions east of the Coln and west of the Hilcot Brook: in other words, the area of approximately 4,400 acres which we take to have constituted the original endowment of the Anglo-Saxon minster.[1]

At the close of the thirteenth century this territory was said to comprise "a large extent of woodland in two places":[2] that is, along the Chedworth border, and on the western side of the main ridge. The name Wood Field, applied to that portion of the common plough-land which extended over the villa-site, suggests that after the Roman period vegetation spread down the hillside and eventually covered the derelict remains of the villa. The same thing happened at Chedworth; but whereas at Withington the site was subsequently cleared for tillage, at Chedworth it was still overgrown with trees in 1864, when a rabbiting party unearthed some fragments of Roman paving while digging for a lost ferret. In thinking back to the Roman period, therefore, we must subtract a good deal of woodland, even of the diminished woodland that exists in Withington today. A Roman traveller from Corinium, approaching Withington by the trackway along the top of the ridge, would gaze across grassy expanses dotted with furze, thorns, and occasional clumps of beech. He would not pass through any forest, for the oolitic limestone of the Cotswold uplands is by nature inhospitable to the oak and ash which probably flourished lower down in the clay soil of the valleys.[3] At

---

[1] Mr H. R. Loyn, *Anglo-Saxon England and the Norman Conquest*, 1962, p. 17, is not convinced by what he calls my "claims" that the bounds of the Saxon estate were "identical" with those of the Roman villa. In fact I am concerned more with area than with boundary lines. But since the eastern, western, and southern boundaries were strongly marked natural features, with other Roman settlements just beyond them, it is difficult to see how else the territory could have been delimited.

[2] *Red Book*, p. 354.

[3] R. P. Beckinsale, 'Vegetation of the Cotteswold Hills', *Proc. Cotteswold Naturalists' Field Club*, xxv, 1935, pp. 283–94; and cf. *Antiquity*, xix, 1945, p. 159.

Withington a line of springs on the eastern slope of the ridge marks the junction of the Inferior Oolite with the Upper Lias clay that spreads over the flat ground between the ridge and the Coln.

§8

Such being the character of the soil, to what uses would it be put by a Roman Briton desirous of exploiting his property to the best advantage?

Since every villa-estate was designed to be, as far as possible, self-sufficient, we may take it that he devoted part of the area to the growing of bread-corn. And there is little room for doubt concerning the ground he would utilize for this purpose. It is possible, indeed, that the matter had been settled long before his time, and that the same ground had been under cultivation, by one method or another, ever since the men of the New Stone Age built their long barrow within half a mile of the villa-site. "Where would you begin to plough if the whole parish lay at your disposal in a virgin state?" When this question was put to a former student of the Royal Agricultural College with twelve years' experience as a working farmer at Withington, he replied without hesitation; and the same reply was given independently by the very well-informed clerk of the parish council. The ground which obviously asks to be ploughed, the only ground in the whole parish of which this can be said, is the level tract of fertile, well-drained, not too stony soil that stretches from the Coln to the north end of the village. It is here that we have already located the plough-land of the earliest Saxon settlement. The field known from the thirteenth to the nineteenth century as the North Field of Withington is the first that would be ploughed and the last that would be suffered to go out of cultivation.

That one part of the ground was left fallow while crops were raised on the other is more than probable, for Roman writers on husbandry had long been recommending the practice.[1] Whether, under Roman management, the Withington field was ploughed in ridges, we cannot tell, but an iron coulter,

[1] Varro I, XLIV, 2 (Loeb ed., p. 274); Virgil, *Georgics* I, 71; Columella II, IX, 4 and 15 (Loeb ed., pp. 144, 154); Pliny, *Nat. Hist.*, XVIII, XLIX, 176 and L, 187 (Loeb ed., V, pp. 298, 300, 306).

found among the remains of a Roman villa at Great Witcombe less than eight miles away, proves by the set of its blade that this mode of ploughing was practised in Roman Gloucestershire.[1] We must also note, for its bearing on the subject of continuity, that Siculus Flaccus describes the intermixture of agricultural holdings as a phenomenon seen in many parts of the Roman world.[2] More than one element of the two-field system, as practised in Anglo-Saxon and Norman England, may therefore have been known in Roman Britain.

If the north field presented itself as the obvious site for tillage, more obviously still did the ridge, the backbone of the estate, offer itself as an ideal pasture-ground for sheep. Its topography alone would justify us in believing that wool-production bulked large in the economy of Roman Withington, even if we did not know how important a place the textile trade occupied in that of Britain as a whole. An inscription dating from the reign of Severus Alexander (222–35) shows that cloaks made of British cloth were being exported to the continent in the first half of the third century.[3] At the end of the century they were an article of commerce sufficiently important to have their price regulated by Diocletian's tariff, and later still we hear of an imperial weaving-mill at Winchester.[4] There were only seventeen such mills in the whole of the western empire, and as this was the only one in Britain, it must have operated on a considerable scale, drawing supplies of wool from all over the province. In a panegyric on the emperor Constantine, Eumenius extols the innumerable sheep-flocks of Britain and their heavy fleeces.[5] So insistent was the demand for wool, that wide areas of chalk-land in Wiltshire which had long been under plough were laid down to grass in this period and converted into sheep-walks.[6] The same economic forces would probably have dictated a similar change in the Cotswolds if the

[1] F. G. Payne, 'The Plough in Ancient Britain', *Archaeological Journal*, CIV, 1948, pp. 96, 97.

[2] The passage is quoted in full by Seebohm, *The English Village Community*, 4th ed., 1890, p. 278 n.

[3] *Corpus Inscriptionum Latinarum*, XIII, pt i, Berlin, 1899, pp. 498, 500, no. 3162.

[4] Collingwood and Myres, *op. cit.*, p. 239.

[5] *Panegyrici Veteres*, London, 1828, III, p. 1356.

[6] Collingwood and Myres, *op. cit.*, pp. 224, 240.

villas of that region had not already, and in all likelihood from the first, specialized in sheep-farming.

The surviving remains of the Cotswold villas amply testify to the degree of comfort and even luxury in which the occupants lived. Less is known of the local market-centres which this flourishing economy called into being; but the streets and houses of the one at Wycomb, two and three-quarter miles north of Withington, extended over more than thirty acres, and the coins found there in hundreds take its history down to the last days of Roman rule. Corinium, the chief town of the district, nine miles away to the south, was the second largest town in Roman Britain, and from A.D. 300 onwards the capital of Britannia Prima.[1] It is evident that the Cotswolds in the fourth century prospered exceedingly, and there are solid reasons for believing that the economic mainstay of the region was an active trade in wool.

What of the social structure? We may take it for granted that the villa-owner kept a staff of slaves as long as the state of the slave-market permitted him to do so. Was there also at Withington a population of tenant farmers, *coloni* settled in households of their own? That Roman Britain had its *coloni* is proved by a reference to them in the Theodosian Code, but until lately archaeologists and historians have been oddly reluctant to assign them local habitations. Collingwood, who believed that villas and villages rarely coexisted, and that the Cotswolds were exclusively occupied by villa-estates, nevertheless held that where villas and villages were mixed in the same district, the villagers were probably *coloni* on the estates of the villa-owners.[2] It may throw some light on this question if we ask what happened elsewhere in the Roman world.[3] African mosaics of the fourth and fifth centuries after Christ display large villas in full working order, with the production of corn left to the *coloni*, who paid rents in kind to the landowner,

[1] *Archaeologia*, LXIX, 1920, p. 189.

[2] Collingwood and Myres, *op. cit.*, pp. 209, 210, 224.

[3] Cf. Rostovtzeff's criticism of Haverfield, that his discussion of the villas would have been more fruitful if he had drawn the legitimate inferences from Gallic and German parallels. — *Social and Economic History of the Roman Empire*, Oxford, 1926, p. 550. "Britain was practically an annexe of Gaul." — *ibid.*, p. 212.

while the more profitable and specialized branches of husbandry were concentrated round the villa itself.[1] Roman Britain shows a marked social and economic affinity with the Rhine lands, especially those on the right bank of the river, where "most of the farms were comparatively large capitalistic agricultural concerns. . . . According to the nature of the land, some of them produced corn, others were ranches, where cattle-breeding was extensively carried on. . . . The native population became, for the most part, tenants and shepherds."[2] Recent investigation of Roman villas in Hampshire has led to the conclusion that "in the late Roman period a series of satellite holdings sprang up around the larger estate or within its boundaries; and this forcibly suggests colonate tenure."[3]

Thus, if the owner of the Withington villa elected to rely for his bread-corn on rents paid in kind by *coloni*, while he kept a staff of shepherds, weavers, and domestic slaves around him at the central establishment and a considerable sheep-flock on the down, we may say that he was conforming to a well-established practice. Nor is it difficult to find a home for the *coloni*. The hamlets, and Foxcote in particular, are likely spots. But it is equally probable that the hamlet-dwellers paid some or all of their rent in wool.[4] We have seen that the main arable area must have lain not in the hamlets but on the future North Field, and this being so, the natural place of domicile for the ploughmen was Upper Withington itself. Classical writers on agriculture recommend the landowner to build his residence at some little distance from the dwellings of the cultivators, and if possible above them, half-way up a hill.[5] At Withington, be-

---

[1] *Ibid.*, p. 629.   [2] *Ibid.*, pp. 212, 213.

[3] S. Applebaum, 'The Distribution of the Romano-British Population in the Basingstoke Area', *Papers and Proceedings of the Hampshire Field Club and Archaeological Society*, XVII, pt ii, 1953, pp. 126–7. The writer adds that he has found traces of a corresponding social pattern on Gallo-Roman estates in the vicinity of Reims.

[4] In later centuries the yardlanders owed the lord of the manor a customary "spinning-fee." — *Red Book*, p. 367 and *passim*.

[5] Varro I, XIII, 7: "Si est collis, nisi quid impedit, ibi potissimum ponatur villa" (Loeb ed., p. 214). Palladius I, VIII, 2: "Ipsius autem praetorii situs sit loco aliquatenus erectiore et sicciore quam caetera." — *Scriptores Rei Rusticae*, ed. Schneider, Leipzig, 1794–7, III, p. 23.

cause of the need for shelter, the site chosen for the villa was only twenty-five feet higher than the village, but in other respects the prescription was followed exactly. Upper Withington, the original village, stands midway between the villa and the North Field. Here the tillers of the soil could live within easy reach of their plough-land, and here a spring, larger and more powerful than the one that supplied the villa, provided them with water, as it still does for the inhabitants of Upper Withington today.[1]

Whether we think of them as slaves or as *coloni*, it is certain that their condition was one of thorough subjection to the owner of the estate. A law of 332 bound the *colonus* and his descendants for ever to the soil. If they showed signs of leaving the demesne they were to be put in irons.[2] They owed labour-service to the landowner, and the state empowered him to collect their taxes. The likeness of their condition to the serf-dom of the Domesday manor has often been noticed, and needs no emphasis here.

§9

Speaking not of Withington only, but of the Cotswold region at large, Haverfield declared that it was pre-eminently the home of stable traditions. "Here, if anywhere, we might expect to find that Romano-British life survived the Saxon flood."[3] Against this must be set the observation that "agrarian history becomes more catastrophic as we trace it backwards." Maitland, the author of this dictum, goes so far as to doubt whether there is any village in England that has not been once, or more than once, a deserted village.[4] And because current opinion is still largely swayed by Maitland's arguments, it insists on postulating a break and a new start even where Haverfield suspected continuity. It requires us, in the first place, to make a desert of Withington. At some time in the fifth or the sixth century the British inhabitants must either perish to a man, or linger only as a diminished remnant.

[1] L. Richardson, *Wells and Springs of Gloucestershire*, London (*Memoirs of the Geological Survey*), 1930, p. 175.

[2] *Codex Theodosianus* V, xv, 1 (ed. Krueger, Berlin, 1923, p. 179).

[3] *Archaeologia*, LXIX, 1920, p. 199.

[4] *Domesday Book and Beyond*, pp. 364, 365.

Organized Christianity must disappear along with the social order of Roman Britain. Into the void thus created we must admit not a trickle but a flood of Anglo-Saxon heathens. The newcomers bring with them a social structure of their own, in which the central and typical figure is the peasant farmer, free by birth and condition, accustomed to speaking his mind on public affairs in popular assemblies, and acknowledging no superior but his king.[1] If we object that these peasants bear little or no resemblance to the *villani* and *bordarii* who confront us in the pages of Domesday Book, we are told that this is because they have been depressed into serfdom or near-serfdom by the introduction of the manorial system later in the Saxon period; and in order to still our doubts, Maitland provides a detailed, though purely hypothetical, account of the steps by which their degradation was, or rather could have been, brought about.[2]

Such being the opposing theses, we have now to determine as best we can which of them is more likely to be true of Withington.

§10

LYSONS makes no mention of coins, but eight Roman coins found on the Withington villa-site are now in the Gloucester City Museum. The latest of them dates from the reign of the emperor Constans (333–50). There is however no reason to suppose that the villa was deserted any sooner than its neighbours. Coins of Gratian (375–83) have been unearthed at Compton Abdale, Combend, and Foxcote, and coins of Honorius (393–423) at Whittington and Wycomb. The Gallic mints which had been the principal source of supply ceased to make new issues after 395, and thereafter local issues, of which

[1] "The basis of Kentish society in Æthelberht's time was obviously the free peasant landholder, without claim to nobility, but subject to no lord but the king. . . . Throughout early English history society in every kingdom rested on men of this type." — Stenton, *Anglo-Saxon England*, pp. 274, 275. The pattern of the Old English social order in historic times "implies that it arose from mass migrations of free peasants, familiar with life in communities, accustomed to discussion in popular assemblies. . . . It is not the manor, but the community of free peasants, which forms the starting-point of English social history." — *ibid.*, p. 310.

[2] Maitland, *op. cit.*, pp. 318–26.

examples have been found at Lydney and Bourton-on-the-Water, took the place of the imperial coinage.[1] Lysons found that one compartment of the fourth-century Orpheus mosaic at Withington had been cut out, and a new border, which from its workmanship he judged to be of considerably later date, had been inserted in its place. Towards the close of the fourth century a hall was built on the east side of the Whittington villa and connected with the house by a corridor seven feet wide and thirty feet long. The fine mosaic pavement of this corridor lay intact, less than twenty inches underground, when the site was excavated a few years ago. Villas at Hucclecote and Bourton-on-the-Water are known to have been repaired at the very end of the fourth century.[2] Therefore, while the evidence is consistent with the supposition that monetary traffic dwindled, and perhaps in places gave way to a system of barter, it lends no support to the idea that the Cotswold villas were generally deserted by 400, or even by 450.

Nor is there any reason to suppose that the villa-estates were broken up when the houses themselves were abandoned. When the owner of a country house today, short of servants and unable to bear the expense of keeping up the fabric, resigns himself to quitting the ancestral home, he may move into a smaller house or into a metropolitan flat, but he does not necessarily put the estate up for sale: that final step may well be deferred until death duties, a form of taxation unknown in Roman Britain, force it upon his heir. So we may picture the Withington villa-owner, in the disturbed conditions of the sub-Roman period, withdrawing to the shelter of Corinium, and thenceforth paying only occasional visits to his old home, but continuing to draw an income from the estate.[3] For want of maintenance, the house would fall gradually into disrepair. It might after a while be invaded by tramps or squatters, who would light fires on the mosaic floors, as they did at Whittington, using the rafters for firewood; and the end of it all would be a conflagration leaving clear traces of itself in the mass of

[1] *Archaeological Journal*, xc, 1933, pp. 282–305, and xcii, 1935, p. 74; BGAS lvi, 1934, pp. 133–9.

[2] BGAS lv, 1933, pp. 329, 366; lvi, 1934, p. 108.

[3] Cf. T. D. Kendrick and C. F. C. Hawkes, *Archaeology in England and Wales*, London, 1932, p. 294.

burnt timber, melted lead, and broken walls that Lysons found when he dug up the site.

Abandoned by the imperial government, the island now lay exposed on all sides to the inroads of the barbarians from oversea. But at some date between 490 and 516 the Britons, who had rallied under the leadership of a certain Ambrosius Aurelianus, inflicted on the Saxons a defeat so crushing that forty or fifty years elapsed before they took up arms again. When Gildas wrote his diatribe, in the second quarter of the sixth century, the interval of peace remained unbroken. The earliest extant statement on the scene of the British victory places it near the mouth of the Severn.[1] If, as seems most likely, it defeated a Saxon attempt to penetrate the Cotswolds from the south, we need look no further for an explanation of the tranquillity that Cirencester and its neighbourhood enjoyed throughout this period.[2] But it would be a mistake to interpret the lull as a mere continuance and preservation of the *status quo*. Rather must we think of it as allowing Saxon colonists to establish themselves in appreciable numbers on the fringes of the region. A large Saxon cemetery at Fairford, in the upper Thames valley but only twelve miles from Withington as the crow flies, is generally accepted by archaeologists as dating from the first half of the sixth century.[3] Other Saxon graves of the same period have been found at Oddington, Kemble, and Avening.[4] To these we may quite probably add the Saxon interments at Foxcote.[5]

Thus at a time when Withington could well have been still producing wool and corn for the benefit of a non-resident British owner, Saxon settlers had already reached the valley of the lower Coln. In the eyes of Saxon war-lords the Cirencester district, with its ample sheep-walks and fertile plough-lands,

[1] An interpolation in one manuscript of Gildas reads: "qui [mons Badonicus] prope Sabrinum ostium habetur." "I feel convinced that the identification of Mons Badonicus with Bath or some point in that neighbourhood is the right one." — E. T. Leeds, *Antiquaries Journal*, XIII, 1933, p. 233n.

[2] Cf. R. H. Hodgkin, *History of the Anglo-Saxons*, Oxford, 1935, I, pp. 112, 122.

[3] G. Baldwin Brown, *The Arts in Early England*, London, 1903–37, III, p. 53; IV, pp. 662–5.

[4] *Ibid.*, IV, pp. 653, 658, 665.   [5] p. 39 *supra*.

offered itself as a rich prize, to be captured as soon as ever fortune should bless their arms again. But the time had not yet come, for Corinium still lay in British hands. The elective administration of the Roman *civitas* had disappeared, and at the time when Gildas wrote a British prince, Aurelius Caninus or Conanus, from his name perhaps a kinsman or descendant of Ambrosius Aurelianus, was reigning in the west midlands.[1] A generation later three princes with Celtic names appear as ruling the territory east of the lower Severn, and it seems more than probable that one of them had Cirencester for his capital.[2]

Then, in 577, a Saxon war-band led by Cuthwine and Ceawlin of Wessex captured Bath, stormed the Cotswold heights at Dyrham, and followed up the rout of the Britons by taking both Corinium and Gloucester. With this victory the dominion of the Cotswolds passed for ever out of British hands. It is probable that Cuthwine and Ceawlin rewarded their chief companions in arms with gifts of British estates. On the other hand, they may have contented themselves with laying the region under tribute.[3] What is certain is that their possession was very far from secure. The Britons might be crushed, but there were other competitors in the field, rival war-lords of Anglo-Saxon blood. In 628 Cirencester witnessed another clash of arms, this time between Cynegils of Wessex and the Mercian Penda. The treaty which ensued removed the Cotswolds permanently from the orbit of Wessex and into that of Mercia. There is every reason to believe that the principality of the Hwicce dates from this time, and was indeed Penda's own creation.[4]

Hitherto we have assumed that Withington in the Roman period was a private estate. It is natural to think of it as the property of a tribal magnate who could appreciate the amenities of Roman civilization. But there is another possibility of which we ought not to lose sight. Haverfield has told us that imperial domains administered by local procurators covered wide tracts in every province; and he found indications, which Collingwood regards as amounting to proof, that one at least of the

---

[1] Collingwood and Myres, *op. cit.*, p. 439n.; H. M. Chadwick and others, *Studies in Early British History*, Cambridge, 1954, pp. 55, 56.

[2] Stenton, *op. cit.*, p. 4; Hodgkin, *op. cit.*, I, p. 178.

[3] As Hodgkin surmises, *op. cit.*, I, p. 191.   [4] Stenton, *op. cit.*, p. 45.

villas in north Somerset belonged to this category.[1] We know that the Roman-British administration was directly interested in the supply of wool. It may be, therefore, that some of the Cotswold villa-estates were imperial property, managed by the emperor's bailiffs or lessees. In that case they could have passed into English hands without any violation of private rights. The Celtic princes who took up the reins after the collapse of imperial rule, and the Anglo-Saxon princes who displaced them, would merely have stepped into the position formerly occupied by the emperor. When we read in Domesday Book that the wool of the Cirencester sheep-flock was expressly reserved to the queen of England, we may begin to suspect that the arrangement had a long history behind it.[2]

In any case, it was not to the interest of either Saxon or Celt to make a desert of the Cotswolds. Why should they destroy the very prize for which they were contending? It is true that markets, in the disturbed conditions of the time, could hardly flourish, and we can well imagine that the trade in wool suffered a temporary eclipse. It is even possible that husbandry, for a generation or more, was reduced to a struggle for bare subsistence. But the chief sufferers, beyond any doubt, were the native aristocracy. Numbers of them probably fell in battle; for the survivors nothing remained, after Dyrham, but to collect such movable wealth as had not been plundered and retire into the still unconquered fastnesses beyond the Severn. The fact that *wealh*, or Welshman, came on Anglo-Saxon lips to be synonymous with slave need not mean, as some writers have supposed, that the conquerors reduced masses of noble and free-born Celts to servitude; rather it suggests that only the lower strata of the population normally remained on the spot when the new lords took possession.[3] For poor shepherds and ploughmen no retreat was possible. When trouble threatened, they might take to the shelter of the woods, but as soon as the danger

[1] F. Haverfield, *The Romanization of Roman Britain*, London, 1923, p. 64; *Victoria County History of Somerset*, I, 1906, pp. 311, 312; Collingwood and Myres, *op. cit.*, p. 224.

[2] DB I, p. 162b.

[3] We are speaking of Mercia, not of Wessex. The laws of Ine give a definite place to "Welsh" peasants and landowners in the social system of Wessex.

passed they would creep back to their fields and pastures and pick up the routine of husbandry again, because the only alternative was to die of hunger.

In that twilit period we may picture the British inhabitants of Withington accustoming themselves to the presence and learning to understand the speech of their new masters, just as their forefathers had perforce learnt to understand Latin. So far as can be seen, the conquerors made no attempt to interfere with their religion. The sacred Chi-Rho monogram, inscribed on four stones in the Chedworth villa, shows that Christianity had long since reached the valley of the Coln. Haverfield felt sure that if Cirencester were excavated as thoroughly as Silchester has been, it would be found to have had its Christian church.[1] The pagan revival of the fourth century was by now a thing of the past. St Patrick, the British-born apostle of Ireland, writing in the next century, takes it for granted that all his fellow-countrymen are Christians; and among the re-proaches which Gildas hurled at the Britons there is no imputa-tion of heathenism. In such a rural spot as Withington a burial-ground, a stone altar and cross, and a well for baptisms might be all the visible furniture of a religion which had now taken on a sternly ascetic cast. The clergy, no longer organized under the urban episcopate of Roman days, worked from monastic centres or hermitages as the spirit moved them. Even if we suppose their ministrations to have become intermittent or to have died away altogether — and in the circumstances of the time a progressive shortage of clergy is more than likely — the example of seventeenth-century Japan proves that Christian villages, bereft of priests and sacraments, could cling to their faith for generations, and this in face of a persecution fiercer than anything the Britons of Gloucestershire were called upon to endure.

In 654, according to the Anglo-Saxon Chronicle, "Penda perished, and the Mercians became Christians." To take the second part of this statement literally would be excessively naïve. When we recall the obstinate heathenism of their kins-

[1]*Archaeologia*, LXIX, 1920, p. 189. The acrostic "Rotas opera tenet Arepo sator," mentioned *ibid.*, p. 198, as having been found inscribed on a wall-plaster in the town, has since been explained as a Christian confession of faith, an anagram of "Pater noster." — BGAS LVII, 1935, p. 157.

men in Denmark and Frisia, the ease and speed with which the Anglo-Saxons were converted requires an explanation. It becomes intelligible if we suppose that the descendants of Woden who reigned over Mercia saw the wisdom of accepting a creed which had never lost its hold over the British population. Their Northumbrian overlords had set the example twenty-seven years before, when Edwin, the king who used to have Roman ensigns borne aloft before him, received baptism at York.[1] Northumbrian and Celtic influences dominated the official Christianity of Mercia for some years after the conversion. It was a former monk of Iona, Finan, bishop of Lindisfarne, who consecrated the first two bishops of Mercia, both of them Irishmen by birth.

The parish church of Withington is dedicated to St Michael the Archangel. No certain inference can be drawn from this fact; but since the cult of St Michael spread from Gaul to Celtic Britain in the seventh century, and since John of Beverley, towards the close of the century, could make his Lenten retreats in a "cemetery of St Michael the Archangel" near Hexham, it is at least possible that the graveyard in which we have pictured the inhabitants of Withington gathering for worship may already have borne the same dedication.[2]

§11

In the fourth generation after the battle of Dyrham, Ethelred of Mercia, co-founder with Oshere of the Withington minster, granted Henbury, down by the Severn shore, to the bishop of Worcester; and his charter of donation states expressly that by Henbury he means the estate of that name "with its ancient boundaries."[3] We have seen reason to believe that the Withington villa-estate also came through the sub-Roman period with its ancient boundaries intact. Its organization as a land-unit devoted mainly to wool-production, and in a lesser degree to

[1] Cf. M. Deanesley, 'Roman Traditionalist Influence among the Anglo-Saxons', EHR LVIII, 1943, pp. 129–46.

[2] Bede, *Historia Ecclesiastica*, ed. Plummer, Oxford, 1896, I, p. 283. An eighth-century charter (CS 246) refers to the church of St Michael at Bishop's Cleeve, Gloucestershire. In the adjoining county of Hereford thirty churches have the archangel as their patron.

[3] "Cum antiquis confiniis." — CS 75.

corn-growing; its population of servile and half-servile husbandmen; its religion; its pattern of fields and trackways: all
these reappear in the same light at the end of the dark interval
as before it.

Where strict proof is unattainable, we must content ourselves with an assessment of probabilities. We must also recognize that any conclusion we reach upon the problem of continuity in Gloucestershire may well be inapplicable to Sussex
or East Anglia. In Gloucestershire, as we have seen, a Celtic
dynasty, established after the collapse of Roman rule, paved the
way for Anglo-Saxon monarchy. The Celtic episcopate of
Diuma and his successors provided a similar halfway-house
between the church of the sub-Roman period and the Anglo-
Roman Christianity of Archbishop Theodore and the bishops
he installed at Worcester. Momentous as these transitions were,
they cannot be described as catastrophic. Above all, they entailed no break in the pastoral and agricultural economy of
villages like Withington.

One feature of the old order did indeed fail to survive. The
Latin, or more probably Welsh, name of Withington is ir-
recoverably lost. This circumstance provides the apostles of discontinuity with an argument which they regard as decisive.
We must however take leave to doubt whether their explanation of the fact is correct, and whether the inference they draw
from it can really counterbalance the mass of probabilities
pointing the other way.[1] It clearly will not do to say, as Mr
Lennard has said, that "the names of the British villages and
the Romano-British villas vanished because the villages and the
villas themselves disappeared."[2] The villas did not disappear.
Of the one at Whittington Mrs O'Neil has observed that "the
ruins of the Roman house must have been visible and known
for centuries."[3] We are perfectly justified in applying the same
remark to Withington and many another Gloucestershire villa.
Furthermore, British place-names were remembered and used
long after the coming of the Saxons. To give one example,

[1] On the fallibility of the argument from place-names in this context, see
Collingwood and Myres, *op. cit.*, p. 427.

[2] *Wirtschaft und Kultur: Festschrift zum 70. Geburtstag von Alfons Dopsch*,
Baden bei Wien, 1938, p. 63.

[3] BGAS LXXI, 1952, p. 23.

Susibre, the British name of a hill sixteen miles from Withington, is used in a Mercian charter dated 718;[1] after that — but how soon after we cannot say — it disappears. The Anglo-Saxon occupation of the Cotswolds was evidently followed by a prolonged bilingual phase; and though the language of the politically dominant race gradually superseded that of the Britons, it did not do so until there had been ample time for British estates to be taken over in working order. Nor must we suppose that the triumph was either complete or wholly one-sided. The Saxon settlers invented a name of their own for the river Coln. This name, Tillath or Tillnoth, appears in the two earliest Withington charters, and in the Anglo-Saxon perambulation of the estate.[2] Then it vanishes, and the Celtic or pre-Celtic name takes its place. If the disappearance of Withington's British name proves a total breach with the Roman and British past, what inference are we to draw from the disappearance of the Saxon river-name?

The argument from place-names is regularly pressed into service by those historians who wish to empty the countryside of its British inhabitants, and thus to make room for a population of free Saxon peasants. That there were free Saxon peasants nobody will deny; the documents bear plentiful witness to their presence both before and after the Norman conquest. The *Rectitudines Singularum Personarum*, an eleventh-century treatise on social classes, refers to them as *geneatas*, and states that the conditions of their tenure vary between one manor and another.[3] If a conjecture about their antecedents is permissible, we may suppose them descended from the rank and file of the Saxon conquerors, the non-noble members of Ceawlin's war-band, or Penda's. We may also, if we are feeling generous, endow each of them with as much as a hide of land. We have already met them in the Domesday and later surveys; they figure there as holding free tenements in Withington, or rather in the hamlets, and serving the lord of the manor when required in the capacity of mounted retainers. There are never

[1] CS 139.
[2] *Tillath* in CS 156; *Tillnoth* in CS 217; *Tilnoth* in CS 299. Ekwall considers it "a most singular name," and thinks it means 'the useful one'. — *English River-Names*, Oxford, 1928, p. 408.
[3] EHD II, p. 813.

more than a few of them in the manor. They form an upper stratum of the peasantry: an *élite* or, as Professor Stenton puts it, a peasant aristocracy.[1]

Were they ever more numerous? If we are to believe the textbooks, they formed at one time — say in the seventh century[2] — the main body of the rural population. The textbooks here follow Maitland, who insists on peopling the countryside with "large masses of free peasants," and refers continually to "a large class of peasant proprietors," "free men who with their own labour tilled their own soil."[3] In course of time, the typical holding of the peasant proprietor somehow becomes reduced from a hide to a quarter-hide, the virgate or yardland of the manorial surveys; and the peasant himself, through a combination of personal misfortune and oppression by territorial magnates like the bishop of Worcester, sinks down to the servile condition in which we find him when the curtain goes up again in the twelfth century.

Such, in brief, is the history of the Anglo-Saxon peasant, as conventionally recounted. The picture it draws of his original state, decline, and fall is now firmly embedded not only in historical literature but even in our dictionaries.[4] And yet no one so far has denied that in the Roman period estates like Withington were peopled chiefly by slaves and *coloni*. No one denies that the yardlanders of the later manor were serfs. Is it plausible to sweep away the servile population of the villa-estate and put in their place a "large mass of free peasants," only to finish up with a tenantry as servile as before? *Entia non sunt multiplicanda praeter necessitatem.* The rule which forbids us to multiply entities without need is just as valid for historical logic as for ontology. Unluckily the Mercian codes of law have

---

[1] Stenton, *op. cit.*, pp. 466, 468.   [2] Maitland, *op. cit.*, p. 326.

[3] *Ibid.*, pp. 221, 223, 323.

[4] See the Oxford English Dictionary, s.v. churl. In defiance of etymology the English Place-Name Society and Ekwall persistently translate the Anglo-Saxon *ceorl* as 'free peasant'. The word really means no more than peasant. As H. M. Chadwick pointed out long ago, it is a generic term, applied in some texts to the free *geneat*, in others to the servile *gebur*, and in others again to both together. — *Studies on Anglo-Saxon Institutions*, Cambridge, 1905, pp. 86, 87, 137. Alfred the Great, in his translation of Orosius, uses *ceorl* as equivalent to *libertinus*, a freedman or manumitted slave. — *King Alfred's Orosius*, ed. H. Sweet, Early Eng. Text Soc., 79, 1883, p. 162.

not survived, and we have no statistical record earlier than Domesday Book. To assess the probabilities, therefore, we must look at other evidence.

It will be remembered that Withington is described in the earliest charters as a "land of twenty *cassati*." For an explanation of this term we can fortunately invoke the highest contemporary authority in Christendom. A Frankish council held in 744 imposed a tax of twelve pence a year on each *casata* for the support of the churches; and Pope Zacharias, writing to congratulate St Boniface on this decree, refers to the tax as "twelve pence from each servile household" (*ab unoquoque conjugio servorum*).[1] The church-tax will be paid, of course, by actual households; but when Withington is described as a land of twenty *cassati*, we are not to suppose that this is a precise enumeration of its inhabitants at any given date: it is an assessment imposed primarily for secular purposes, a 'rateable value', as it were, expressed in terms of the population the estate is deemed capable of supporting. Thus, when granting Fladbury to the bishop of Worcester, Ethelred of Mercia says in so many words that it is a land with a *capacity* of forty-four *cassati*.[2] But church and state alike in the eighth century take it for granted that the villages are peopled, not exclusively indeed, but mainly and typically by husbandmen of servile condition.

Against this generalization Maitland hinted, rather than affirmed, that the word perhaps took on a different meaning when it crossed the English Channel. He also urged other objections which need not be discussed here.[3] It is enough to note that they were wholly negative in character, and that even

---

[1] E. Lesne, *Histoire de la Propriété Ecclésiastique en France*, II, Lille, 1922 p. 43. The usual form in Anglo-Saxon charters is *cassati*, *cassatos*, with variants *casatos* (CS 103, 113, 245) and genitive *cassatuum* (CS 100, 155); but the feminine is also found, e.g. *casatas* (CS 82), *cassatas* (CS 85, 87, 230), and once at least a neuter (*sunt* XVI *casata*, CS 197).

[2] "terram XLIIII cassatorum capacem," CS 76.

[3] *Domesday Book and Beyond*, pp. 327–40. As proof that continental terminology was inapplicable to Anglo-Saxon conditions, Vinogradoff, *Growth of the Manor*, p. 243, adduces the expression *terra unius familiae*, which, he says, is not used in the same sense abroad, but "alternates with hide and *hiwisc* in the Anglo-Saxon charters." This is quite untrue. Of the 1,354 texts in Birch's *Cartularium*, only three (CS 179, 180, and the doubtful 696) describe an estate in terms of *familiae*.

if they could be sustained, they would fall very far short of demonstrating the preponderance of those free landowning peasants with whom Maitland wished to populate the country-side. Vinogradoff, in his *Villainage in England*, tried to build up a more positive argument. Scraps of manorial usage and of legal theory, culled from a variety of sources, all of post-Norman date, provided the bulk of his evidence.[1] The fact on which he laid most stress was the privileged condition of the peasants on the ancient demesnes of the crown: a status which Vinogradoff believed to have "roots extending far into Anglo-Saxon antiquity."[2] It is safe to say that no one believes this now, for Professor Hoyt has shown beyond possibility of contradiction that the ancient demesne and the privileges of its tenants were never heard of before the twelfth century.[3]

In a later work Vinogradoff returned to the subject, armed with a new item of evidence. This was a passage in the Domesday of Worcestershire. The passage states that the abbey of Pershore was entitled to receive church-scot at Martinmas from three hundred hides, at the rate of one load of corn from every hide in which a franklin, or free peasant, dwelt. If the franklin had more than one hide, he was not to be liable for the rest. Upon this Vinogradoff observes: "There are few passages in Domesday so replete with information as this . . . The repartition of church-scot is very characteristic; it is imposed on the hides, and it is assumed that these hides are normally held by franklins, every one being possessed of one hide or more. The exemption of the extra hides in a franklin's possession supposes two things — firstly, that the tax was levied from the free households as such, and secondly, that the accumulation of

---

[1] Bracton holds that a villein can bring a civil action against his lord; this must be "a survival of a time when some part of the peasantry had not been surrendered to the lord's discretion." — *op. cit.*, p. 75. The privileges of ancient demesne are another survival of primitive freedom. — *ibid.*, pp. 89–126. The hundred looks like "an organization based on the freedom of the mass of the people." — *ibid.*, p. 195. Domesday Book ignores the free customs of [later] Kent: therefore there may well have been equally free customs in other shires of which Domesday tells us nothing. — *ibid.*, p. 208. For Vinogradoff's own summary of these arguments, see *ibid.*, p. 218.

[2] P. Vinogradoff, *English Society in the Eleventh Century*, p. 474.

[3] R. S. Hoyt, *The Royal Demesne in English Constitutional History*, Ithaca (N.Y.), 1950, especially pp. 50, 51, 173, 180–92, 204–7.

several hides in one free household was an exception at the time when the tax arose. Anyhow[!], we see clearly the framework of ancient English society in the west underlying the superstructure of the landlordships which towers over it. It is composed of households of the size of one hide on the average," and the heads of these households are free peasant proprietors.[1]

Is it necessary to point out that the passage will not bear this weight of inference? When the customs of Withington were put into writing about a hundred years after Domesday, it was recorded that in the harvest season every hide was to find one wagon for the carriage of the bishop's hay and corn.[2] Does this mean that the bishop's tenants occupied, or had formerly occupied, holdings of one hide apiece? Clearly not, for the same record expresses all other tenurial obligations in terms of yardlands. The typical holding was therefore only a quarter-hide, and the solitary reference to a hide means nothing more than that every four yardlanders were expected to provide one wagon between them. Very probably they took it in turns.[3] The fuller statement of customs drawn up in 1299 records the obligation of sundry free tenants to pay church-scot. It also tells us that each customary tenant owed church-scot at the rate of one crannock of wheat from every yardland.[4] Thus the liability rested on both free and servile tenants. And it had done so for centuries: the fact emerges clearly from the Worcester-shire Domesday. There we read that the bishop is entitled to church-scot at the rate of one load of the best corn from each hide of land, *"free or villein."*[5] In the corresponding entry for Pershore the villein hides are not mentioned because two of the three hundred hides in question belong to another abbey, Westminster, and it is taken for granted that each abbot will

[1] *English Society in the Eleventh Century*, p. 419.   [2] *Red Book*, p. 367.
[3] Cf. *ibid.*, pp. 293, 352, where the obligation of the yardlanders of Tredington and Bishop's Cleeve to provide cart-loads of firewood and wagons for the hay-crop is assessed by half-hides.
[4] *Ibid.*, p. 357.
[5] DB I, p. 174a. Similarly the church of Lambourn claimed a sester of corn as church-scot from every *geneat*, and the same quantity from every *gebur*. — R p. 240. Cf. also the Countess Goda's gift to Winchcombe Abbey of the church-scot from 25 villein yardlands at Hawling. — *Landboc sive Registrum Mon. de Winchelcumba*, ed. D. Royce, Exeter, 1903, I, p. 219.

collect the tax from his own villeins.[1] Any churchman could be trusted to make his serf pay this due, but it needed a royal charter or a legislative enactment to impose the liability upon freeholders. The author of the *Rectitudines* makes this plain. After enumerating the fundamental obligations from which not even the highest and freest landowner is exempt, he continues: "On many estates further dues arise *on the king's order.*" And among these "further dues" he expressly mentions church-scot.[2]

It is instructive to compare Vinogradoff's manipulation of the Domesday record and later evidence with the candid admission of a more recent scholar. In his valuable study of early Kentish institutions J. E. A. Jolliffe says nothing of the slaves and the *laetas* or freedmen who appear in the earliest Kentish laws. If words are to bear their normal meaning, these lowly toilers must have constituted the real "basis" of rural society in seventh-century Kent. By sedulously ignoring their existence, Jolliffe was able to convince himself and many of his readers that "most men were free," that the free peasants formed "the main stock of the folk," and that "from this basis in the group of folk-free kinsmen all society rose as by the natural growth of a physical body."[3] Jolliffe returned to the subject in a later essay; but now, when he contemplated the serfdom of central England, with its organization bespeaking a landlordship which had existed from the beginning, he felt constrained to admit that it stood out as "the most formidable obstacle to the acceptance of organized freedom as the sole basis of English history." Finding it "hard to look upon the midland manor as the product of evolution, and equally hard to envisage the society of lords and serfs who could have created such a settlement in the sixth century," he gave up the problem as insoluble.[4]

And yet perhaps a solution is not unattainable. At present the

---

[1] Cf. the Northumbrian Priests' Law, § 59, which provides that if any villager fails to pay Peter's Pence, his landlord is to pay it for him and impound the villager's ox. — EHD I, p. 438.

[2] EHD II, p. 813, where church-scot is translated as "church dues."

[3] J. E. A. Jolliffe, *Pre-Feudal England*, Oxford, 1933, pp. 40, 71, 120.

[4] *Oxford Essays in Medieval History presented to H. E. Salter*, Oxford, 1934, pp. 27, 28.

social history of Anglo-Saxon England stands in obvious and urgent need of revision. When the task is undertaken, it will be advisable to focus attention in the first instance not on the upper ranks of the peasantry, but on the rural proletariat, the *wealas*, *theowas*, and *geburas*. Given, as a legacy from the sub-Roman period, a labouring population of unfree, Celtic-speaking natives, the question arises: over how many generations would their stock be likely to perpetuate itself? No intelligent slave-owner has ever allowed his slaves to breed without restriction. If the native stock dwindled, its place could be filled easily enough by captives of the same blood and speech as the dominant race, for the Anglo-Saxon kingdoms were frequently at war with one another, and had no compunction about enslaving their prisoners.[1] Might not a gradual but complete replacement of this sort account for the predominantly Anglo-Saxon character of our place-names? And then, as we trace the lines of social evolution down into the later Saxon period and beyond it, we must ask how far the fully developed theory and practice of villeinage reflects the influence of the servile midlands, and how far that of the possibly freer south and east?

To any scholar ambitious of bringing new light into this dark tract of history the estates of the see of Worcester, with their continuity of ownership and wealth of records extending over some twelve hundred years, offer themselves as a most promising field of investigation. A detailed study of the group as a whole, using the modern technique of local history, would certainly uncover many secrets, and might resolve some at least of those perplexities with which the beginnings of English society are still surrounded.[2]

[1] Cf. the letter of Brihtwold, archbishop of Canterbury, to the bishop of Sherborne, concerning the ransom of a Kentish girl who had been carried off to Wessex and enslaved, probably during Ine's conflict with the men of Kent. — EHD I, p. 731.

[2] There are of course many sites beyond the Worcester orbit which might well repay study. Cassington in Oxfordshire has been suggested by Dr W. G. Hoskins, and two Surrey villages, Ashtead and Ewell, by Mr R. C. W. Cox.

MERCIANS AND WELSH

IT IS all too easy for us to overlook the historical importance of Mercia. There are no records from the midland kingdom to set beside the annals and chronicles that have come down to us from Wessex. The Mercian law-codes have perished. In the turmoil of the Danish invasions it was not Mercia but Wessex that proved its capacity for survival and lived on to unite all England under a single monarchy. The last king of Mercia disappeared from history towards the close of the ninth century; a descendant of the West Saxon royal line occupies the English throne today. And yet if there had been no Mercian realm, our history might have taken a very different course. Wessex provided the spring-board, but Alfred the Great and his successors could hardly have made such triumphant headway against the Danes if they had not found in the midlands the shattered remnants of a once powerful English state, and made of them a series of stepping-stones towards the reconquest of the Danish provinces.

In one important respect Mercia differed from its Northumbrian and West Saxon rivals. The fighting kings of Wessex gradually pushed their dominion westward all the way to Land's End. The corresponding movement in the north cannot be traced in detail, but Stenton has adduced the ancient place-names of Cumberland and Lancashire as suggesting that King Æthelfrith of Northumbria (592–616) could have ridden from the Solway to the Mersey through territory occupied by his own people.[1] Alone of the three kingdoms, Mercia never reached the western sea. Hence it was always exposed to the danger of a war on two fronts. That this weakness might in the end be fatal is obvious; what is not so clear is why the Britons waited so long to make their final stand. In the end, as we know, they arrested the Mercian advance decisively enough to leave the frontier between Wales and England a permanent

[1] F. M. Stenton, *Anglo-Saxon England*, p. 78.

line on our maps to this day; but how came they ever to let their enemies cross the Severn?

In one of his last contributions to early English history that excellent scholar and archaeologist F. T. Wainwright spoke of it as "inevitable" that the Mercians and the Welsh should be enemies. "This relationship," according to him, "had been determined by proximity since the time when they first came into contact with each other."[1] Wainwright's dictum stands in marked contrast with what he himself had written twenty years before when discussing the Anglian settlement of Lancashire. Then he was quite ready to believe that in the earliest phase of the settlement the two races, Britons and English, dwelt side by side in peace.[2] No one who has ever stood at the point where Offa's Dyke comes to a dramatic finish on top of a cliff one hundred feet above the Severn after crossing miles and miles of difficult country between the Severn and the Dee is likely to under-estimate the force of Mercian-Welsh antagonism. And very recently we have been told that "in any consideration of the relations between the English and the Welsh in the Marches of Wales it is customary and almost inevitable to begin with Offa's Dyke."[3] But the Dyke was built in the last years of the eighth century, by which time Mercia was the dominant power in south Britain. Perhaps Offa's predecessors had not always been at odds with the Welsh. Would it not be wiser to begin at the beginning?

Until the second quarter of the seventh century the Mercians, an obscure people settled in the valley of the Trent, politically dependent upon the northern kingdom of Deira, had made no mark whatever upon English history. Bede refers in passing to one of their kings; otherwise we should hardly know of their existence.[4] But in 628, led by an adventurer named Penda, who was probably a member of their royal house, they broke into the region of the lower Severn. This had been conquered in 577 by the men of Wessex, but Penda succeeded in driving the West Saxons out. One consequence of his victory was the establishment of an Anglian principality, the kingdom of the

---

[1] *The Anglo-Saxons*, ed. P. Clemoes, 1959, p. 66.
[2] *Trans. Historic Soc. of Lancashire and Cheshire*, XCIII, 1941, pp. 28, 29.
[3] *Angles and Britons*, Cardiff, 1963, p. 85.
[4] Bede, *Hist. Eccl.*, II, 14; Nennius, in EHD I, p. 238.

Hwicce, with a ruling family which for the next hundred and fifty years reigned over Gloucestershire, Worcestershire, and part of Warwickshire as Mercian under-kings.[1] In 633 Penda turned northward, and in alliance with Cadwallon of Gwynedd, the most powerful Welsh king of the day, ravaged Deira and slew its king.

This campaign, and the unrecorded parleys which led up to it, inaugurated a Mercian-Welsh relationship which held good for the remainder of the century. Throughout a lifetime of strenuous warfare Penda never fought against the Welsh. Heathen as he was, claiming descent from Woden, he allied himself with the Christian Welsh because in his eyes as in theirs the real enemies were the Anglian dynasts of Northumbria. His Deiran overlord, King Edwin, had annexed the British kingdom of Elmet and invaded north Wales. While his reign lasted, Edwin was by far the most powerful ruler in the island. In public he made a point of having the insignia of Roman office borne aloft before him, and in 627 he caused himself to be baptized by a Roman missionary in the Roman city of York. To the Welsh princes it may well have seemed that this barbarian, whose forebears had been hired by theirs to guard the north-east coast, was presumptuously setting himself up as the equal or more than the equal of the civilized heirs of Rome. After Edwin's overthrow by the combined forces of Penda and Cadwallon, Oswald of Bernicia defeated Cadwallon and united the two Northumbrian kingdoms under his own sway. But in 641 Penda defeated Oswald at the battle of Maserfelth, a place better known as Oswestry. The results of this battle will appear in the sequel.

Geoffrey of Monmouth represents Cadwallon as debating with his counsellors whether or not to attack Oswald's brother and successor Oswiu with Penda's help. The issue is decided by the arguments of Margadud, king of Dyfed, who speaks as follows. "My lord, seeing that it has been your intention to drive the whole English race out of Britain, why turn aside now from your purpose and suffer them to live in peace in our midst? Come now! at least allow them to fall out among them-

[1] H. P. R. Finberg, *The Early Charters of the West Midlands*, Leicester, 1961, pp. 167–80.

selves and slay one another until they shall have exterminated themselves from our country ... Give Penda leave without more ado to make war upon Oswiu, so that they may destroy each other in civil strife and our island be rid of them for good and all."[1]

That Margadud delivered himself of this oration is more than we have any call to believe. Nevertheless the sentiments put into his mouth by the great romancer in all probability reflect faithfully enough the views of Cadwallon and his advisers. Why should they reject the services of a heathen rascal who had got together a useful war-band and was more than willing to cut the throats of his fellow barbarians? It might even be worth while to reward him. The presence of Anglian settlers on the Welsh border might be irksome, but at least it would help to keep the Northumbrians out. Moreover, a good Welshman, by the grace of God and if necessary with the help of a deathbed repentance, could look forward to an eternity free from any contact with these ruffians. For Penda, unimpressed by what he saw of Christianity among the Welsh, remained a heathen to the last, though he saw the expediency of allowing his children to receive baptism. It is not altogether surprising that the next generation of Mercians took their Christianity from other than Welsh sources — from Ireland and from Iona, either directly or through Lindisfarne.

In 655 Oswiu of Northumbria routed the confederate host led by Penda and the king of Gwynedd in a great battle which left the Mercian war-lord dead upon the field. By that time Penda had established a chain of principalities across the midlands, none of them powerful enough in itself to alarm his Welsh allies, but linked by family ties and united under Penda's own military command. He had set up his eldest son Peada as king over the Middle Angles. His creation of the kingdom of the Hwicce has already been mentioned. The history of this kingdom need not detain us now; it has been reconstructed in outline elsewhere from a series of charters long preserved at Worcester Cathedral. Had the church of Hereford kept its early records equally well, we should probably know much

---

[1] *The Historia Regum Britanniae of Geoffrey of Monmouth*, ed. A. Griscom, 1929, pp. 527, 528.

more than we do about a third Anglian principality, the kingdom of the Magonsæte. But Hereford Cathedral was sacked and burnt in 1055; it is therefore not surprising that until recently the kingdom and its rulers were little more than names. Since its territory embraced Herefordshire and Shropshire, it is obviously of cardinal importance in the early history of the Welsh border. Fortunately a little fresh light has been thrown upon it by documents which until recently escaped the notice of historians.

The new material comes to us from Much Wenlock. Here, about the year 680, a convent of monks and nuns was established on a site purchased from Merewalh, the first recorded king of the Magonsæte; and in due time Merewalh's daughter Mildburg became its abbess. The community preserved its corporate identity through all the vicissitudes of the next four hundred years, but was disbanded shortly after 1066 by the Norman earl of Shrewsbury, who installed in its place a colony of Cluniac monks from La Charité-sur-Loire. A year or two later the Cluniacs engaged Goscelin, the most competent professional hagiographer of the day, to write the life of Mildburg. Goscelin collected the ancient traditions of the house from survivors of the pre-Norman community, and transcribed *verbatim* a document called St Mildburg's Testament. This includes the substance of five charters drawn up in Mildburg's lifetime. Some of the charters are given in full, and stand up well to every critical test. The remainder of the Life is still unpublished.[1] It is largely a narrative of miraculous occurrences, eked out with pious rhetoric; but the strictly biographical particulars of Mildburg and her family, based as they are upon authentic charters and the oral traditions of an ancient corporate body, deserve respect, the more so as at no point do they conflict with other evidence.

Goscelin tells us that Mildburg's father Merewalh was Penda's third son. On this point local tradition supports the tenth-century genealogy of the Mercian kings in the *Liber Vitae* of Hyde. It is necessary to emphasize the fact that Merewalh's descent from Penda is vouched for by the very sources

[1] BM Add. MS. 34,633. For a critical edition of the Testament see H. P. R. Finberg, *op. cit.*, pp. 197–216.

on which we depend for knowledge of his existence. Yet the relationship has been called in question by no less an authority than Sir Frank Stenton. He objects, first, that no other names beginning with M occur in the Mercian family tree. To this it may be answered that other names in the genealogy, names which no one questions, have initials which occur only once: for instance, Thingfrith, father of Offa the Great. Stenton remarks, further, that the names current in Merewalh's family — Merchelm, Mildfrith, Mildburg, Mildthryth, Mildgith, and Merefin — alliterate with the name Magonsætan, given to the people settled round Magana, now Maund, seven miles south-east of Leominster. He thinks this "suggests very strongly that they had a claim to rule in their own right over this people, and that originally they were independent of the Mercian kings."[1] But in fact the name Magonsætan is first recorded in 811,[2] and there is no evidence that it was used in Merewalh's time; indeed, the older sources name the people of his realm the "western Hecani."[3] Moreover, the argument cuts both ways, for according to Ekwall the first element in Merchelm, the name of Merewalh's eldest son, is *Merce*, meaning Mercians.[4] We know now that all the other recorded members of the family were Merewalh's children, and Stenton has himself remarked that "the practice of giving to a child a name which alliterates with that of his father was common among the Germanic peoples."[5]

Goscelin states that Merewalh remained a pagan like his father until 660, when a Northumbrian missionary named Eadfrith made a Christian of him. The king then founded a church at Leominster, where he was residing at the time, and placed Eadfrith in charge of it. Subsequently he established a number of other churches, and, as we have seen, provided a site at Wenlock for the monastery of which his daughter became abbess.

From the foregoing details it is clear that the territory over which Merewalh reigned extended from the Wye to the

---

[1] *Anglo-Saxon England*, p. 47n. [2] CS 332.
[3] H. P. R. Finberg, *op. cit.*, p. 217n.
[4] *Oxford Dictionary of English Place-Names*, s.v. Marchamley.
[5] Royal Commission on Historical Monuments, *Herefordshire*, III, 1934, p. lvi.

Wrekin. On the east it presumably marched with the kingdom of the Hwicce, which was co-extensive with the diocese of Worcester. Analogy suggests that the kingdom of the Western Hecani or Magonsæte coincided with the diocese of Hereford; and if so, it was bounded on the west by the forests of Clun and Radnor. Stenton has called attention to the archaic place-name Burlingjobb, borne by a hamlet near Radnor, a name "as ancient in type as any place-name in the western midlands," and, as such, good evidence of very early Anglian settlement in what is now Radnorshire.[1]

The only signs of defensive work along this western frontier are eight short dykes which have been examined by Sir Cyril Fox. Five of these are thrown across the ridgeways which lead from the central highlands of Wales towards the English midlands; each of the other three is sited at the western end of a valley suitable for arable or pastoral husbandry. It is not certain that they are older than Offa's Dyke, and Fox considers them to represent private efforts rather than a political frontier.[2]

Now the existence on the Welsh border of a little kingdom ruled by an Anglian dynasty as early as the second half of the seventh century is a fact deserving close attention. It has implications which have not been squarely faced by our historians. In particular, there is the problem of its origin. We hear of no earlier king than Merewalh. What circumstances had set him up as ruler over this delectable countryside?

The Roman-British canton or *civitas* of the Cornovii must have included some if not all of the territory which later became Merewalh's, for its capital lay at Viroconium, only seven miles from Wenlock. After the collapse of Roman administration a British kingdom of Powys established itself in central Wales and Shropshire.[3] One of its princes lost his life at the battle of Chester (*c.* 613); then silence falls over Powys until the ninth century.[4] In the meantime, Oswald of Northumbria

[1] *Anglo-Saxon England*, p. 212.
[2] C. Fox, *Offa's Dyke*, 1955, pp. 160–68.
[3] H. M. Chadwick attributes the foundation of the kingdom to Vortigern, and believes that it was originally coextensive with the *civitas Cornoviorum*. — *Studies in Early British History*, Cambridge, 1954, p. 47.
[4] G. P. Jones, 'Notes on the Political History of Early Powys', *Archaeologia Cambrensis*, LXXXV, 1930, pp. 131–43.

was defeated by Penda and Cadwallon at the battle of Maserfelth in 641; and in the following generation we find a son of
Penda reigning in Shropshire.

Sir John Lloyd, in his classic *History of Wales*, says: "No
record has been preserved of the English conquest of Cheshire,
Shropshire, or Herefordshire."[1] But is it certain that any such
conquest took place? In our picture of the Anglian settlement
have we left enough room for political bargaining and treaty
arrangements? May not the silence remarked by Lloyd be
explicable in some such terms?

If the traditional identification of Maserfelth with Oswestry
is correct — and there seems no reason to doubt it — we
can at any rate see what the Northumbrian king was doing
there. He was engaged in what would nowadays be called a
preventive campaign, designed to split the dangerous coalition
between Mercians and Welsh. He failed, and it looks as if the
establishment of Merewalh's principality followed soon after
his defeat. Since the political history of Powys at this period is
altogether blank, we cannot know how far its rulers acquiesced
in the loss of Shropshire. They may have considered that
a small and relatively weak Anglian principality on their
eastern frontier would be no danger to themselves but
would ensure the continued assistance of Penda and his
heirs against the still formidable Northumbrian power.
All that can be said with assurance is that Cadwallon of
Gwynedd, the paramount Welsh ruler at the time, was in
quite a strong enough position to strike a bargain with his
Mercian ally, even if necessary at the expense of a Welsh
neighbour.

The population over which King Merewalh ruled must
have been predominantly Welsh in blood and speech. Some
three miles beyond the frontier dividing his principality from
that of the Hwicce is a village named Pensax, or 'hill of the
Saxons'. A place-name like that clearly bespeaks a surrounding
population of Welsh-speaking Britons. Wininicas, the original
name of the place acquired from Merewalh for the building
of his daughter's minster, has for its first element the Welsh

---

[1] Lloyd, *History of Wales from the Earliest Times to the Edwardian Conquest*,
1911, I, p. 195.

gwyn, meaning 'white', and the same element reappears in the wholly Welsh name Wenlock ('white monastery') which superseded it in the tenth century.[1] A study of the dialect peculiar to the border shires until recently has shown that the linguistic frontier between English and Welsh ran from a point between Ellesmere and Oswestry to Upton Magna, about two miles east of Shrewsbury, thence along the Severn to Bewdley, and thence to Much Cowarne, eight miles northeast of Hereford. West of this line the dialect bears marked peculiarities which can only be explained by the descent of its speakers from speakers of Welsh. The English of the region, says the author of the study quoted here, "was always a Welsh English."[2]

It appears that when the foundations had been laid at Wenlock, an abbess with a Frankish name, Liobsynde, was brought in to supervise the beginnings of conventual life until such time as the king's young daughter Mildburg should be experienced enough to take charge. The endowment consisted at this time of 97 hides round Wenlock, 5 hides at Magana (now Maund), 30 hides in the region of "Lydas" (probably Lyde in Herefordshire), and — significantly — 12 hides by the River Monnow. This last was not to be the minster's only Welsh possession. Goscelin states that Mildburg used frequently to visit a property she had at a place called Lanchmylien, where she was held in great veneration by the natives both during and after her lifetime. This place can be securely identified with the "Lanbylien" of the *Taxatio Ecclesiastica*, now Llanfillo, a village five miles north-east of Brecon. The parish church there is one of the comparatively rare Welsh churches dedicated to an Anglo-Saxon saint, and the only one dedicated to St Mildburg. The modern form of the place-name bears out the suggestion of the learned Bollandist Père Grosjean that for "Lanbylien" we should read Lanbylieu, and that in this *lan* Mildburg has supplanted an original Welsh patroness, Belyeu or Belyau, one of

[1] Since the publication of my *Early Charters of the West Midlands* it has been ascertained that "Wininicas" and "Wininicensis" are the correct readings of the place-name both in CS 587 and in the Life of Mildburg. The footnote on p. 201 of that work, therefore, requires correction.

[2] Alexander J. Ellis, 'On the Delimitation of the English and Welsh Languages', *Y Cymmrodor*, v, 1882, pp. 173–208, especially pp. 185–8.

the legendary daughters of the king from whom Brecon derives its name.[1]

The picture that begins to emerge of conditions on the Welsh border in the second half of the seventh century is clearly not one of unrelenting hostility between Welsh and English. An Anglian dynasty reigning over a preponderantly Welsh-speaking population, planting English settlers in what is now Radnorshire, and endowing the minster at Wenlock with lands in the valley of the Monnow, could scarcely have maintained itself in the teeth of Welsh opposition. Nor do we hear of any opposition from Wales; on the contrary, the records point to a state of peaceful coexistence along the border, with intervals of comradeship in battle against the Northumbrian foe.

After the death of Penda and an interregnum lasting three years, his son Wulfhere succeeded to the Mercian kingship. At different times Wulfhere fought against the Northumbrians, the West Saxons, and the Jutes of Hampshire. His successor Ethelred, another son of Penda, fought the Northumbrians and the men of Kent. Neither of these kings was ever rash enough to engage in a war on two fronts. At no time did they behave as if there were any danger of a stab in the back from Wales.

Meanwhile their kinsmen went on reigning undisturbed in the border country. Merewalh left two sons, Merchelm, whose name survives in *Marcham*ley, a village five miles east of Wem, and Mildfrith. It seems that these two succeeded their father and reigned jointly over his principality, for together they executed a charter at some date before 704 granting 63 hides of land in various parts of Shropshire to the minster at Wenlock. Mildfrith, who apparently outlived his brother, was remembered by the clergy of Hereford as the founder of their cathedral church, and he was certainly buried there.[2] It is probable that the ecclesiastical centre of the principality had been at Leominster until Mildfrith fixed the see where it has ever since remained.

A charter ostensibly granted by King Wulfhere in 664 to the newly founded abbey of Medeshamstede names four places in

---

[1] *Analecta Bollandiana*, LXXIX, 1961, p. 165, anticipated by J. Fisher in *Trans. Hon. Soc. Cymmrodorion*, 1906-7, p. 107.

[2] H. P. R. Finberg, *op. cit.*, pp. 221-23.

Shropshire among the possessions of the house.[1] The charter is unquestionably spurious, but Stenton has argued convincingly that its list of possessions must be founded upon early and authentic records.[2] Medeshamstede, the later Peterborough, seems to have been the principal centre of clerical education in seventh-century Mercia, and to have sent out missionaries in all directions. Cosford, Shifnal, Wattlesborough, and Lizard, the four Shropshire places named in the charter, are certainly a long way from Peterborough, but Mildburg's convent at Wenlock is now known to have been a daughter-house of the famous East Anglian monastery founded by St Botulf in 654. Evidently the Anglians of Shropshire were prepared to look far afield for clergy of their own race and speech.

The charter by which the abbot of St Botulf's put Mildburg in possession of the Wenlock endowments was confirmed by her uncle, Ethelred of Mercia, and in the charter by which Merchelm and Mildfrith increased the endowments Ethelred's consent is underlined. By 704, when Ethelred relinquished his throne and retired into a monastery, Mercia had ceased to be the loose confederation of principalities which Penda had bequeathed to his successors. With its western flank secured by a good understanding with the Welsh, it was now a strong centralized monarchy, destined soon to become the paramount power in southern England. The growth of the central authority entailed a corresponding diminution in the status of the minor dynasties. There are charters in which it is possible to see traces of a system by which a *comes*, attached to a local ruler's court, exercised a restraining influence in the interests of the central power, rather like the British 'residents' accredited before 1947 to the Indian maharajahs. Thus, in 693, Oshere, king of the Hwicce, makes a grant of land "with the consent of my *comes* Cutbert." The same Cutbert later witnesses two grants by Oshere's sons, in one text being styled "*comes* of the Hwicce."[3] It is unlikely that the centralizing process was accomplished

---

[1] CS 22. The list is repeated in CS 48, ascribed to Ethelred of Mercia.

[2] 'Medeshamstede and its Colonies', in *Historical Essays in honour of James Tait*, Manchester, 1933, pp. 313–15.

[3] CS 85, 116, 122. Cf. CS 111, a grant of land in Middlesex by Suæbred, king of Essex, with whom is associated "Pæogthath cum licentia Ædelredi regis comis" (*sic*).

without friction. The unexplained and apparently unavenged murder of Ethelred's queen Osthryth in 697 may have been somehow connected with it, for Osthryth was a kinswoman of the Hwiccian royal family.[1] That dynasty outlived its neighbours, but in a charter of 777 Offa the Great of Mercia styles its last representative "my under-king, ealdorman, that is, of his own people of the Hwicce."[2] Merewalh's line was already extinct, it seems, for Mildfrith is the last recorded *regulus* of the Magonsæte. Thenceforth these principalities were provinces administered by ealdormen who may or may not have been of royal descent, but who certainly owed their position to the choice of the Mercian king.

The history of the Welsh border, then, during the first half-century of English-Welsh contact, is one of peaceful evolution. This is a fact which cannot be too strongly emphasized, for it has been almost universally ignored. The Welsh of Brecon clearly did not regard St Mildburg as an alien enemy. Her fellow-countrymen, naturally disinclined to listen to homilies in Welsh, might send a long way for English preachers, but some of them must have understood and even spoken Welsh. The name Wealhstod, borne by a bishop of Hereford contemporary with St Mildburg, signifies 'interpreter', especially at first an interpreter of Welsh. The Mercian settlers in Shropshire took over such Welsh names of villages and hamlets as Ercall, Hodnet, Lizard, Prees; and, as Professor Kenneth Jackson has remarked, while names of hills and rivers might have been picked up from a few survivors, the adoption of British settlement-names implies the continued existence of British rural communities.[3] It may well have taken centuries for English to become the predominant speech.

Above all, the adventurers from Penda's war-band who took up holdings west of the Severn with the consent of his Welsh allies are quite unlikely to have revolutionized the agrarian

[1] H. P. R. Finberg, *op. cit.*, pp. 176–7.   [2] CS 223.

[3] On the name Wealhstod Professor J. R. R. Tolkien remarks that it could not have come into use as a baptismal name until it had become familiar as denoting the occupation of a professional linguist. — *Angles and Britons*, pp. 23, 24. On Welsh place-names in Shropshire see B. G. Charles, *ibid.*, p. 86 *et seq.*; and on the significance of such survivals, K. Jackson, *ibid.*, p. 74.

economy or remodelled to any significant extent the morphology of villages and hamlets. We have no reason to believe that they could have introduced a system of husbandry different from the one they found there even if they had wished to do so. As late as Domesday the great royal manor of Leominster preserved the characteristic Welsh form of rural organization, which indeed persisted on both sides of the border well into the thirteenth century.[1]

It is perhaps desirable at this point to ask what, if anything, can be learnt about the earliest phase of border history from Welsh sources.

In the Legend of St Monacella, or Melangell, we read that Brochwel Ysgithrog, prince of Powys and earl of Chester, held his court in a city called Pengwern, now Shrewsbury, his residence being where the church of St Chad now stands. This Legend has been printed from the manuscript collections of the Elizabethan antiquary David Powell.[2] Since it refers to St Chad's as a collegiate church, it must have been put into writing before 1547, but how much earlier we do not know. Recently it has been discussed by Mr C. A. Ralegh Radford, who shows that the saint belongs to the later eighth rather than the early seventh century, and that the whole of the opening passage relating to Brochwel and his court at Pengwern is "an antiquarian gloss, based on the speculations of Welsh scholars of the sixteenth century."[3] The idea that Shrewsbury was once called Pengwern can however be traced back to the thirteenth century. It is found in the writings of Giraldus Cambrensis; but he places the royal residence not at St Chad's but on the site of Shrewsbury Castle.[4] And it is still accepted by some modern authorities, including, apparently, Ekwall. Against it is the fact that Shrewsbury had, and has, another Welsh name, Amwythig, which can also be traced back to the thirteenth century

[1] Cf. G. R. J. Jones, 'The Pattern of Settlement on the Welsh Border', *Agricultural History Review*, VIII, 1960, pp. 66–81, especially pp. 78 *et seq.*

[2] *Archaeologia Cambrensis*, III, 1848, p. 139.

[3] C. A. Ralegh Radford and W. J. Hemp, 'Pennant Melangell: The Church and the Shrine', *Archaeologia Cambrensis*, CVIII, 1959, pp. 83, 85.

[4] *Itinerarium Kambriae*, in *Opera*, Rolls ser. 21, VI, p. 81; *Descriptio Kambriae*, *ibid.*, p. 169.

and may be older still.[1] Nor does the suggestion that Shrewsbury was a Welsh capital in the seventh century find any support from archaeology. Although the site is a very likely one for a hill-fort of the Early Iron Age, no object recognizably of Iron Age character has been found in or near it; the Romans appear to have by-passed the place; and no finds of the post-Roman British period have been recognized. Apart from a Saxon bronze pin, which Mr G. C. Dunning assigns to the eighth or ninth century, there is no evidence of settled occupation at Shrewsbury until it makes its first appearance under its English name in a Wenlock charter dated 901.[2]

The name Pengwern is found in certain Welsh poems for which the oldest written source is the fourteenth-century manuscript known as the Red Book of Hergest. The poems are elegies on a Welsh chieftain named Cynddylan, who is represented as having lost his life in battle against the English, and as lying buried at Baschurch, a village seven miles northwest of Shrewsbury. His sister Heledd bewails his fate, and the desolation which has overtaken the hall of Cynddylan at Pengwern. The eminent Welsh scholar Sir Ifor Williams, who has produced the definitive edition of these poems, finds in them traces of an orthography older than the Norman Conquest, and he guesses — to use his own word — that they were composed about the middle of the ninth century.[3] According to him — and it is fortunate that the point has been made by a Welsh critic — the Cynddylan poems are not historical compositions, but the verse elements in a saga which at one time also contained prose: a saga inspired by patriotic motives at a time when the fortunes of Powys were at their lowest ebb.

[1] *Brut y Tywysogion*, ed. T. Jones, Cardiff, 1955, pp. 36, 40, 42, 48, 56, 74, 188, etc. Dr G. Melville Richards, of the Department of Celtic Studies in the University of Liverpool, informs me that 'Amwythig' seems to be based on the old Welsh verb *amwyn*, preterite *amwyth*, 'fight', 'defend', with the general meaning of 'fortification' or 'defensive stronghold'.

[2] Lily F. Chitty, 'Prehistoric and Other Early Finds in the Borough of Shrewsbury', *Trans. Shropshire Arch. Soc.*, LIV, 1951–2, pp. 122, 126, 127, 129, 138, 139.

[3] Ifor Williams, 'The Poems of Llywarch Hen', *Proc. British Academy*, XVIII, 1932, pp. 273, 295, 297, 299; *Canu Llywarch Hen*, Cardiff, 1935, pp. xxxvii, lxxiii, lxxviii. (I am indebted to my colleague Mr I. E. Roberts for help with these references to the Welsh edition.)

Now we may — indeed we must — accept this judgement; but since patriotic sagas often embody folk-memories founded upon fact, it behoves us to look at this one more closely. In the longest of the Cynddylan elegies there is a stanza (III) which describes the hero as one of those who assisted at the field of Cogwy.[1] Cogwy is the Welsh name, found also in Nennius, of Maserfelth, or Oswestry, the battle in which Penda defeated the Northumbrian invasion led by St Oswald. It follows that Cynddylan, if he existed, belonged to the heyday of the Mercian-Welsh alliance. The English against whom he fought must therefore have been Northumbrians, and he fought them side by side with Penda's war-band. This is borne out by another elegy, unfortunately extant only in a highly corrupt text, which represents Cynddylan as taking part in a successful cattle raid somewhere near Lichfield, and as being always very ready when called upon by the son of Pyd: that is, apparently, by Penda, son of Pybba.[2] As for his dwelling-place, Miss L. F. Chitty has plausibly suggested that The Berth, a hill-fort near Baschurch, may be the site of Cynddylan's Pengwern.[3] It seems probable that the identification of Pengwern with Shrewsbury is nothing more than a bad guess on the part of Giraldus and his contemporaries.

One other Welsh document deserves our passing attention. This is a Life of Saint Beuno written in Welsh in 1346.[4] There are indications that it is an abbreviation or paraphrase of an older Life written in Latin. Beuno was a contemporary of Cadwallon and Penda. His biographer describes him as establishing himself for a time with his disciples at Berriew, on the west bank of the Severn. One day the saint heard somebody on the other side of the river hunting a hare and encouraging the hounds by shouting *Kergia, Kergia*.[5] This told St Beuno what it

[1] *Canu Llywarch Hen*, p. 48.

[2] Ifor Williams, 'Marwnad Cynddylan', *Bulletin of the Board of Celtic Studies*, VI, 1932, pp. 134–41.

[3] *Archaeological Journal*, CXIII, 1956, p. 182. One might suggest, as an alternative, Pengwern near Llangollen.

[4] Translated by A. W. Wade-Evans in *Archaeologia Cambrensis*, LXXXV, 1930, pp. 315–41; the passage quoted is on p. 316.

[5] Cf. the passage in the Legend of St Monacella, where the Welsh prince Brochwel is described as hunting the hare, and shouting to his dogs "Prendite, caniculi, prendite." — *Arch. Camb.*, III, 1848, p. 139.

certainly would not have told us — that the stranger was an Englishman. Thereupon he called his disciples and said: "Put on your clothes, my sons, and your footwear, and let us leave this place. The nation of the man of strange speech, whose cry I heard inciting his dogs, will overcome this place, and it will be theirs, and they will keep it in their possession."

If this anecdote is to be taken at all seriously, what does it tell us about conditions on the border in the mid-seventh century? Allowing St Beuno full credit for his prophetic insight into the distant future, we cannot help observing that the contemporary Englishman is depicted, not as burning and slaying at the head of a victorious war-band, but as peacefully enjoying the pleasures of the chase; and that although the Welsh saint thinks fit to decamp with most of his followers, he leaves one disciple behind at Berriew, apparently without any fear that he may be dooming that disciple to premature extinction at the hands of a brutal invader.

It will be seen that Welsh tradition throws only a flickering light on this obscure period. But such hints as can be gathered from native poetry and legend are consistent with the picture drawn in these pages, of an Anglian settlement not imposed initially by force of arms.

After 678, when a Mercian host commanded by Ethelred won a decisive victory over Ecgfrith of Northumbria, the Welsh princes had no further reason to dread attack from the north. Henceforward Mercia itself was actually or potentially the more dangerous English power. It seems, however, that peaceful relations were maintained until the last of Penda's sons withdrew from the scene. But the Life of St Guthlac, a Mercian nobleman of high rank who incidentally had lived among the Britons and knew their language, tells us that in the reign of Coenred (704–9) hostilities broke out at last. They continued intermittently, with varying fortunes, throughout the eighth century. Finally Offa built his famous dyke to settle the frontier, leaving to the Welsh some portions of the territory which in earlier, more peaceful, days the Mercians had made their own.[1]

[1] C. Fox, *op. cit.*, pp. xx, xxi; Stenton, *op. cit.*, p. 212.

That century of bloody warfare has coloured all later history and legend. Yet the two generations of peaceful coexistence which preceded it left marks that could not be quite effaced. The tide of battle might flow backwards and forwards over the Welsh March; farmsteads might be burnt and livestock seized by raiders; but the pattern of settlement continually reasserted itself. Mildburg's community at Wenlock, though it lost its Welsh properties, maintained its corporate existence down to the Norman Conquest. An unbroken succession of bishops ruled the diocese of Hereford, preserving in its boundaries the outline of Merewalh's forgotten kingdom.

YNYSWITRIN

IN THE course of his researches among the archives of Glastonbury Abbey William of Malmesbury came across a document of which he gives the following account.

"Concerning the land of Ynswitrin [sic],
given to Glastonbury in the time of the conversion of the English
to the Faith.

"In the year of Our Lord's Incarnation 601 a king of Dumnonia granted the land called Yneswitrin to the Old Church which is situated there, at the request of Abbot Worgret, namely five hides. 'I, Bishop Mauuron, wrote this charter. I, Worgret, abbot of the aforesaid place, have undersigned it.' The age of the document prevents us from knowing who that king was, but we may infer that he was a Briton from his calling Glastonbury Yneswitrin in his own tongue, for we all know that this is the British name they use for Glastonbury. Abbot Worgret, whose name smacks of British barbarism, was succeeded by Lademund, and he by Bregoretd [*sic*]. The dates of their tenure of office are uncertain, but their names and titles are plainly set forth in a painting near the altar in the larger church."[1]

Elsewhere in his "libellus" or tractate on the antiquity of Glastonbury William of Malmesbury speaks of Worgret,

[1] "Anno Dominicae Incarnacionis sexcentesimo primo rex Domnoniae terram, quae appellatur Yneswitrin, ad Ecclesiam vetustam concessit, quae ibi sita est, ob peticionem Worgret abbatis, in quinque cassatis. Ego Mauuron episcopus hanc cartam scripsi. Ego Worgret, ejusdem loci abbas, subscripsi. Quis iste rex fuerit scedulae vetustas negat scire. Verumptamen, quod Britannus fuerit, hinc praesumi potest, quod Glastonia lingua sua Yneswitrin appellavit; sic enim eam Britannice vocari apud eos constat. Worgret autem abbati, cujus nomen Britannicam barbariem redolet, successit Lademund, et ei Bregoretd. Praelacionis eorum tempora sunt in obscuro, set nomina illorum et dignitates in majori Ecclesia, prodente secus altare pictura, sunt in propatulo." — *Adami de Domerham* [= AD] *Historia de Rebus Gestis Glastoniensibus*, ed. T. Hearne, Oxford, 1727, p. 48.

Lademund, and Bregored as the only British abbots whose names have survived.[1] Others, before his visit, had led the way in searching for pre-English names. In the first quarter of the eleventh century the Irish who conducted a school for the sons of the nobility at Glastonbury did their best — or worst. A certain abbot named Beonna lay buried at Meare, three miles from the abbey. Beonna is a well-recorded Anglo-Saxon name, borne among others by an abbot of Medeshamstede (789 × 805) and a bishop of Hereford (824 × 832),[2] but the Irish boldly identified the Beonna of Meare with their own St Benen, a disciple and successor of St Patrick. An inscription on his tomb, copied by William of Malmesbury, speaks of this identification in rather non-committal terms, but in 1091 the abbot's remains were solemnly translated to Glastonbury, and by that time the English Beonna, latinized as Benignus, was firmly established as one of the Celtic saints who were alleged to have made Glastonbury illustrious long before the English occupation of Somerset.[3]

William of Malmesbury also describes two monuments that stood a few feet from the old church at the edge of the monks' cemetery. The shorter of the two contained four panels, on which could be read the names: Bishop Hedde, Bregored, and Beorward.[4] Of these, Hædde became bishop of Wessex in 676 and died in 705; and Beorward or Beorwald — for the historian gives both forms on the same page — may be either Beorhtwald who was abbot in 670,[5] or, as William of Malmesbury believed, the Beor(n)wald who was in office between 705 and 712.[6] Between these two churchmen with unquestionably

---

[1] AD p. 46.

[2] The name occurs frequently in the *Liber Vitae* of Durham. "Beonna's thorn-tree" occurs as a landmark in CS 480, and "Beonna's ford," now Binneford in Sandford, Devon, in CS 1331.

[3] The language of the Bollandists in this connection is unsparing. "Cum ipsum S. Benigni magistrum, D. Patricium, Glastoniae vitam explevisse Glastonienses mendaciis non parcentes asseruerint, S. Benigni quoque nomen in praeclara illa falsorum corruptorumque scriptorum ac monumentorum officina nonnunquam esse usurpatum nemo profecto mirabitur qui in celeberrimi monasterii moribus non plane peregrinus sit." — *Acta Sanctorum*, November, IV (Brussels, 1925), p. 169. For the Irish school at Glastonbury see *Memorials of St Dunstan*, ed. Stubbs, Rolls ser. 63, pp. 10, 74, 75.

[4] AD p. 45.   [5] CS 25.   [6] CS 113; EHD I, p. 731.

Anglo-Saxon names comes Bregored, the supposedly Celtic abbot named in the passage already cited. An early Welsh element *Bri-* occurs in the personal name Briavel, and *guored* or *guared* is a common second element in Middle Welsh personal names. It is just possible, therefore, that Bregored is a corrupt form of a British name.[1] But if we take it as it stands, both its elements, *Bregu*, or *Brego*, and *ræd*, are plainly Teutonic. The former occurs in Breguswith, the mother of St Hilda, and Bregowine, archbishop of Canterbury from 761 to 764; the latter in Aldred, Ethelred, and other well-known names. Of Bregored's predecessor in office, Lademund, all that can be said is that his name has an undoubtedly Teutonic ending.[2] As for Worgret, it figures on the map today as the name of a hamlet near Wareham in Dorset. Ekwall derives it from the Old English *weargrōd*, meaning gallows.[3] This may seem an unlikely appellation for an abbot of Glastonbury, and since there are many names having as their first element the Primitive Welsh or Primitive Cornish *Wor-* (later *Guor-*, *Gur-*), it may be that Worgret is in truth a Celtic personal name.[4] But if so, it does not follow that the abbot who bore it lived before the Saxon conquest. A churchman named Bectune, whose name is not obviously Anglo-Saxon, and another whose name, Catwali, is obviously British, were ruling an abbey in Dorset long after that shire and Somerset had fallen under English rule.[5]

With these facts in mind we may now examine the charter which Abbot Worgret procured from a nameless king of Dumnonia. The first question to be asked is what grounds

[1] I am indebted here to a personal communication from Professor Ekwall.

[2] It may be a corruption of Leudemund (Liutmund, Leutmund, Ludimunt; see E. Förstemann, *Altdeutsches Namenbuch*), or even, as Professor Ekwall has suggested to me, of Bademund, which, in the form Badumund, occurs very frequently in the Durham *Liber Vitae*.

[3] E. Ekwall, *Studies on English Place- and Personal Names*, Lund, 1931, p. 91.

[4] I have to thank Professor K. H. Jackson for a note on this point. Worgret is superficially not unlike Wurgeat, the name of a Welsh prince who attests two of Athelstan's charters (CS 663, dated 928, and 689, dated 932). The name Guruaret occurs among the Bodmin manumissions. — Oliver, *Monasticon Dioecesis Exoniensis*, p. 433, no. 45.

[5] CS 107, 186.

William of Malmesbury had for giving A.D. 601 as the date of the grant. Scholars are now generally agreed that written land-grants were an innovation brought in by Archbishop Theodore (668–90) and his companions.[1] Even if we admit, in the face of this consensus, that a genuine Dumnonian charter might have been issued before Theodore's time, we can be quite certain that it would not have been dated A.D. 601, for the era of the Incarnation was not used in charters before the middle of the seventh century. It found its way into documents and historical writings after 664, when St Wilfrid at the synod of Whitby induced the Northumbrian church to accept the Easter tables compiled by Dionysius Exiguus.[2] The British clergy of the south-west were still resisting the change forty years later.[3]

In his *Gesta Regum* William of Malmesbury cites the grant of Ynyswitrin to "the Old Church," and goes on to say: "It is proper to remark how ancient that church must be which even then was called old." If he means that the words "ecclesia vetusta" occurred in the text of the charter, this would be proof positive that it was not drawn up before the reign of Ine (688–726), for the primitive wattled church at Glastonbury only became known as the "old church" when Ine built alongside it a new church dedicated to SS. Peter and Paul.[4] But the *Gesta Regum* in its final form is later than the work *On the Antiquity of Glastonbury*, so it would be unwise to lay much stress upon what may be merely an afterthought on the historian's part.

On the other hand, the language of William of Malmesbury leaves no room for doubt that what he saw was not a memorandum in a gospel-book nor a monumental inscription, but a formal charter. It may have been a copy and not the original, but it was so ancient as to be legible only in part. The name of the grantor could not be made out. Two of the attestations,

---

[1] F. M. Stenton, *Anglo-Saxon England*, p. 141; *The Latin Charters of the Anglo-Saxon Period*, Oxford, 1955, p. 30; W. Levison, *England and the Continent in the Eighth Century*, Oxford, 1946, p. 232; D. Whitelock in EHD I, p. 343; E. John, *Land Tenure in Early England*, Leicester, 1960, p. 1.

[2] R. L. Poole, *Studies in Chronology and History*, Oxford, 1934, pp. 33, 34.

[3] Haddan and Stubbs, *Councils and Ecclesiastical Documents*, III, pp. 268–73.

[4] *Gesta Regum*, ed. Stubbs, Rolls ser. 90, pp. 29, 36.

however, could be read and were transcribed by the historian. "I, Bishop Mauuron [or Mauvron?] wrote this charter. I, Worgret, abbot of the aforesaid place, have undersigned it." These attestations have an authentic look; at least they are not obviously fabricated. Mauuron is certainly not an Anglo-Saxon name. The practice of including with the signatures a statement that one of the signatories himself wrote or composed the document is found in several charters ranging in date from 680 to 704.[1] Not all of these can be accepted as they stand, but this usage is one of their least doubtful features. It occurs regularly in Frankish charters, and may well have been introduced into southern England by Leuthere, the Frankish bishop of Wessex (670–6), or by St Wilfrid, who had lived in Gaul, and who, incidentally, was himself a benefactor of Glastonbury.[2] The formula "Ego A subscripsi" occurs commonly enough in genuine charters of the seventh and eighth centuries.[3]

In examining a charter of which only two attestations have survived, the canons of textual and diplomatic criticism avail us little. So far as they can be applied, they suggest that the Ynyswitrin document was not a crude fabrication, like the Great Privilege of Ine or the still more imaginative Charter of St Patrick which inventive pens at Glastonbury produced some time after the historian's visit, but a genuine land-grant. The attestations, however, and all that we know of written land-grants generally in this country, give good grounds for believing that the grant of Ynyswitrin has been antedated by at least three quarters of a century, probably more. And if so, it belongs to the period when Glastonbury was already subject to the Anglo-Saxon kings of Wessex. Is it at all likely that an abbot in that period would have received a grant of land from a British king?

As it happens, we can answer this question affirmatively. The

---

[1] CS 37 (A.D. 675), 50 (A.D. 680), 61 (A.D. 681), 62 (A.D. 672 for 682), 100 (A.D. 687 for 699), 103 (A.D. 701), 107 (A.D. 704).

[2] W. Levison, *op. cit.*, pp. 227, 228. On Wilfrid's gift of Clewer to the abbey, see J. Armitage Robinson, *Somerset Historical Essays*, 1921, p. 32.

[3] Levison, p. 176; cf. CS 78 (A.D. 692), 101 (A.D. 699), 113 (Ine to the abbot of Glastonbury, A.D. 705). The words "ob peticionem Worgret abbatis" may well represent a clause in the original text beginning "rogatus a ..." such as occurs in several charters of the period, e.g. CS 37, 50, 58, 60, 64, 77.

church of Sherborne appears to have been what Glastonbury claimed to be, an old Celtic foundation, which Cenwalh and later kings of Wessex took under their protection. A list of its royal benefactors, from Cenwalh onwards, was compiled or copied in the fourteenth century from obviously ancient sources; and among other precious facts it records that "King Gerontius gave five hides at Macuir by the Tamar," that is, at Maker, on the western shore of Plymouth Sound. The benefactor in this instance was that King Geraint of Cornwall to whom St Aldhelm, some time before 705, addressed a celebrated letter, and against whom Ine went to war in 710. At a time when the kingdom of Dumnonia, or West-Wales as the English called it, was rapidly losing ground to its aggressive English neighbour, its king may well have deemed it politic to conciliate the principal churches of Wessex.[1] Or he may have been moved by simple piety. Whatever the motive, it is clear that if a king of Dumnonia could give five hides of land to Sherborne, he or another ruler of the same kingdom could equally well give a five-hide estate to Glastonbury.

That Geraint's was the name which could no longer be read in the Ynyswitrin charter must remain a mere surmise, though a highly probable one. There is at least no reason for doubting that the text seen by William of Malmesbury represented a genuine grant by a Cornu-British king. It was drafted by a Cornish bishop whose name is elsewhere unrecorded. The date was not 601, but much more probably *circa* 700 or even later. It is just possible that on a faded and tattered parchment the date DCCI was honestly misread as DCI.[2]

One question remains, and that the most difficult to answer. Where was Ynyswitrin?

A Welsh poem refers to "Ynys wydrin" as the home of Sir Richard Herbert, who was executed in 1469. Bradney, the historian of Monmouthshire, identifies it with the place now known as Coldbrook, a mile or so from Abergavenny.[3] Since

[1] See p. 100 below.

[2] On the possibility that such a date might occur in a genuine charter, see R. L. Poole, *op. cit.*, p. 34.

[3] *Report on Manuscripts in the Welsh Language*, Hist. MSS. Comm., 48, II, p. 148, no. 108; Bradney, *History of Monmouthshire*, I, p. 185. I am indebted for these references to Dr G. Melville Richards.

this lay in the kingdom of Gwent, not in Dumnonia, we may disregard it, except as evidence that Ynyswitrin could be a genuine British place-name.[1] *Ynys* or *inis* is Welsh for island, not necessarily an island in the sea, but any piece of land wholly or partly surrounded with water. It is often followed by a personal name, and some modern scholars have interpreted *witrin* as such a name.[2] Not so the monks of Glastonbury. They took *witrin* to be the Welsh *gwydrin*, meaning 'glassy', and associated it with the first syllable of the English name *Glaston-bury*. It followed that both names denoted the same hallowed spot in Somerset.

This piece of linguistic puerility appears to have been adopted by William of Malmesbury — that is, if we take his text as it stands. William further reports, as a matter of common knowledge ("constat"), that Ynyswitrin was the usual name for Glastonbury among the Britons. By these he means, presumably, the Britons of Cornwall and Wales; it is unlikely that any native Welsh-speaking inhabitants remained in twelfth-century Somerset. But did he know their language, and had he ever travelled west of the Tamar or the Severn? There is no sign of it in his writings; indeed, he never conceals his low opinion of the Welsh and of their "barbaric" tongue.[3] The suspicion arises that this particular sentence ("sic enim eam Britannice vocari apud eos constat"), if not the whole mis-identification, may be one of the many passages which have been interpolated into William's original text.[4]

Suspicion deepens when we turn to the corresponding passage in the Life of Gildas written for the abbey by Caradoc of

[1] It has however been suggested that the Dumnonian kings may at one time have ruled on both sides of the Severn Sea. — *Studies in Early British History*, ed. N. K. Chadwick, Cambridge, 1954, p. 53.

[2] H. Williams in Cymmrodorion Record Series, III, 1901, p. 410; R. J. Thomas, *Enwau Afonydd a Nentydd Cymru*, 1938, p. 180, quoted by A. G. C. Turner in *Proc. Somerset Arch. & Nat. Hist. Soc.*, XCV, 1950, p. 117.

[3] Cf. his remarks about Athelstan's dealings with the Britons of Exeter ("urbem quam contaminatae gentis repurgio defaecaverat"), *Gesta Regum*, p. 148, and about Abbot Worgret ("cujus nomen Britannicam barbariem redolet"), AD p. 48.

[4] It is noticeable that the passage "Verumptamen . . . constat" could be deleted without injury to the structure and context of the paragraph in which it occurs.

Llancarfan. "This utterly unhistorical *Vita*," says J. S. P. Tatlock, "is a part of that campaign of propaganda in behalf of the ancient renown and the early British associations of this enterprising English house which continued with such success through the twelfth century."[1] To satisfy his patrons, Caradoc — alone among the biographers of Gildas — brings his hero to Somerset in the time of King Arthur and describes him as spending the last years of his life there. He says that Glastonbury means a 'city of glass' and was originally named in the British tongue — ("Glastonia, id est Urbs Vitrea, quae nomen sumsit a vitro, est urbs nomine primitus in Britannico sermone — "). The sentence is obviously incomplete: it should end with a British place-name. In the earliest extant manuscript of the Life an erasure has been made after "sermone," and the first four words of the following sentence ("Obsessa est itaque ab") are written over the erasure in the same hand.[2] The Life then continues without any further etymology, true or false, and ends with a flourish of pious rhetoric: "cuius anima requievit et requiescit ac requiescet in caelesti requie. Amen." But between the Amen and a verse colophon proclaiming Caradoc's authorship, some one — not necessarily Caradoc himself — has awkwardly inserted a postscript stating that "Glastonbury was of old called Ynisgutrin, and is still called so by the native Britons."[3] This afterthought seems to be, like the rest of the Life, pure fiction. I can find no independent evidence that the Britons then or earlier called Glastonbury either Ynisgutrin or Ynyswitrin.

During the twelfth century the monks of Glastonbury played with three successive explanations of the English place-name.

[1] *Speculum*, XIII, 1938, p. 141.

[2] Corpus Christi, Cambridge, MS. 139, fo. 180b. The librarian of Corpus Christi, Dr R. Vaughan, has been good enough to examine the passage under ultra-violet light, but he informs me that the erased characters are irrecoverable.

[3] "Ynisgutrin nominata fuit antiquitus Glastonia et adhuc nominatur a Britannis indigenis." The Durham manuscript of the Life (Cathedral Library, MS. B 11, 35, written perhaps in the third quarter of the twelfth century) omits the verse colophon. I have to thank the librarian, Miss M. Johnson, for information about this MS. The Life cannot be said to have been properly edited as yet. The best printed text is Mommsen's in *Mon. Germ. Hist., Auctores Antiquissimi*, XIII, *Chronica Minora* III, 1898.

The first rested, so far as can be seen, on no more solid basis than a misinterpretation of the name Yneswitrin found in the Dumnonian charter. This misinterpretation shows fairly clear signs of having been foisted into the texts of William of Malmesbury's *De Antiquitate* and Caradoc's *Vita Gildae*. The second gained currency when King Arthur was incorporated into the legendary history of the abbey. Arthur brought with him an alternative British place-name, Avalon. This seems to have been the name of a Celtic paradise, an Isle of the Blest where departed spirits enjoyed eternal happiness; but it now acquired an earthly location in the damp surroundings of mid-Somerset. There it has been firmly established ever since 1191, when the monks dug up a coffin full of gigantic bones and found with it — so they declared — a leaden cross inscribed: "Here lies buried the renowned King Arthur, in the isle of Avalon."[1]

The third, and in all probability the correct, etymology traced the first element in Glaston-bury back to a personal name. In the amplified text of William of Malmesbury the eponym is said to have been a descendant of Cunedda named Glasteing, who travelled from the west of Britain through the Middle Angles to the site of Glastonbury. There he settled, and the isle became the permanent home of his posterity.[2] Welsh genealogies give his name in the more correct form Glast, and reveal faint vestiges of a tradition that Glast and his followers came from the vicinity of Lichfield.[3] To the folk-name Glastingas, or rather to its genitive plural Glastinga, the English

[1] J. Armitage Robinson, *Two Glastonbury Legends*, Cambridge, 1962, pp. 1–27, 58. There is at present no conclusive archaeological evidence of a monastic establishment at Glastonbury before the seventh century. The oldest feature that can be associated with the monastery is a bank and ditch running north and south across the west end of the choir and the chapter-house. Mr C. A. Ralegh Radford thinks this may represent the *vallum* of a Celtic monastery, like that at Tintagel, but no datable relics have been found in it, and it may not be older than *c.* 700. — *Proc. Somerset Arch. & Nat. Hist. Soc.*, CVI, 1962, p. 32.

[2] AD p. 16.

[3] BM MS. Harl. 3859, ed. E. Phillimore in *Y Cymmrodor*, IX, 1888, p. 180; Ifor Williams, 'Glasinfryn', *Trans. Caernarvonshire Historical Soc.*, IX, 1948, p. 106. (The last-named article is written in modern Welsh. I have to thank Professor T. Jones Pierce for remedying *pro hac vice* my ignorance of that tongue.)

added, at first, the termination *ieg*, meaning island, and subsequently *byrig*, in the sense of a fortified enclosure.[1]

In the seven centuries which have elapsed since the monks of Glastonbury launched their publicity campaign, the false identification of Ynyswitrin has permeated the literature of the subject, and it is now so firmly lodged in so many minds that no criticism is ever likely to expel it. Yet it has to face one very obvious objection. The grant of Ynyswitrin is made to a monastic community ruled by Abbot Worgret and settled at Glastonbury. The community must already have possessed the site of its church and enough land round it to provide the monks with sustenance, however meagre. Why then should anybody make them a grant of what they already had? Why, in short, give Glastonbury to Glastonbury?

It is even more pertinent to ask in whose jurisdiction the site of the abbey lay. The Roman canton or *civitas* of the Durotriges stretched across most of Somerset and Dorset. That of their western neighbours, the Dumnonii, is unlikely to have

---

[1] A. G. C. Turner, *loc. cit.*, suggests *glasstan*, the Cornish word for oaktrees, as the first element; but this would hardly yield *glastinga*. Ekwall, in the *Oxford Dictionary of English Place-Names*, prefers the Old Celtic *glasto*, meaning woad, and is sufficiently impressed by what has been written about Ynyswitrin to point out that the Latin *vitrum* also means woad. This would indeed be a significant coincidence if there were any valid reason for supposing that both names referred to the same place; but we have seen that there is none, and in any case why should the spot have had two synonymous Celtic names? There is a further objection: Professor K. H. Jackson informs me that the *st* in words like *glasto* had already become *ss* long before the sixth century; cf. his *Language and History in Early Britain*, Edinburgh, 1953, p. 533. The early forms of Glastonbury are as follows:

Glastingai 678 (lost charter, AD p. 49); Glastingaea, Glastingay 704 (CS 109); Glasteie, Glastingeie 725 (CS 142); Glastingei 744 or 745 (CS 169).

Glastingaburg 672 for 682 (CS 62); Glæstingabyrig 688 (marginal note in A-text of the Anglo-Saxon Chronicle, which Plummer, II, p. xxvi, believes to have been added by the original scribe in the late 9th century); Glastingaburghe 702 × 706 (CS 112); Glastingburi, Glastingburg' 725 (CS 143); Glastingaburi 729 (CS 147); Glestingaburg 732 × 755 (*Mon. Germ. Hist., Epistolae Selectae*, ed. Tangl, 1916, no. 101); Glastingaburgh 744 (CS 168).

All of the foregoing are taken from copies made after a lapse of centuries, and sometimes no doubt modernized by the copyists. Hence they provide no conclusive answer to the real problem: when and why did the isle of the Glastings become a 'bury'? If a guess may be hazarded, it was perhaps after the new building in Ine's reign. [See, further, p. 94.]

extended farther east than the Parrett, if as far, and the same may be said of the British kingdom of Dumnonia which took its place. By 600 the English had begun to settle in mid-Somerset, and by 700 they had conquered the whole of Devon. At no possible time, therefore, within the period of dated land-charters can Glastonbury have been in the gift of a Dumnonian king.[1]

From these historical considerations it follows that the real Ynyswitrin must have lain west of the Parrett, and in all probability west of the Tamar. The name, unfortunately, is not to be found on the map of Cornwall today, but then neither is Dinnurrin, which we know to have been the seat of the Cornish bishopric in the ninth century.[2] Cornish place-names have undergone much transformation, and even when the English Place-Name Society brings out its long-delayed volume on the county the essential clue may still be lacking. It is indeed possible that the true Ynyswitrin will for ever elude our search. But one suggestion may be offered here, very tentatively. Some four miles north-west of Maker, the place which King Geraint gave to Sherborne, is a spot named Ince. It lies on the north bank of the Lynher, near the confluence of that river and the Tamar. Ince is clearly the Celtic *ynys*; in one or other of its forms it is a common element in Cornish place-names. It answers to the Old English *ig* or *ieg*, which has the same meaning. Now it is on record that King Ine gave an estate at "Linig, by the Tamar," to Glastonbury. This was presumably after his victorious campaign against Geraint in 710. Linig is another lost name, but judging from its assessment of twenty hides, the property was much more extensive than the five-hide estate at Ynyswitrin. As is shown elsewhere in this book, it

[1] See the combination of archaeological, documentary, and topographical evidence marshalled by Dr W. G. Hoskins in *The Westward Expansion of Wessex*, Leicester, 1960, pp. 1–22. Even before this paper appeared, Professor Stenton argued that the English had occupied the whole of Somerset long before the end of the seventh century. — *Anglo-Saxon England*, p. 63. It is now obvious that the "ibi" in "quae ibi sita est," and the phrase "ejusdem loci abbas" further on, must have referred in the original charter not to Ynyswitrin, as Malmesbury perhaps thought, but to Glastonbury, the name of which probably occurred in that part of the text which had become illegible.

[2] CS 527.

comprised a tract of land between the Lynher and the Tamar, extending as far north as the parish of St Dominick.[1] If the true Ynyswitrin lay in this part of Cornwall, it would be not unnatural for Ine to celebrate his victory by confirming a gift made originally, on this hypothesis, by Geraint, and enlarging it for the benefit of his favoured abbey.

[1] See pp. 100–02 below.

ADDENDUM. Dr A. M. Everitt has kindly drawn my attention to the article on the Kentish place-name Glassenbury in J. K. Wallenberg's *Place-Names of Kent*, Uppsala, 1934, p. 320. The fourteenth-century forms of this name are identical with the early forms of Glastonbury. Wallenberg suggests that both names may be derived from a Germanic base and signify people living near a stream, or, since Middle High German *glast* means brilliant, radiant, resplendent, "the splendid folk."

SHERBORNE, GLASTONBURY, AND THE EXPANSION OF WESSEX[1]

A MONASTIC historian, engaged in collecting materials for a cartulary or chronicle of his abbey, would sometimes find among the archives documents which had ceased to be of any practical use. They might be crumbling to pieces, or faded, or written in an undecipherable script. Or they might refer to transactions which had long since been undone: leases which had expired, original grants of property which the monastery, for one reason or another, had ceased to own. Tenacious of their rights as monastic corporations usually were, there were losses which even they had to admit were irrevocable. In such cases the original charters no longer served as title-deeds. To copy them out in full might well seem a waste of time; but if the scribe ignored them altogether, past glories would be forgotten and benefactors might be robbed of the commemoration due to them. The best course open to a conscientious scribe was to make an abstract or epitome, recording the names of the grantors and adding brief particulars of the lands or relics or precious vessels they had given to the abbey. By this means a good deal of historical fact would be preserved with the least possible expenditure of time and parchment. The historical value of the charters which have come down to us in full has never been in doubt, though scholars are well aware that some of them are crude fabrications, others genuine but faultily transcribed, or touched up in places to help the defence of threatened rights, while others again are more or less clumsy reconstructions of lost originals. By contrast with this mixed collection, a series of bald statements in the form: A gave the abbey an estate at B, need not excite suspicion to anything like the same extent. For in the first place, the monk who wrote the statements down was not

[1] Based upon a paper read to the Royal Historical Society, 11 October 1952.

trying to prove anything, not asserting any claim. The record is disinterested; we may presume that it was written in good faith, that the scribe, having nothing to gain by making an unsupported statement, did not invent it, but took it from documents which he believed to be genuine. We cannot be sure that he interpreted his documents correctly, and of course he may have been mistaken about their genuineness. The canons of textual criticism cannot be applied here; we have therefore to test the statements by other criteria. Do they conflict with anything that is certainly known from other sources? Can they be fitted convincingly into the general history of the time? If they pass these tests, we shall not be unduly perturbed by minor discrepancies. For example, when we read that an estate at X, given by King Y in the ninth century, consisted of ten hides, and then find that in Domesday Book X is rated at only six hides, this will not strike us as a fatal objection, for part of the estate may have been alienated in the meantime, and we know that many assessments were lowered by royal favour. We may encounter difficulties in identifying places named in the record, but such difficulties may often be solved by reference to the later history of a manor, or to some detail like the dedication of the parish church, for ecclesiastical property tended to remain ecclesiastical though it might pass from one church to another, and we know how commonly, in the seventh and eighth centuries, churches of Anglo-Saxon foundation were dedicated to saints of the New Testament.[1] On the general question of these fragmentary records, William of Malmesbury has some judicious observations. "Although the number and extent of the properties I have listed here as belonging to one house may seem incredible, yet I have no doubt that all these, and many more which I omit because the particulars are uncertain, were really given to the abbey of Glastonbury. It need occasion no surprise if some manors are recorded as having been granted, either really or nominally, by more than one grantor. Sometimes the names are not clear; sometimes properties given long ago were taken away and later restored; and in other cases, one owner gave part of a manor and some one else the rest, but the whole may have been ascribed to one giver."

[1] On this see W. Levison, *England and the Continent in the Eighth Century*, Oxford, 1946, pp. 34–36, 259–65.

This was written in 1129 or thereabouts, when the great chronicler spent some time at Glastonbury studying the archives and monumental inscriptions of the abbey. He found there a large number of original charters and early copies. He also found a *Landbok*, or *Liber Terrarum*, compiled apparently towards the close of the tenth century, and containing transcripts of one hundred and thirty-six royal and other charters. After thoroughly exploring this material, he wrote his well-known tractate *De Antiquitate Glastoniensis Ecclesie*. This was printed in 1727 by Thomas Hearne from a manuscript in the library of Trinity College, Cambridge.[1] The Glastonbury *Landbok*, still extant in the time of Abbot Monyngton (1341–1374), has since disappeared. Fortunately some one who examined it in 1247 took the trouble to copy out its table of contents, under the heading *Cartae contentae in libro terrarum Glastoniae*, and this epitome is now bound up in the same Trinity College manuscript with the *De Antiquitate*. It too was printed by Hearne.[2]

The church of Sherborne did not, like Glastonbury, lay claim to a fabulous antiquity, but its authentic records go back to the earliest days of West Saxon Christianity. Towards the close of the fourteenth century they were epitomized by a monk of the house under the heading *Incipiunt nomina regum ejusdem ecclesie fundatorum*. The word *fundator* here, as usually in monastic texts, means 'principal benefactor'. There follows a list of royal names, in an order far from chronological; and to each king's name is appended a brief statement of the lands he gave to Sherborne. This memorial, with other Sherborne documents, is bound up in a volume which formerly belonged to Sir Robert Cotton and is now in the British Museum. It has been printed almost in full by Dugdale.[3]

---

[1] MS. 724, written in mid-thirteenth century. For a full description see M. R. James's *Catalogue*, II, p. 198. As printed by Hearne, the *De Antiquitate* occupies pp. 1–122 of his *Adami de Domerham Historia de Rebus Gestis Glastoniensibus*, Oxford, 1727. In subsequent footnotes I refer to this work as AD.

[2] In *Johannis . . . Glastoniensis Chronica sive Historia de Rebus Glastoniensibus*, Oxford, 1726, pp. 370–75. In subsequent footnotes I refer to it as JG.

[3] Dugdale, *Monasticon*, I, 1817, p. 337, from Cotton MS. Faustina A II, fo. 24. As the reading of several names is open to question, I have found it necessary to consult the manuscript.

In both cases the records thus preserved for us in summary form include a number of documents of which the text is lost. The purpose of this essay is to examine them, in conjunction with other evidence, on the chance that they may throw some light on the process of expansion by which the sovereignty of Wessex was carried westward from the forest of Selwood to Land's End.

Great obscurity surrounds the origin of Sherborne. A charter of Cenwalh, king of Wessex, dated 671, is transcribed in one of its registers and printed in the *Cartularium*.[1] It purports to have been issued with the consent of Wulfhere, king of Mercia, and Archbishop Laurence of Canterbury; and it refers to Sherborne as an episcopal see (*pontificalis officii sedes*). As Laurence died in 619, and no bishopric existed at Sherborne until 705, the document cannot be accepted as it stands. For more trustworthy information, and for a clue to the early history of the monastic house, a clue which the local historians have disregarded, we turn to the Cotton MS. There we find Cenwalh named at the head of the list of benefactors, with the added information that he gave "Lanprobi," an estate of a hundred hides. In this name we recognize the ordinary Celtic prefix for a church or an ecclesiastical estate, followed by the name of an early saint and martyr, Probus, whose cult seems to have been well established among the Britons of the south-west, for there is a Lanprobus in Cornwall also, in Domesday Book called Lanbrabois, now simply Probus. The Dorset *lan* which Cenwalh gave is almost certainly identical with the "Propeschirche" named among the possessions of Sherborne in 1145 and with the *capella sancti Probi* mentioned in a papal bull of 1163. Its exact situation is not known.[2] The English name Sherborne is primarily a stream-name. It may well be that Lanprobus is the older British name of the monastic property on which the town was afterwards built.

The same Cenwalh figures as the earliest English benefactor of

---

[1] CS 26.

[2] The bull of 1163 refers to "ecclesiam sanctae Mariae Magdalenae sitam juxta castrum Sherborne, cum capellis sancti Michaelis et sancti Probi" (Dugdale, I, p. 339); cf. J. Hutchins, *History of Dorset*, 1861–70, IV, p. 257, and J. Fowler, *Mediaeval Sherborne*, 1951, p. 107.

Glastonbury. In 670, at the instance of Archbishop Theodore, he gave two hides at Ferramere, now Meare, to Beorhtwald, the first abbot of Glastonbury who bore an English name.[1] This was twelve years after the battle of Penselwood, which has often been regarded as having opened Somerset east of the river Parrett to English settlement. Sir Frank Stenton, however, considers it probable that the victory carried the West Saxons at least as far as the Blackdown Hills on the border of Devon,[2] and if we can trust a charter dated 672 which conveys to Glastonbury land within four miles of Taunton, the probability becomes a virtual certainty.[3]

Cenwalh, once he had made up his mind to embrace Christianity, strongly supported Roman usages. The records already cited show him acting in concert with Archbishop Theodore, reorganizing British churches on Anglo-Roman lines, placing English abbots in charge of them, and increasing their endowments.

The next king but one, Centwine, is described by his contemporary, St Aldhelm, as a generous benefactor of new churches. The same authority says that Centwine defeated his enemies in three great battles.[4] We are not told who these enemies were, but there can be little doubt that they were the Britons of Dumnonia, and that the battles were fought in what is now Devon. The late J. J. Alexander, a local scholar who made a careful study of the subject, was of opinion that by 685, the end of Centwine's reign, the English had advanced no further westward than the river Dart, and that although Ine, in 710, conquered north Devon and even penetrated into the northernmost tip of Cornwall, the conquest of south Devon remained incomplete until the wars of Cuthred and Cynewulf, halfway through the eighth century.[5] Professor Stenton, who remarks that "few questions in Early English history are more obscure," considers it probable that Devon was conquered in the reign of Ine (688–726), and that for the next hundred years the river Tamar formed the dividing line between Wessex and

[1] AD p. 49; CS 25.
[2] F. M. Stenton, *Anglo-Saxon England*, Oxford, 1943, p. 63.
[3] CS 62. The date should perhaps be corrected to 682.
[4] Stenton, *op. cit.*, p. 67.
[5] DA LXXII, 1940, p. 107, and LXXIII, 1941, p. 95.

Cornwall.[1] Where so much is doubtful, any shred of evidence becomes important; and a Glastonbury record, preserved in outline by William of Malmesbury, will perhaps assist us to clear up the problem.

In order that we may view the record in its historical setting, it is necessary to recall the well-known letter which Aldhelm, while abbot of Malmesbury, addressed to the reigning king of Dumnonia, Geraint, and to the clergy of his realm. Beginning with some remarks upon the theological dissensions then raging among the Britons, Aldhelm urges them, with solemn warnings against the perils of schism, to regulate the shape of their tonsures and the date of Easter in accordance with Roman usage. He then goes on to inveigh at some length against the Britons on the other side of the Bristol Channel, whose behaviour towards their English neighbours he describes as both uncharitable and heretical.[2] It is difficult to see why this criticism of the north-Welsh should have been directed to a Cornish address, unless the epistle was designed as a contribution to the process nowadays called 'softening up'. We may acquit Aldhelm of deliberately writing war-propaganda for the government of Wessex, but there is an undertone of implication that if misfortune should ensue, the Cornishmen would have only their schismatic selves to thank for it. It is hardly fanciful to see in what followed a gesture of appeasement by the weaker party. For Geraint next appears in the unnatural guise of benefactor to an English church. He gave Sherborne five hides at Macuir, now Maker, on the western shore of the Tamar estuary. But if the Cornish king hoped to buy off the enemy, he was disappointed, for in 710 war broke out again. In preparation for this campaign, Ine evidently mobilized the whole strength of the West Saxon kingdom and its allies. He was assisted by Nunna, king of Sussex, and the victorious issue of the struggle is attested by the record that Ine gave Abbot Beornwald of Glastonbury "twenty hides by the Tamar: to wit, Linig."[3]

[1] Stenton, *op. cit.*, p. 72; *The Place-Names of Devon*, Cambridge, 1931–32, pp. xiv, xviii.
[2] A. W. Haddan and W. Stubbs, *Councils and Ecclesiastical Documents*, Oxford, 1869–71, III, pp. 268–73.
[3] AD p. 97.

Where was Linig? The termination -*ig* is of common occurrence in place-names; it signifies an island, and not merely an island in the modern sense, but any piece of land nearly surrounded by water. The other element is apparently based on the Welsh root *lei*, to flow; according to Ekwall, it occurs in the river-names Lyne (Northumberland), Leen (Notts), Lynor

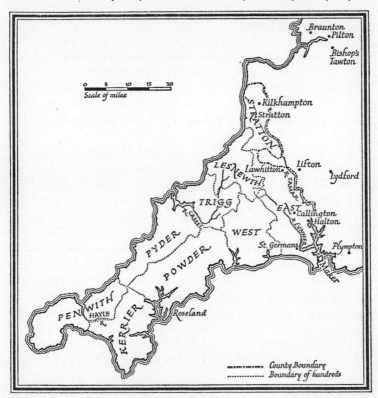

(Devon), and Lynher (Cornwall).[1] Etymology therefore suggests that the twenty hides of Linig are to be located between the Lynher and the Tamar. Turning to the map, we find that the district east of the Lynher is studded with English place-names, but on the west bank Celtic names predominate. Further, the ecclesiastical traditions of the district point to an intimate, though transient, connection with Glastonbury at this

[1] E. Ekwall, *The Concise Oxford Dictionary of English Place-Names*, Oxford, 1960, pp. 294, 309, 310.

very period. In the parish of St Dominick there was a chapel of St Ildract or Indract, the saint whose tomb at Glastonbury, on the left of the high altar, was one of the most striking objects in the abbey church. The eponym of the parish is the Celtic Domnech, Latinized as Dominica, one of the companions of St Indract: indeed, according to one version of the tale, his sister. The local legend, as recorded by John of Tynemouth about the middle of the fourteenth century, relates that in the reign of Ine of Wessex, Indract, with Dominica and nine other companions, landed in the Tamar estuary and established a settlement there, complete with chapel and fishpond. Here they "lived a most strict life in the service of God for a long time." Afterwards, leaving Dominica behind, Indract and the others abandoned the settlement and went on pilgrimage to Rome. On their return to Britain they were murdered by robbers a few miles west of Glastonbury. The details of this legend may be unhistorical, but in so far as it points to the existence, during Ine's reign, of a monastic settlement at or near St Dominick, there seems no reason why it should not be true, and this establishment may well have been a daughter-cell of Glastonbury.[1]

Thus several lines of evidence converge to indicate that the campaign of 710 left Ine in a position to dispose of land west of the Tamar, where only a few years previously his opponent, Geraint of Cornwall, had ruled in full sovereignty. And this being so, it is impossible to hold that any appreciable part of Devon still lay, at this date, outside the control of Wessex. For the true conqueror of Devon we must look back to Centwine. The three victorious campaigns of which Aldhelm speaks as falling within Centwine's reign (676–85) had evidently left the kings of Wessex in a position of such mastery over the whole of

[1] For an admirable discussion of the hagiographical evidence, see G. H. Doble, *St Indract and St Dominic*, 'Cornish Saints' Series, no. 48, 1944. John of Tynemouth says that Indract's party landed at "Tamerunta." Whether we identify this landing-place with Trematon on the Cornish side of the Tamar, or with Tamerton Foliot on the Devonshire bank, it seems clear that the little colony established itself in the parish of St Dominick. The chapel stood near Halton, at one end of a spur-way leading northwestward from the shore of the Tamar to Callington and beyond; see the instructive map, prepared by Sir Cyril Fox, of the ridgeways in the 'Linig' district. — *Antiquaries Journal*, XXXII, 1952, p. 68.

Devon that less than thirty years later they could invade and overrun a considerable part of Cornwall.[1]

It would almost certainly be a mistake to think of these conflicts in terms of a war between two modern states, like France and Germany, and of territorial annexation by the victor. In all probability the first English invaders of West-Wales were colonists in search of new land to cultivate, pioneers resembling the much later backwoodsmen of the North American forest. Their infiltration may well have begun and continued for some time before the first recorded clash of arms. The native Britons perhaps looked on at first with sullen acquiescence while bands of Saxon colonists hacked out for themselves new clearings in the densely wooded combes, or occupied low-lying riverside grounds which the Celts had failed to cultivate. But sooner or later the process would give rise to what the jargon of diplomacy today styles 'incidents', and the stronger power would then intervene to protect its colonists. There is no need, then, to suppose that all the campaigns of Centwine and Ine were offensives, deliberately mounted with the object of extending the sovereignty of Wessex. On some occasions they may equally well have been defensive actions undertaken to protect the colonists against attack by hostile neighbours. Political annexation would follow, as the aftermath of victory.

The silence of the Anglo-Saxon Chronicle respecting the next clash on the western front is explained by the fact that it ended in the defeat of Wessex. It is the *Annales Cambriae* which inform us that in 722 the Britons won a victory at "Hehil apud Cornuenses." Whether, with Ekwall, we locate this battle on the Camel estuary, or with Stenton, on the river Hayle, it is clear that the English advance received a serious check.[2] Sherborne received no further benefactions in Cornwall until Egbert's reign. There may even have been some loss of territory lately won, for nothing more is heard of the Glastonbury settlement at Linig. According to the legend, Indract and his

---

[1] For further evidence cf. W. G. Hoskins, *The Westward Expansion of Wessex*, Leicester University Press, 1960.

[2] Ekwall, *op. cit.*, p. 228; Stenton, *op. cit.*, p. 72. Other and less probable suggestions have been put forward, such as Hele Bridge in Marhamchurch and Hele in Jacobstow. — DA LXV, 1933, p. 372; PND p. xviii. On the whole, the Camel seems the likeliest identification.

companions finally withdrew from the shores of the Tamar because one of the brethren took to stealing fish in order to augment the daily ration, thus emptying the fishpond. We may suspect that other and more potent causes were at work.

Meanwhile the settlement of Devon went on, helped forward by royal grants to the churches of Wessex. In 705 Ine founded an episcopal see at Sherborne and appointed Aldhelm as its first bishop, with jurisdiction over all the English churches west of Selwood. In 729 Æthelheard of Wessex gave to Glastonbury ten hides in the valley of the Torridge.[1] Ten years later he gave twenty hides at "Cridie" to Bishop Forthhere of Sherborne for the foundation of the minster that was later known as Crediton.[2]

According to the Chronicle, Æthelheard's successor Cuthred fought against "the Welsh" in 743 and 753. It is probable that the later of these battles took place in Devon or Cornwall.[3] Of Cynewulf, the next king but one (757–86), the Chronicle relates that he was very frequently in action against the Welsh, and he himself, in a charter dated 766, expresses some remorse for his severities against the Cornish enemy.[4] By this time Devon was formally organized as one of the shires of Wessex under a *prefectus* or ealdorman of its own, though it may still have included organized groups of Britons living under West-Welsh law.[5]

In 802, the first year of his reign, Egbert enfranchised the Glastonbury estate on the Torridge, and enlarged it by the gift of another five hides.[6] In 815 he invaded Cornwall and harried

---

[1] AD pp. 61, 97; JG p. 105.

[2] *The Crawford Collection of Early Charters and Documents*, ed. A. S. Napier and W. H. Stevenson, Oxford, 1895, pp. 1–5.

[3] The earlier was fought in alliance with Æthelbald of Mercia, and therefore perhaps against the north-Welsh; but in 752 Cuthred threw off the Mercian yoke.

[4] "... pro expiatione delictorum meorum, necnon, quod verbo dolendum est, pro aliqua vexatione inimicorum nostrorum Cornubiorum gentis." — CS 200.

[5] CS 200 is attested by seven *prefecti*, CS 224 and 225 by six, though in 224 their title is omitted. The shires of Wessex at this date were Berkshire, Hampshire, Wiltshire, Dorset, Somerset, Devon, and perhaps the Isle of Wight.

[6] AD p. 68. In the *Liber Terrarum* this donation is linked with Æthelheard's earlier gift in the same district by two consecutive entries: "Æthelardus de Torric. Ecgbirhtus de libertate ejusdem." — JG p. 371.

it from one end to the other. Ten years later a Cornish raid across the Tamar was repulsed at "Gafulford," now Galford in the parish of Lew Trenchard. Finally, in 838 the Britons made common cause with a great host of Danish marauders, but were routed by Egbert at the battle of Hingston Down. So much we learn from the Chronicle. What the Chronicle does not make sufficiently clear is that these victories left the king of Wessex in a position of undisputed mastery over the whole of Cornwall. They also enriched him with large domains beyond the Tamar, of which he gave a tenth to the Church.[1] The Cornish bishop, Kenstec, was now compelled to acknowledge the archbishop of Canterbury as his canonical superior.[2] But it seems that Kenstec's office was allowed to die with him, for his submission had not brought peace to the Cornish Church, nor reconciled his flock to Anglo-Roman usages. We are told — from a Saxon source — that "so far as they were able, they withstood the truth," and that the bishop of Sherborne was therefore commissioned to visit Cornwall annually and "uproot their errors."[3] By way of subsidizing this missionary work, Egbert added to the Sherborne endowments three estates in Cornwall: "Polltun," now Pawton, a manor which included six or seven parishes and parts of four more, between Bodmin and Padstow;[4] "Cællwic," elsewhere called "Cælling," probably identifiable with Kelly in Egloshayle;[5] and "Landwithan," now Lawhitton, which comprised Launceston and four neighbouring parishes.

For a reason that will appear in the sequel, the gift of the three manors was long remembered at Crediton and Exeter, and was recorded in two documents with which historians are now familiar.[6] But what has apparently passed unnoticed hitherto is that this was not by any means the full tale of Egbert's benefactions. The Sherborne list of founders informs us

---

[1] *Crawford Charters*, pp. 18, 107.   [2] CS 527.   [3] CS 614.

[4] Six whole parishes, according to Charles Henderson (*Cornish Church Guide*, Truro, 1925, p. 65); seven, according to the same authority on another page (*ibid.*, p. 25).

[5] Henderson, *op. cit.*, p. 87. Later bishops had a manor in Egloshayle named Bernere. The older identification of Cællwic with Callington has been shown to be untenable: cf. *Devon & Cornwall Notes & Queries*, XXVII, 1956–8, p. 225.

[6] *Crawford Charters*, p. 106; CS 614.

that he gave that church twelve hides at "Kelk" and eighteen hides at "Ros" and "Macor." Macor is clearly Maker, the estate formerly given to Sherborne by King Geraint,[1] and the record here probably implies a confirmation of existing title or a regrant of property which had been lost in the interim. "Kelk" is the original Cornish name of the place in north Cornwall to which, under Saxon occupation, the Old English suffix -hæmatun was added; it is now Kilkhampton.[2] "Ros" is the Celtic word for promontory; it stands here for the district known today as Roseland. The church of this district, Eglosros as it is called in Domesday Book, stood at Philleigh, and in this donation of Egbert's we may in all probability see the origin of what was afterwards known as the manor of Tregear, a vast episcopal domain comprising the parishes of St Antony, St Just, Gerrans, Philleigh, and St Michael Penkivel, together with parts of Feock and Ruan Lanihorne.[3]

It will be observed that at the date of Egbert's donation Kilkhampton had not yet had an English suffix added to its name. Due weight must be given to this circumstance in considering the question how far the defeat of 722 had checked the process of English settlement in Cornwall. In the modern Cornish hundred of East, which borders on the Tamar, we find that of 625 names for which early forms have been collected, as many as 325 are English. The proportion in the southern division of the hundred, roughly between the Lynher and the sea, is 40 per cent, and in the northern, between the Inny and the Ottery, 45; but in the middle division the average is 65, and it rises above 80 in the parishes of St Mellion, St Dominick, Calstock, and Stoke Climsland, the district where Glastonbury had acquired a temporary foothold in Ine's reign. But taken as a whole, the figures are in marked contrast with those for Stratton, the northernmost hundred of Cornwall. Throughout this hundred the proportion of English names is over 90 per cent.[4]

[1] Ekwall cites the Old Breton *macoer* and the Welsh *magwyr* as identical with this place-name (*op. cit.*, p. 311). There is also a Magor in Camborne. — J. E. B. Gover, 'Cornish Place-Names', *Antiquity*, II, 1928, p. 325.

[2] Ekwall, *op. cit.*, p. 275.

[3] G. H. Doble, *St Gerent*, 'Cornish Saints' Series, 41, 1938, pp. 21, 22.

[4] J. J. Alexander, in DA LXV, pp. 371, 372, and LXVI, pp. 298, 299, from statistics supplied by J. E. B. Gover.

The topographical and documentary evidence, therefore, is consistent with the supposition that the reverse at Hehil retarded English settlement across the lower Tamar, and even perhaps led to a withdrawal from positions previously occupied, but that in north Cornwall its effects were slighter and less permanent. The contrast between the overwhelming preponderance of English place-names in the far north, and their relative paucity in the south, would hardly have been so marked if the whole process of settlement had required to be started afresh after Egbert's conquest.

The lesser density of settlement across the lower Tamar helps to explain the political arrangements that were instituted, now or soon afterwards, by the government of Wessex. Kings of the native dynasty continued to reign in Cornwall; the *Annales Cambriae* record the death of one of them, named Dumgarth, in 875. For the Celtic inhabitants the tribal code of West-Wales was perhaps not yet superseded by the law of Wessex. To keep the English colonists in order, the king of Wessex appointed two high-reeves. These officials collected their king's dues in money and in kind; they probably also heard local pleas in a judicial capacity and acted as commanders in warlike emergencies.[1] One of them fixed his headquarters at Stratton, and took charge of all the English settlements in the district of Trigg: that is, in the modern hundreds of Trigg, Lesnewth, and Stratton. The sparser settlements to the south were administered from Lifton, a royal manor just across the Tamar on the Devonshire side.[2]

From the next king, Æthelwulf (839–55), Glastonbury received a grant of "Occemund," now Monk Okehampton,[3] and from his successor, Æthelbald (855–60), ten hides at "Brannoc-mynstre." There is no Brannocminster on the map today, but the Celtic name Brannoc occurs in Branscombe, on the south coast, and also in Braunton, the burial-place of St Brannoc, to

[1] Cf. H. M. Cam, *Liberties and Communities in Medieval England*, Cambridge, 1944, pp. 84–6; Stenton, *op. cit.*, pp. 297, 475.

[2] As appears from Alfred's will (below, p. 108). See also p. 166 for evidence that the connection between Lifton and Cornwall persisted, though in an attenuated form, well into the thirteenth century.

[3] AD pp. 69, 99; JG pp. 42, 108, 371. For the identification, cf. PND p. 154, and Ekwall, *op. cit.*, p. 349.

whom the parish church is dedicated.[1] Branscombe is ruled out, for Æthelbald's donation, we are told, was *ad capturam isiciorum*, and *isicius* means a freshwater fish, most probably salmon.[2] This seems decisive in favour of Braunton, where in the thirteenth century rents were paid in salmon, and where salmon-fishing is still carried on today, at the mouth of the river Taw. Here, then, we have the earliest known reference to a local industry which has kept its economic importance down to the present time.

Æthelbald's brother and successor Æthelbert (860–66) gave Sherborne eight hides at "Tauistoke." This may be either Tawstock in north Devon, or Tavistock in the south; the probabilities are in favour of Tawstock. When Alfred the Great drew up his will, *c.* 881, he directed that the lands in Trigg, dependent upon Stratton ("thæs landes æt Strætneat on Triconscire"), should go to Edward the Elder. To his younger son, Æthelweard, he assigned "Liwtune [Lifton] and the lands belonging thereto, that is, all that I have among the West-Welsh except Trigg."[3] The lesser density of English settlement in the south of the peninsula is reflected in the document known as the Burghal Hidage. Of the 500 hides charged with the up-keep and manning of the two westernmost strongholds, 360 were assigned to Pilton, the northern *burh* near Barnstaple, and only 140 to Lydford, which is eight miles east of Lifton.[4] But that colonization now extended to the Tamar, if not farther, is proved by the fact that Sherborne possessed a minster with a considerable estate at Plympton on the eastern shore. This property Edward the Elder took into his own hands, giving Sherborne three Somerset manors in exchange.[5] His motive was probably the same as when he acquired Portchester in 904 by exchange with Bishop Denewulf of Winchester;[6] he wished to secure the two greatest harbours on the south coast against Viking invaders. The same policy may well have led him to

[1] PND p. 32; DA LXX, 1938, p. 273.

[2] AD pp. 69, 70, 99; JG pp. 42, 109, 371. In the first chapter of his *Ecclesiastical History*, Bede says that the rivers of Britain are particularly abundant in *issicii* and eels. Stapleton translates this "lampreys," but Henry of Huntingdon, who repeats the statement in Bede's words, elsewhere uses *murena* for the lamprey. — *Historia Anglorum*, ed. T. Arnold, Rolls ser. 74, pp. 5, 254.

[3] CS 553. For the identification of Liwtune, see DA LXX, 1938, pp. 104–10.

[4] CS 1335. [5] CS 610. [6] CS 613.

acquire Maker, on the opposite shore of the Tamar. At any rate, by 1066 Maker had passed from Sherborne to the crown, and had been annexed to the Devonshire hundred of Walkhampton. It remained in the county of Devon, anomalously, until 1844.

Already in the lifetime of Alfred the Great it had become clear that the partition of the vast Sherborne diocese could not be long deferred. A preliminary move in that direction had indeed been made. Asser, the Welsh ecclesiastic who wrote Alfred's life, relates that Alfred "gave" him "Exeter, with all the diocesan territory (*parochia*) belonging to it in Devon and Cornwall."[1] This statement has often been discussed, and not infrequently misunderstood. By "Exeter" here Asser means the monastery in that city where the boy Wynfrid, better known as St Boniface, went to school. The endowments of this monastery were used to provide Asser with an income while he exercised episcopal functions in Devon and Cornwall, not as a bishop with a diocese of his own, but as an auxiliary to the bishop of Sherborne. Strictly speaking, his position was uncanonical. Ever since the fourth century canon law had insisted that there should be only one bishop in each diocese, with his cathedral in some urban centre, and with no *chorepiscopus* deputizing for him in the rural districts. Nevertheless, the needs of aged and infirm prelates, and of those responsible for very large territories, could ultimately be met only by the appointment of deputy bishops. Willibrord, the apostle of Frisia, was assisted in his last years by a *chorepiscopus*, and Boniface himself, although Pope Zacharias at first refused him permission, finally obtained similar assistance. The example of these great Anglo-Saxon missionaries was decisive; the number of *chorepiscopi* grew quickly, both in their native country and in the Frankish Church, until in the middle of the ninth century the compilers of the Pseudo-Isidorian Decretals made a fresh attempt to drive the institution out of the Church.[2] More than one passage in the ecclesiastical history of south-west England which has perplexed earlier writers can be explained by the presence of these *chorepiscopi*. Asser, until he was himself promoted to the see of

[1] Asser, *Life of King Alfred*, ed. W. H. Stevenson, Oxford, 1904, pp. 68, 321.

[2] W. Levison, *England and the Continent in the Eighth Century*, pp. 65–8.

Sherborne, acted as *chorepiscopus* in Devon and Cornwall. Tradition has preserved the names of two other bishops, Wærstan and Putta, who followed him, with their headquarters at Bishop's Tawton.[1]

In 909, on the death of Asser, the existing diocese of Sherborne was formally divided into three. Dorset remained to Sherborne; Somerset was made into a new bishopric, with its see at Wells; and Devon and Cornwall into another, under a diocesan bishop who fixed his see at Crediton. It was natural that on taking over this part of the Sherborne jurisdiction, the bishop of Crediton should also take possession of the endowments that had been given for its maintenance.

Some twenty years later the work begun by Egbert was completed by Athelstan. William of Malmesbury, the only chronicler who has reported these events, states that Athelstan, after asserting his supremacy over the Welsh princes, turned against the Cornish Britons, "and attacked them with great energy, compelling them to withdraw from Exeter, which until that time they had inhabited on a footing of legal equality with the English. He then fixed the left bank of the Tamar as the shire boundary, just as he had made the Wye the boundary for the north Britons."[2] In another passage William of Malmesbury recognizes that Cornwall had been "subjugated" by Egbert a hundred years before.[3] We have seen how complete that subjugation was; it enabled Egbert to annex large domains to the Wessex crown-land, and to make handsome gifts to his Church. On the other hand, it has already been suggested that while the English settlers in Cornwall were governed by the laws of Wessex, the Britons, even in Devon, may have remained subject to their own West-Welsh law and custom. The name of one hamlet, Walreddon near Tavistock, has been taken to mean 'community of Britons', and there may have been autonomous groups elsewhere in Devon, even in Exeter itself,

---

[1] The tradition concerning the Tawton bishops was first put in writing *c.* 1580 by John Hooker of Exeter, who is not likely to have invented it. Hooker had access to episcopal records now lost. Cf. J. R. Chanter, 'Tawton — the First Saxon Bishopric of Devonshire', DA VII, 1875, pp. 179–96; but Chanter has not perceived that Wærstan and Putta were only *chorepiscopi.*

[2] *Gesta Regum*, ed. W. Stubbs, Rolls ser. 90, p. 148.   [3] *Ibid.*, p. 106.

where the parishes of St Petroc and St Kerrian, with their Celtic dedications, have been supposed by some authorities to be the site of a British enclave.[1] This seems to be the most reasonable construction that can be placed on the statement just quoted from William of Malmesbury, that there were Britons inhabiting Exeter *aequo jure* with the English.[2]

The name of a Cornish king, Ricatus, has been found on a cross at Penzance which is unlikely to be earlier than the beginning of the tenth century.[3] But it seems certain that the dynasty came to an end about this time, and its extinction probably gave the signal for measures designed by Athelstan to bring Cornwall more fully into the politico-ecclesiastical orbit of Wessex. There can be no doubt that Athelstan devoted much attention to south-western affairs. He held several councils in Devon, notably at Exeter in 928 and at Lifton in 931. At some date before 1066 the six tribal divisions or 'small shires' of Cornwall — Trigg, Pyder, Powder, Wifel, Winne, and Penwith — were reorganized as hundreds on the English model. This transformation may well have been the work of Athelstan,[4] and coupled with the imposition of Wessex law over the whole peninsula, it may have provoked resistance serious enough to call for military action.

We are better informed concerning Athelstan's dealings with the Cornish Church. A charter is extant which records his gift of seven parcels of land to the church of St Buryan. The text of the charter as we have it is unsatisfactory, and its date (943) is manifestly wrong, but it is probably based on a genuine original.[5] Tradition also names Athelstan as a benefactor to the

[1] T. Kerslake, 'The Celt and the Teuton in Exeter', *Archaeological Journal*, xxx, 1873, pp. 211–25. Kerslake added four more parishes, St Pancras, St Paul, All Hallows in Goldsmith Street, and St Mary Arches, though admitting that these dedications might be English.

[2] See, further, pp. 122–24 below.

[3] H. O'Neill Hencken, *The Archaeology of Cornwall and Scilly*, 1932, p. 248; R. A. S. Macalister, *Corpus Inscriptionum Insularum Celticarum*, Dublin, 1945–49, II, p. 181.

[4] Hundreds cannot be traced in England before Edmund's reign (939–46), but there is reason to believe that they were then already an established institution. — Stenton, *op. cit.*, p. 296.

[5] CS 785. For a useful discussion of the textual difficulties, marred only by the writer's belief in Athelstan's mythical expedition to Scilly, see C. Croft,

churches of Bodmin, Padstow, and Probus.[1] With more certainty it can be stated that he attached a large endowment to St
Germans, and made it the seat of a bishop, at the same time
appointing a bishop with a British name, Conan, to officiate
west of the Tamar.[2] This was in 926, according to a charter
which Leland saw, but which has since disappeared.[3] For his
further support, the Cornish bishop was allowed to enjoy
the usufruct of three manors, Lawhitton, "Cællwic," and
Pawton, which had devolved from Sherborne to the bishop of
Crediton.

If Athelstan had wished to draw a boundary-line between the
Celtic-speaking natives and the English-speaking colonists who
had settled in Cornwall, the Lynher rather than the Tamar
would have been the obvious frontier. By fixing the Tamar as
the shire-boundary he made a substantial concession to native
sentiment. His benefactions to Cornish churches, and his
appointment of a Cornish bishop, were dictated by the same
policy. In the final impression, Athelstan stands out not as a
victorious war-lord marching in triumph down the peninsula,
but as a statesman blending firmness with conciliation, and
thereby perfecting a work that has endured unquestioned from
his day to ours.

A succession of eminent authorities have interpreted Athelstan's appointment of Bishop Conan to St Germans as the

'King Athelstan and the Parish of St Buryan', *Devon & Cornwall Notes &
Queries*, XXIII, 1949, pp. 337–42. Henderson says that "Athelstan established a
college of secular canons on the site of the hermitage of St Beriana" (*Cornish
Church Guide*, p. 67). The charter does indeed refer to *clerici* there, but says
nothing to suggest that they were of recent institution.

[1] Henderson, *op. cit.*, pp. 59, 174, 187. E. H. Pedler, *The Anglo-Saxon
Episcopate of Cornwall*, 1860, p. 72*n.*, remarks that "in former times there
seems to have been a prevailing desire in Cornwall to claim an origin from
king Æthelstan." Thus a gift of Newton St Petroc, Devon, to the church of
Bodmin, really made by Eadred (946–55), was ascribed to Athelstan, and a
charter was concocted to support the attribution (CS 725; cf. Pedler, *op. cit.*,
p. 152). These ascriptions at least testify to the enduring and beneficent
quality of Athelstan's work.

[2] Or, as Dunstan put it, "as far as the Tamar flowed." — *Crawford Charters*,
p. 19.

[3] Haddan and Stubbs, *op. cit.*, I, p. 671; the editors remark that Leland
wavers between 926 and 936, but the former is certainly right, for Bishop
Conan attests charters in 931, 932, and 934 (*ibid.*, p. 676).

creation of a regular diocesan see for Cornwall.[1] In reality, as
the sequel shows, Conan was merely a *chorepiscopus* acting for
the bishop of Crediton, who remained in paramount charge of
the undivided bishopric, and, while giving up the revenue from
three manors, retained possession of the other episcopal estates
in Cornwall. An entry in the Bodmin Gospels records a number
of manumissions carried out there "for King Eadred and Bishop
Æthelgar" of Crediton.[2] When Conan died, Eadred's council
advised that the arrangement respecting the three manors
should be continued for his successor's benefit; and the same
decision was taken *c.* 963 when Bishop Wulfsige was appointed
to St Germans. But on the death of Wulfsige the bishop of
Crediton put in a claim to the estates. Æthelred II then referred
the matter to Archbishop Dunstan of Canterbury, who wrote a
letter in reply, tracing the history of the three manors back to
Egbert's conquest. The archbishop ends by giving his opinion
that the manors ought by right to go to the bishop at St
Germans, or, as he styles him, the "shire-bishop."[3] He evidently
felt that the time was ripe for detaching Cornwall from the
diocese of Crediton; and a few years later the government came
round to this view. In 994 Æthelred gave Bishop Ealdred of St
Germans a charter establishing a see in Cornwall with full
diocesan jurisdiction. The charter decrees that Ealdred's bishopric shall be "free, and subject to him and all his successors, so
that he may govern and rule his diocese as the other bishops of
my realm do theirs."[4]

The ecclesiastical autonomy thus tardily conceded was destined to be short-lived. It led to a conflict of interest between
Crediton and St Germans, in which Crediton was finally victorious. Lyfing, bishop of that see, who stood high in favour

---

[1] Stenton, *op. cit.*, p. 433; Henderson, *op. cit.*, p. 98; Stubbs, *ibid.*, p. 20;
Stevenson, in *Crawford Charters*, p. 104.

[2] Haddan and Stubbs, I, p. 679.

[3] *Crawford Charters*, p. 19. Neither this letter, nor the well-known
narrative in the Leofric Missal, refers to any part of the episcopal domain
except the three estates in question; that is why scholars until now have not
appreciated the full extent of Egbert's benefactions or of the Crediton property in Cornwall.

[4] Dugdale, II, p. 535. The charter appears to contemplate the removal of
the see from St Germans to Bodmin, as a precaution against Danish raiders.
On this see further p. 170 below.

with Cnut, persuaded him to let him hold St Germans as well as Crediton. His successor, Leofric, also held both sees, but the union remained merely personal until 1050. Then Leofric sent one of his clergy, named Landbert, to Rome, with the object of enlisting papal support for a move which he had planned. The envoy represented to the pope that Crediton was a mere *villula*, and as such far less suitable for an episcopal see than the fortified city of Exeter. The highest authorities of the Church had always frowned upon bishops who set up their cathedrals in rural centres. Leo IX was therefore easily persuaded to approve the transfer and to recommend it to King Edward. In his negotiations with the government at home Leofric stated the case rather differently. He urged that as a result of the Danish invasions both his bishoprics were impoverished, and that Exeter, the only town of any strength in the two shires, was also the seat of an old monastery, now much decayed, the property of which would make a useful addition to his resources. It was true that the monastery had lost all its possessions except one small estate at Ide, but it had claims to a number of others, claims which Leofric was ultimately to succeed in making good. These arguments convinced King Edward, who presently came down to Exeter, and in the presence of the queen and the whole court solemnly installed Leofric in the old monastic church. A royal charter was then promulgated, fixing the episcopal see there and annexing the monastery to the bishopric. At the same time the charter decreed that from henceforth the two bishoprics of Devon and Cornwall should be amalgamated. It cannot be taken for granted that the pope would have agreed to this amalgamation, if he had been asked. The evidence suggests that he had been neatly circumvented.[1] For pluralism, then as now the obvious expedient for a church

[1] The full account of the negotiations given in the Leofric Missal, fos. 3–5, is printed by Haddan and Stubbs, I, p. 691, and Edward's charter in *Ordnance Survey Facsimiles of Anglo-Saxon Manuscripts*, ed. W. B. Sanders, 1878–84, II, Exeter, no. 13. The terms of the charter ("hoc tamen notum papae domino in primis Leoni facio ipsiusque attestatione confirmo") referring to the amalgamation of the bishoprics, and the absence of any allusion to the subject either in the account of Landbert's mission or in the pope's letter, are pretty clear indications that it had not been discussed at Rome. For the fifteen estates formerly belonging to the Exeter minster and recovered by Leofric, see Dugdale, II, p. 527.

in financial straits, was prohibited by canon law; and by this union of bishoprics Leofric had ceased to be a pluralist. With that stigma removed, and with his see established in an urban centre, his position was canonically unimpeachable.

By way of epilogue, a few words may be added on the descent of the estates with which this study has been concerned. By 1066 many of them had been taken over by other churches, while some had passed wholly or partly into lay hands. The bishop of Exeter, as successor in title to the bishops of Crediton and St Germans, held Roseland, Pawton, and Lawhitton; but Launceston, originally included in Lawhitton, had passed to Harold, that notorious despoiler of churches, who also held Kilkhampton.[1] Maker and "Brannocminster" belonged to the king, the latter having been exchanged by Glastonbury in 973 for property in Somerset.[2] A layman named Wulfnoth held two other Glastonbury manors, Brampford Speke and Monk Okehampton.[3]

The shrinkage of the old Sherborne endowments is sufficiently explained by the division of the bishoprics. It seems clear that the kings of the Old English line exercised far-reaching powers of resumption, which enabled them, when they saw fit, to redistribute the endowments of the churches. But the process was not relished in episcopal circles, and from the twelfth century onwards the bishops withstood any further repartition of their endowments. Hence the perpetuation of such absurdly large and over-wealthy bishoprics as Exeter and Lincoln.

[1] I follow Henderson in identifying the Trigel of the Exon Domesday with Tregear in Roseland. — VCH *Cornwall*, part viii, pp. 68, 103. For Kilkhampton and Launceston, see *ibid.*, pp. 65, 72.

[2] CS 1294.

[3] Brampford: CS 799; Ekwall, *op. cit.*, p. 60; DA lxx, 1938, pp. 253–75; AD p. 102; JG p. 377; DB iv, p. 123. Monk Okehampton: DB iv, p. 267.

HYPLE'S OLD LAND

AN INTERESTING 'land-book' issued by Edward the Martyr in 976 lay unpublished in the chapter archives at Exeter until 1881. Two years later it was discussed in some detail by J. B. Davidson. Since then little or nothing has been done to work out its implications in detail. The late Mrs F. Rose-Troup dealt with this charter among others in the last paper she wrote for the Devonshire Association, but the paper opens with a melancholy reference to the writer's failing health and eyesight, and, with all respect to the memory of a devoted worker, it must be said that her notes on this particular document are the least useful section of a paper which does not show her at her best.[1]

Davidson perceived that the land with which the charter is concerned lay for the most part in the parish of Cheriton Bishop. Had he lived to see the publication of the Crawford charters, which at that time still lay in private hands, he would not have failed to notice also how remarkably the geography of this charter dovetails into that of the earliest Devon land-book of which the full text has survived. As this is possibly a fact of great significance, it will be worth while to examine the evidence in detail.

We shall never know exactly when the Anglo-Saxons first began to settle in the Dumnonian peninsula, but their political and military control of what is now Devonshire can hardly have been complete before the reign of Centwine (676–85). The earliest known act of English sovereignty within its borders is a grant by King Æthelheard of Wessex to Glastonbury abbey of ten hides in the valley of the Torridge. This charter is not extant now, but according to the Glastonbury chroniclers it was dated 729. Ten years later the same Æthelheard granted twenty hides to Bishop Forthhere of Sherborne for the endowment of a new minster. The minster was to be established at

[1] DA LXXIV, 1942, pp. 237–61.

Crediton, and its endowment consisted of a large territory in the heart of Devon. A tenth-century copy of the charter describes the boundary in minute detail. Beginning at Creedy Bridge, it runs past Norton to Nether Exe, and down the Exe to the junction of that river with the Creedy, then westward to the Lilly Brook, and thence to the "Green Way," now known as Crediton Lane, which forms the eastern boundary of Cheriton Bishop (Grid reference 796956).[1] It then proceeds as follows:

From Green Way to Wolf-pit;

i.e. from Crediton Lane westward and down through Colihole (a natural and perfect lair for a wolf) to the bottom of the valley.

from Wolf-pit upstream to where the brooks meet;

near East Ford (789955).

then up the middle of the ridge;

probably up Ford Hill (780959).

along the ridge to the path;

the road from Yeoford, which is reached perhaps midway between Three Gate Cross and Caddiford Cross (773959).

from the path straight to the alder;

apparently moving a short distance away from the path, which may not then have taken exactly the same course as now.

southward over to the precipice;

just above Lewdon (769950).

from the precipice to the head of Birch-combe;

near Cross Farm (765944).

from the head of Birch-combe to Hana's ford;

westward down Crosshill Lane to the ford just north of Staddon Plantation (760947). It is tempting to see a trace of Hana in the farm now called *Honey*ford, less than a mile away to the south; but the earliest recorded form of this name appears to be Honyworthi, from *hunig* and *worthig*, meaning honey-farm (PND p. 430).

thence to Broad Ash;

[1] The topography can be followed on sheets SX 69, 78, 79 of the 2½-inch Ordnance Survey.

? near Wilson, originally Wulfgar's *tun*, and lately rechristened Wulfgar's Farm (756953).

from Broad Ash to the head of Fox-combe;

where the parish boundary starts going downhill to the Yeo (749952).

thence to Stanford (the stone ford) on the Yeo;

where the road from Hittisleigh Cross passes over the Yeo (741946).

from Stanford to the alder-thicket;

? near Easton Cross (723942).

from the alder-thicket to the landslip;

a steep declivity north of the road, halfway between Fursham Cross and Chapple (710938). Greenwood's map of Devon, published in 1827, shows that the parish boundary of Drewsteignton formerly turned aside from the Hittisleigh road just before Fursham Cross and passed straight across the head of the "landslip."

thence to Green Down.

following the line of the old Drewsteignton boundary as shown by Greenwood, who however has transposed Flood (which he calls "Blowder"!) and Chapple. Returning to the Hittisleigh road near Chapple, the boundary turns southward past Flood, and reaches the main road at a point slightly east of Grendon (710928), which is the Green Down of the charter.

From Green Down on the highway

A.30, the main road from Exeter to Okehampton.

to Putta's post;

probably at Harepath Cross (718924), where a side-track leads off to *Puddi*combe. The earliest recorded form of this name is *Pode*combe, and the authors of PND therefore question its association with the Putta of this charter (p. 403 *n.*), but cf. the analogous development of Puddington (*ibid.*, p. 389).

thence to Beornwynn's tree;

from Beornwynn's tree to Stanford on the Yeo;

This ford is omitted in one copy of the bounds. If correctly inserted, it should probably be identified with the ford at Vete (736915). Yeo, a common stream-name in Devon, means simply 'water'.

thence to Bucga's ford;

by Greystone, where the road crosses another brook (749916), an affluent of the one which now forms the boundary between Cheriton Bishop and Drewsteignton. This boundary stream, like the ford over its tributary, appears to have been named after Bucga, for in 1285 it was known as Boggebrok (PND p. 431). Between the two streams is a farm now called Lower *Budbrook*.

from Bucga's ford to Brunwold's tree;

? at Narracott (757915).

thence to Ash-combe;

the site of Coombe Hall (761912).

from Ash-combe to Wonbrook;

Greenwood's map takes the parish boundary of Drewsteignton over the Budbrook at Coombe Hall and across the ridge to the next valley. Here it touches a stream which rises near Cheriton Cross. This must be the Wonbrook (777916). It flows down past a farm called Woodbrook, which is probably not a corruption of the older name, but an alternative introduced some time before 1244, when it makes its first recorded appearance.

along the stream to the Teign;

down the Woodbrook *alias* Wonbrook to its junction with the Budbrook, and thence to the Teign (778900).

upstream on the Teign to Path-ford;

where A.382 crosses the Teign (713893). This is now called Dogmarsh Bridge, but the original name survives on both sides of the river in the corrupt forms Parford and (Great) Pafford.

thence to Franca's combe;

A footpath along the north bank leads gently uphill. Franca has been forgotten, but the path runs up past a farm which may have been his; it is now known as Coombe (720897).

from Franca's combe to the head of Drascombe;

via Bowden Farm, and going westward, either along the road from Drewsteignton or by the field-path, now disused, which led from Bowden to Stone Farm. The head of the combe is reached just above Underdown (707910).

thence to Deormere;

the lake now known as Bradford or Bradmere Pool (700910).

from Deormere to the Longstone;

There are still a number of longstones in the vicinity of Spinsters' Rock (see the illustrations in DA LXII, 1930, plates XXV–XXVII), and there may formerly have been others nearer to Whiddon Down.

thence to the head of Hurra's combe;

The spelling Hurracombe survived until the seventeenth century (PND p. 446); it is now Hollycombe. Greenwood's map shows the Drewsteignton boundary crossing the main road about 500 yards west of Whiddon Down and returning to it from the head of the combe, which is near Martin, i.e. *mære tun*, the 'boundary farm' (690925).

from the head of Hurra's combe to Rush-ford on the Nymet;

going down the combe to Hollycombe Ford on the river Troney (723970), which in this charter is called the Nymet (cf. *Crawford Charters*, p. 58, PND p. 348). The boundary then runs down that stream. Rush-ford is probably the ford at Quince Cross, near the meeting of the Bow, Hittisleigh (formerly Drewsteignton), and Spreyton parish boundaries.

thence to Hillerton.

Hillerton Cross (720981).[1]

From Hillerton Cross the boundary runs north-eastward, apparently skirting the parish of Morchard Bishop, to Binneford in Stockleigh English, and thence back to the starting-point at Creedy Bridge. Its most striking feature, and the one to which I would call particular attention, is the détour it makes in order to reach the Teign, which is its southern limit. A glance at the map-diagram will make this clear. After travelling westward for six miles north of Cheriton Bishop, the boundary curves round that parish and proceeds about four miles in the opposite direction, taking in a great part of Drewsteignton, before striking northward on its way back to Creedy Bridge. There were evidently cogent reasons for including Drewsteignton in the grant. But the most obvious way to do this was to draw the boundary down Crediton Lane to the main road (A.30) and thence down the Woodbrook to the Teign. By

---

[1] The framework for the interpretation of this boundary was provided by W. H. Stevenson (*Crawford Charters*, pp. 53–60), who identified the Green Way, the river Yeo, Grendon, the Exeter–Okehampton highway, Budbrook, the Teign, Parford, Drascombe, Deormere, Hollycombe, and Hillerton. After exploring this boundary and that of Treable, for the most part on foot, I have filled in the intermediate points, and ventured to correct Stevenson's notes on the Woodbrook and Rush-ford.

closing, in this way, a gap of little more than three miles, a détour of ten would have been avoided. The fact that this course was not taken suggests that there were also cogent reasons for excluding Cheriton Bishop. What were those reasons? Did King Æthelheard wish to keep Cheriton for himself? or to bestow it on one of his thegns? The soil is thin and poor; it is

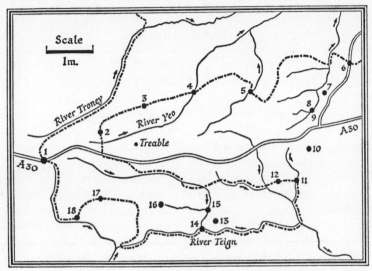

Crediton boundary ········   Boundary-points in the Treable charter ●

not the famous 'red earth' of the Crediton district. At the same time, the estate assigned to the new minster consisted of a very large territory, something like a dozen parishes, and everywhere but here its boundary was fairly straightforward. It is difficult to think of any topographical or other peculiarity which might have prompted this careful exclusion of Cheriton if it was Æthelheard's to deal with as he pleased. The most likely explanation is that it was not his: that, in other words, it belonged to some individual or group of people with whose property the king of Wessex did not feel free to interfere.

Let us remind ourselves at this point that the sovereignty of Devon had but lately passed into Anglo-Saxon hands. There are good grounds for believing that not all the native Cornu-Britons were immediately dispossessed. Celtic place-names, though infrequent, are to be found in every part of Devon. Sir Frank Stenton, while emphasizing the preponderance of English names, and regarding it as proof that no considerable remnant of British population remained to complicate the life of the invaders, is nevertheless prepared to believe that certain Celtic names may indicate the presence here and there of Britons who succeeded in maintaining their national identity for some time after the English conquest. Of such names Walreddon, near Tavistock, is perhaps the most striking example; it has been interpreted as *Weala-ræden*, a community of Britons.[1] Turning now to Cheriton Bishop, we find, within the area which Æthelheard so deliberately excluded from the grant of 739, a farm named Treable. In the thirteenth century this name was written as Tryfebel.[2] It is obviously compounded of the Cornu-British *trev*, meaning homestead, and a British personal name. The boundary of Treable, as I hope to show, coincided very closely with that of the property which Æthelheard refrained from giving to the minster. From these circumstances it seems clear that certain Cornu-British inhabitants of Cheriton Bishop preserved their racial and linguistic identity long enough to ensure the survival of a Celtic place-name amid a predominantly Anglo-Saxon nomenclature.

How long did this state of things continue? To answer that question, we have to pass over an interval of nearly two hundred years. We come then to the reign of Athelstan, and to the famous though somewhat cryptic passage in which William of Malmesbury narrates the measures taken by that king against the Cornu-Britons. William is a late authority for Athelstan's reign, but he had access to materials which are now lost.[3] He tells us that Athelstan, after asserting his supremacy over the Welsh princes, turned against the Cornu-Britons, "and attacked them with great energy, compelling them to withdraw from Exeter, which until that time they had inhabited on a footing of legal equality with the English. He then fixed the left bank of the Tamar as the shire boundary, just as he had made the Wye the boundary for the north Britons. Having cleansed the city of its defilement by wiping out that filthy

[1] PND pp. xx–xxiii.   [2] *Ibid.*, p. 429.
[3] Stenton, *Anglo-Saxon England*, Oxford, 1943, p. 335*n*.

race, he fortified it with towers and surrounded it with a wall of square-hewn stone."[1]

If William of Malmesbury meant his readers to understand that Exeter was previously unwalled, we must reject that part of his statement, for Mr C. A. Ralegh Radford has declared that the courses of ashlar William observed in the city wall "bear the unmistakable imprint of Imperial Rome."[2] The utmost that can be said with probability is that Athelstan may have repaired and strengthened the ancient Roman wall. But the rest of the narrative fits in very well with what we know from other sources. Down to the beginning of the tenth century a dynasty of native kings survived in Cornwall, with a status perhaps roughly similar to that of the greater Indian princes under British-Indian rule. That the Anglo-Saxon colonists of Devon and Cornwall had been governed by the law of Wessex from the first is hardly open to doubt, but the Britons of Cornwall, under their native dynasty, may have continued to regulate their affairs in accordance with west-Welsh tribal law and custom; and it is not difficult to believe that groups of Cornu-Britons in Devon itself may have been permitted to do so too, like those inhabitants of Caerleon who, much later, are described in Domesday Book as "living under Welsh law."[3] This is the most reasonable construction that can be placed on William of Malmesbury's statement that until Athelstan removed them, there were Britons inhabiting Exeter *aequo jure* with the English. It has been suggested that the parishes of St Petrock and St Kerrian, with their Celtic dedications, formed the nucleus of this British *enclave*.[4] At the same time, it is clear that there must have been other groups of Cornu-Britons up and down the county. Indeed, the chronicler implies as much;

---

[1] "Inde digressus, in Occidentales Britones se convertit, qui Cornewalenses vocantur. . . . Illos quoque impigre adorsus, ab Excestra, quam ad id temporis aequo cum Anglis jure inhabitarant, cedere compulit, terminum provinciae suae citra Tambram fluvium statuens, sicut Aquilonalibus Britannis amnem Waiam limitem posuerat. Urbem igitur illam, quam contaminatae gentis repurgio defaecaverat, turribus munivit, muro ex quadratis lapidibus cinxit." — William of Malmesbury, *Gesta Regum*, ed. Stubbs, Rolls ser. 90, p. 148.

[2] DA LXXIX, 1947, p. 23.   [3] DB I, p. 185c.

[4] T. Kerslake, 'The Celt and the Teuton in Exeter', *Archaeological Journal*, XXX, 1873, pp. 211–25.

elliptical as his statement is, it includes a reference to the Tamar which would be unintelligible had no British communities existed between the Tamar and the Exe. Athelstan's measures clearly affected Devon and Cornwall as a whole. The Cornish dynasty being now extinct, the time had come to organize Cornwall as an English shire, and to impose Wessex law upon the whole peninsula. Such measures may have provoked serious and active discontent, with Exeter as the centre of disturbance. If so, the repairing of the city wall marked the end of the revolt. The narrative seems to imply that in order to guard against further disaffection, a number of Cornu-Britons were removed from Exeter and other spots in Devon, and re-settled west of the Tamar.

The deportation of minorities is not unknown at the present day. Before, however, we accuse Athelstan of carrying out a piece of 'social engineering' in a manner worthy of our own more brutal century, there are two points that we should bear in mind. One is that there had been a considerable Anglo-Saxon settlement in Cornwall. There are parishes in east Cornwall where English place-names are as much in the majority as anywhere in Devon. For a racial and linguistic frontier the Lynher would have been more obviously suitable than the Tamar. Between the two streams lay territory which the men of Wessex had made their own. By including this in Cornwall, and fixing the shire boundary along the Tamar, Athelstan was making a substantial concession to Cornish sentiment. Further, by establishing a Cornish bishop at St Germans, and by his benefactions to other Cornish churches, he went out of his way to conciliate his British subjects, and it was as a benefactor rather than a triumphant war-lord that they remembered him in later times.

To return now to Cheriton Bishop. We have seen that Æthelheard, in 739, carefully excluded it from his grant to the church of Crediton. The place-name Treable, occurring within the excluded area, suggests that he did so because he was unable or unwilling to disturb its Cornu-British inhabitants. The survival of this Celtic name amid the predominantly Anglo-Saxon toponymy of the neighbourhood implies that these inhabitants remained in possession to a comparatively late date, and William of Malmesbury encourages us to believe that they were still there at the beginning of Athelstan's reign. Then they were deported and re-settled in Cornwall. If this is a correct interpretation of the evidence, Cheriton Bishop must have passed into the king's hand before 939, and remained there until Athelstan or one of his successors thought fit to grant it away.

In point of fact, when Cheriton does make its next appearance in the records, it is in the king's hand. By the charter of 976 King Edward grants it to his "faithful vassal" Ælfsige. He calls the estate "Hyple's old land," and describes its boundary. To Mrs Rose-Troup the expression "Hyple's old land" meant that Hyple had been the owner in an already distant past.[1] To my mind it implies the opposite: that he was the last man in possession before the estate was taken into the king's hand, and that his ownership fell within living memory, say within the fifty years previous to Edward's grant.[2] As for the name Hyple, it has already been pointed out that the second element in Trefebel, the modern Treable, is a Celtic personal name. According to Ekwall, the name is *Ebell*, corresponding to the Gaulish Epillus.[3] It is possible that by 976 some confusion had arisen between this name and an Old English name like Ipela, but even so its identity with the Hyple of the charter is plain enough.[4]

The boundary of Hyple's old land runs as follows:

1. First, from Three Posts

> an artificial boundary-mark at or near the spot described in the Crediton charter as "the head of Hurra's combe," i.e. just north of the Exeter–Okehampton highway, and slightly to the west of Whiddon Down (690925).

[1] DA LXXIV, 1942, p. 255.

[2] The Stoke Canon charter (CS 723) refers to "four acres west of the Exe, opposite Edferth's old land." Bosworth-Toller, Supplement, s.v. *eald-land*, takes this to mean 'land which has been left untilled for some time', and cites the later dialectal use of old-land or olland in this sense. The area covered by the Treable charter is well over six thousand acres. Much of it was probably woodland in 976, with a clearing round Treable itself, which may have been allowed to fall out of cultivation after the removal of the last British owner.

[3] PND p. 429.

[4] The interchange of *b* and *p* is a regular feature of the Cornu-British dialect. In the Bodmin Gospels *presbiter* becomes *prespiter*.

due east[1]

along the road to Hittisleigh.

2. as far as Gate Well [or Goat's Well];

at Flood, one of the sources of the Yeo (706933).

3. thence east along Rough Down

past the "land-slip" and "alder-thicket" mentioned in the Crediton charter. The modern names Fursham and Fursdon (Furze Down) indicate a rough, scrub-covered expanse (721942).

4. as far as Stanford.

where the road from Hittisleigh Cross passes over the Yeo (741946). This is the first Stanford of the Crediton charter (see above, p. 118).

5. From Stanford east to Lamford.

passing by the two intermediate points named in the Crediton charter, to "Hana's ford" on the Staddon-Caddiford brook (760947). By 976 the ford has changed its name to Lamford. The Domesday form *Lantfort* suggests that the first element is *land*, and that the meaning is 'boundary ford'; cf. Ekwall, *op. cit.*, p. 285, s.v. Lambrook.

6. From Lamford east to The Way.

the Green Way of the Crediton charter, now Crediton Lane (796956). A number of intermediate points are passed over in silence. The eastward direction carries the boundary up Crosshill Lane to the top of the ridge. Greenwood's map shows a lane passing due east from Cross Farm through Mounson to Crediton Lane; and the charter either takes this course or follows the less direct route established by the Crediton charter.

7. Along The Way to the old ditch;

The boundary goes down Crediton Lane past Twisted Oak, then turns aside into the lane that runs down between Venbridge House and Gorwyn. Part of this lane is what an Abbotsham charter of c. 1174 describes as a "twofold ditch," i.e. a hollow way running between two earthen banks (786943).

---

[1] Here and elsewhere the MS. has *iest* for *east*. This peculiar use of the initial *i* has its parallels in the Exeter Book, where the name Eadgifu, in the record of a manumission, becomes Iedue, and Ealdgyth is written Ialdit. — *The Exeter Book of Old English Poetry*, Facsimile edition, London, 1933, p. 52, *n.* 70a.

8. **south along the ditch to Rooks Fen**

now called Gorwyn, i.e. Gore-fenn, the muddy fen (PND p. 430).

9. **to where the Rushbrook discharges itself.**

The verb *utsceotan* and the noun *utscyte* signify the outfall where one stream flows into another. In this case the two brooks meet just north of Gorwyn Farm (782940).

10. **Thence due south to the big ridge over Middle Hill.**

The name Middlehill is now applied to a house near Melhuish Wood, a mile and a quarter east of Cheriton Cross. A line drawn southward from Gorwyn brings us across the main road to a cart-track leading from Cheriton Cross to Melhuish Barton. This track runs along Middle Hill, properly so called. Just beyond it is "the big ridge": a narrow-crested hill, the summit of which is marked at present by a line of trees (780926). With or without trees Windmill Hill, as it is called on the old six-inch map, would form a conspicuous object in the landscape. The word translated "ridge" here is *wale*, accusative of OE *walu*, meaning literally weal, but applicable to any long narrow projecting object.

11. **Thence south to the old ditch**

beside the lane which runs up from Fulford past Greenlane Farm and Listondown Barn. Formerly it continued westward down the valley (780916).

12. **and along the ditch as far as Ecca's homestead.**

The MS. has *ieccan stoc*. For a parallel to the initial *i*, cf. the spelling *iest* for *east*, noted above. Ecca's property is now represented by *Egg*beer and Lower *Egg*beer. The boundary crosses the valley and goes up to Lower Eggbeer, following the line of the old Cheriton–Drewsteignton boundary as shown on Greenwood's map. A guide-post situated at or near the cross-roads just above the farm would stand out conspicuously on the sky-line (770917).

13. **Then south to the middle of the old earthwork.**

The direction is really south-westward. A footpath through Broomspire Park Copse leads, or used to lead, down the valley to the Budbrook, which is crossed by a footbridge near Coombe Hall (the "Ash-combe" of the older charter). There is a choice of paths from this point to the "old earthwork," i.e. the great prehistoric fortress known as Prestonbury Castle (747900).

14. [Then] due south as far as Cuca's Brook;

> Looking back from the summit of Prestonbury, the points here suggested for Ecca's *stoc* and the crest of Middle Hill stand out in perfect visual alinement. Cuca's Brook is evidently the second Yeo of the Crediton charter, i.e. the stream that flows into the Teign just below Fingle Bridge (742899).

15. up along Cuca's Brook to where the little streamlet discharges itself;

> at the edge of Drewston Wood (745904).

16. up on the little streamlet as far as[1] its source;

> near Cross Farm in Drewsteignton (730907).

17. thence west to Frythestan's ditch;

> via Bowden and Stone Farm. Frythestan's ditch was presumably the boundary of his farm, and I take it to have been on the line of the road leading past Spinsters' Rock down to Sandsgate (702908).

18. west on the ditch as far as Rushbrook;

> the brook which flows past Sandsgate and into the Teign at Dogmarsh Bridge (698903). On the Ordnance map it is called White Water. The older and more appropriate name has left its trace in *Rush*ford Barton and *Rush*ford Wood. This brook still forms the parish boundary of Drewsteignton.

(1). up on Rushbrook as far as Three Posts.

> back to the starting-point near Whiddon Down (690925).

It will be perceived that if this interpretation is correct, the northern boundary coincided almost exactly with the Crediton boundary described in the charter of 739. The southern boundaries overlapped to some extent in the parish of Drewsteignton. That some territorial adjustment should have taken place in the course of two hundred years is hardly matter for surprise. It is on record that the canons of Crediton did not maintain their hold on all of the territory assigned to them by Æthelheard: witness the fourth Crawford charter, from which we learn that by 930 three hides in Sandford were back in the king's hand. The name Preston (priests' farm) perhaps commemorates their former presence, but by 1066 they had ceased to own any portion of Drewsteignton.

[1] reading *oð ða*; the MS. has *oða*.

Neither did "Hyple's old land" remain intact. Its original outlines, however, are still visible in Domesday Book. By 1066 it had been divided between two thegns, Leofgar and Ælfstan, and its manorial name had been changed to Lamford. Leofgar's was the southern and smaller portion; it comprised Eggbeer and what was afterwards known as Little Lamford, the modern Lambert. Ælfstan's portion is entered in Domesday Book as the four manors of Lantford, Midelanda, Ceritona, and Cuma. After the Norman Conquest these manors passed to the Honour of Gloucester, and from their later descent and subdivision it appears that they comprised Treable, Easton, (Great) Lamford, Staddon, Wolgereston *alias* Wilson, Medland, Cheriton, and Coombe Hall.[1] Treable, or Trev-ebell, survived in living use as the name of a farm near the western limit of the property, where the original Celtic homestead presumably stood.[2]

The argument set forth here does not pretend to be conclusive, but it offers a working hypothesis for the investigation of Celtic Devon. It suggests that the Celtic place-names we find scattered up and down the county have survived because they represent properties that remained in Cornu-British hands until the reign of Athelstan. They may or may not be the names of later manors; we have seen how the manorial name could shift from Celtic Treable to Old English Lamford. Not until the thirteenth century does the Celtic name re-emerge in written record. Many other names of British origin may well have undergone a similar eclipse. We cannot tell how many Cornu-Britons were absorbed into the Anglo-Saxon settlements, nor why some were left in quiet possession of their ancestral acres until the tenth century. It is at any rate clear that they were a far from negligible element in the population of Devon.

One last remark. Much of what I have written here and elsewhere is based on the two volumes which the English Place-Name Society devoted to this county. These are quite invaluable aids to research, as one discovers very quickly by contrast when one tries to work on the history of some county

---

[1] DA xliv, 1912, pp. 334–7.

[2] A bronze coin of Hadrian's reign has been unearthed near Treable. For this information I am indebted to Lady Fox. In all probability the site of the old farmstead would repay excavation.

which the society has not yet touched. Hence any criticism must be coupled with an expression of deep and lasting gratitude to the authors. But the authors themselves are well aware that the work needs revision at certain points; and it seems to me to betray, here and there, an Anglo-Saxon bias. The element -*pen* will serve to illustrate the point. In names like Pinhoe and Penn Moor the authors willingly recognize the Cornish word for head, top, summit, promontory; but in a number of other place-names they prefer the Old English *penn*, meaning enclosure, sheep-pen. They prefer it even where the lie of the land favours the Celtic alternative, as it does at Ipplepen. This village stands on a hill; its -*pen* is almost certainly Cornish; and I do not see why the first element should not be derived, like the Hyple of our charter, from a Celtic personal name. I believe, in short, that Ipplepen should be added to the list of Celtic survivals. If so, its interest is all the greater because of its proximity to Denbury; that is, *Devena-burh*, the 'stronghold of the men of Devon', a site which, for all the rich promise of its name, has not yet stirred any archaeologist to action. But enough has been said to indicate that in the topography of these early charters there are discoveries to be made, of a nature that will amply reward the student.

THE CHURLS OF HURSTBOURNE

IN THE course of his enquiry into the origins of the
English manor Seebohm quoted two custumals. The first,
which he attributed to the reign of Eadwig, was a custumal
of Tidenham in Gloucestershire. The other, relating to the
village now called Hurstbourne Priors in Hampshire, occurs in
a charter dated 900. These two documents give precise details
of the obligations incumbent upon peasants in a strictly
manorial economy. In this respect they stand almost alone, for
Anglo-Saxon England has left us no multiple surveys corresponding to the Frankish *polyptiques*. They fully deserve the
attention Seebohm concentrated on them.[1]

Seebohm's book, *The English Village Community*, possesses
every characteristic of a historical masterpiece but one: it
totally lacks charm of style. This deficiency its author shared
with his friend and critic, Vinogradoff; but his other great contemporary, Frederic William Maitland, was a brilliant writer,
and his *Domesday Book and Beyond*, largely written by way of
rejoinder to Seebohm, so far outshone the latter's work in dis-
tinction of style and subtlety of argument that Maitland's views
have won general acceptance. However, the study of our early
charters has not stood still in the last sixty years. It may be
profitable to re-examine Maitland's arguments, and in doing so
to look more closely at the documents involved.

The Tidenham custumal occurs in a cartulary of St Peter's
minster at Bath, written in the middle of the twelfth century.[2]
This manuscript includes copies of several royal land-grants,
beginning with a charter dated 956, by which King Eadwig
granted thirty hides at Tidenham to the minster. The next

[1] F. Seebohm, *The English Village Community*, 4th ed., 1890, pp. 148–64.
For the best edition of the two custumals, with English translation, see
R CIX, CX.
[2] Corpus Christi College, Cambridge, MS. 111, pp. 53–131; printed in
Two Chartularies of . . . Bath, ed. W. Hunt, Somerset Record Society, VII,
1893.

sixteen pages are taken up with charters relating to lands in Oxfordshire, Somerset, and Gloucestershire. Then comes the custumal, headed *Divisiones et Consuetudines Dyddanham*, and immediately after it a lease of Tidenham granted by the abbot and convent of Bath to Archbishop Stigand for his lifetime. This is undated, but from internal evidence it must have been granted between 1061 and 1065.[1] The arrangement of the cartulary does not bear out Seebohm's association of the custumal with Eadwig's charter of 956; as Maitland showed, it suggests rather a possible connection with Stigand's lease. Elsewhere Maitland admitted that the argument was not conclusive;[2] and Mr T. H. Aston has recently pointed out that since the abbey never regained possession of Tidenham, only one firm conclusion is possible: that the custumal was drawn up at some date between 956 and 1065.[3]

Stigand, the great pluralist, was not only archbishop of Canterbury but also bishop of Winchester, and as such head of St Swithun's, the Old Minster, to which Hurstbourne Priors belonged. It is natural, therefore, to ask whether we may see in him a possible link between the two custumals. If so, that of Hurstbourne would have been foisted into a much older document. But while it is easily conceivable that the monks of Bath should have recorded the customs of Tidenham in the expectation that the manor and its husbandmen would revert to them after Stigand's death, no such motive can be postulated in the case of Hurstbourne. There is nothing to suggest that Stigand ever had any special or personal connection with this estate. From the Domesday record it appears that he and the clergy of the Old Minster gave a lease of Bransbury to another churchman, and that Stigand leased one of his own episcopal manors to the abbot of Ely. From the same source we learn that he held East Meon, a large manor belonging to the Old Minster, until the day of his death. But of Hurstbourne the record says flatly that "it was always in the hands of the Minster."[4]

[1] R p. 469.
[2] *Domesday Book and Beyond*, Cambridge, 1907, p. 330; *Collected Papers*, III, p. 19.
[3] *Transactions of the Royal Historical Society*, 5th ser., VIII, 1958, p. 67n.
[4] VCH *Hants.*, I, pp. 452a, 462a, 465a, 467a.

A sequence of documents enables us to view the custumal of this Hampshire estate in historical perspective. In the last quarter of the eighth century an ealdorman named Hemele acquired 36 hides of land, 26 of which lay at Hurstbourne, from Beorhtric, king of Wessex, in exchange for 34 hides by the River Meon.[1] He then gave Hurstbourne to the church of Abingdon, laying Beorhtric's charter upon Our Lady's altar there.[2] In the next reign, according to information which comes to us both from Winchester and from Abingdon, King Egbert recovered Hurstbourne, giving Marcham, near Abingdon, to the church in exchange.[3] When Egbert died, Hurstbourne passed to his son Æthelwulf. Æthelwulf in turn bequeathed it by will to his son Alfred for his lifetime, with remainder to the church of Winchester. He also left 50 hides at Chisledon in Wiltshire to Alfred on the same terms.[4] When Alfred succeeded to the kingdom, another exchange was effected; the Winchester clergy gave up 100 hides at Cholsey to the king in return for Chisledon and Hurstbourne, which by this time was assessed at 60 hides. But presently, finding themselves unable to pay the heavy sum required to buy peace from the Vikings, they asked Alfred to pay it for them and to take back Chisledon and Hurstbourne: which he did.[5] When the time came for him to make his will, he left the two estates to the Old Minster in accordance with his father's injunction, adding thereto a separate property of his own near Hurstbourne.

Of the charter which Hemele laid upon the altar at Abingdon, Stenton has declared that apart from one incongruous phrase the text as we have it "may reasonably be accepted as a genuine land-book of King Beorhtric."[6] The Abingdon chronicle reproduces another charter by which Egbert gives the

[1] CS 258, from the Abingdon chronicle.

[2] *Chronicon Monasterii de Abingdon*, ed. J. Stevenson, Rolls ser. 2, I, p. 28. The chronicler has blundered here. He states that Hemele gave "villam de Mene," but goes on to show that it was the charter exchanging the land by the Meon for Hurstbourne which he laid upon the altar.

[3] *Ibid.*, p. 33; CS 413; CS 592. On the validity of this evidence, see further, below.

[4] Ha pp. 17, 51; CS 592, 594.   [5] CS 565.

[6] F. M. Stenton, *The Early History of the Abbey of Abingdon*, Reading, 1913, p. 29.

monastery 50 hides at Marcham in 835.[1] This makes no mention of Hurstbourne, and internal evidence, according to Stenton, is such as to condemn the charter, at least in its present form.[2] There is however no reason to doubt that the exchange took place. Ever since Offa's victory at Bensington in 779 Berkshire had lain under Mercian rule and in the diocese of Leicester. In 829 Egbert of Wessex made himself master of all England south of the Humber, but Mercian sovereignty was re-established in the following year; and even though the kings of Wessex may have retained their personal estates in Berkshire throughout these conflicts, by 835 Egbert may well have been glad to rid himself of a property in so debatable a border shire by exchanging it for one in the heart of Wessex.[3] The fact of the exchange is confirmed by the Hurstbourne charter of 900, the evidence of which is not the less impressive, indeed more so, for being veiled under a textual corruption. As the original charter has not survived, we depend upon a copy in the Codex Wintoniensis. There we read that "Ecgberht Rex comparavit... Hysseburnan Aðelred uno episcopo et ab illa familia æt Abbandune, deditque pro illa L manentes in... Merchamme." No bishop named Æthelred is recorded from Egbert's reign, and "uno" here is meaningless as it stands, but it gives us a clue to the original reading. This must surely have been "ab illo Reðuno episcopo," meaning Rethun, abbot of Abingdon until 814 and thereafter bishop of Leicester.[4]

---

[1] CS 413. [2] Stenton, *op. cit.*, p. 30.

[3] In 965 King Edgar executed a charter bestowing Marcham on the restored monastery at Abingdon (CS 1169). This is hardly sufficient ground for holding, with Stenton (*op. cit.*, p. 30), that "not until the reign of Edgar did the church of Abingdon obtain possession of Marcham." Between 835 and 965 the monastery went through many vicissitudes, and Edgar's charter may well have been a restitution of land once held but lost in the troubled interval.

[4] Reðhun presbiter abbas, CS 343, 348, both dated 814. As bishop he figures in CS 355 (Hrethunus, Rethunus); 356, 357, 358 (Reathunus, Ræðhun, Ræthunus, all three dated 816); 359 (Redhun, 817); 370 (Redhun, 822); 378, 379 (Reðhun, Hræðhun, 824); 384 (Reðhun, 825); 386, 387 (Hræþhun, Reduuin, 825); 413 (Rethun, 835); 416 (Ræþhun, 836); 421 (Ræðhun, 838–9). To these may be added the spurious or doubtful CS 296, 352, 366, 461, 850, and 1046. For "ab illo" here, cf. "ab illa familia" in the same clause; also "ille Aðulf rex," "ille Ælfred rex" in the companion charter, CS 594.

Thus the descent of Hurstbourne from Egbert to Alfred is attested by three charters and confirmed by Alfred's will. The first of the three charters, CS 565, records the exchange of Hurstbourne for Cholsey and the bargain over Hurstbourne and Chisledon. It has come down to us in a slightly distorted form: Bishop Ealhfrith of Winchester appears as "Alfreðus," and in the attestations of the king's two sons the copyist has misread "fs" (=*filius*) as "fr" (=*frater*); otherwise it has no objectionable features.[1] The second charter, CS 592, has the textual corruption to which attention has already been drawn. Here, as often elsewhere, a copyist's blunder furnishes presumptive evidence of an authentic original. The formulas of this Hurstbourne charter seem unexceptionable.[2] A further point in its favour is that the king states, among other reasons for granting it, that the older title-deed of the estate is missing. Quite true, and we know why it could not be found: it was still at Abingdon. The third, CS 594, is the charter with the Hurstbourne custumal, which must now be examined in the light of Maitland's criticisms.

Alfred died on the 26th of October 899. Less than twelve months later his son and successor, Edward the Elder, proceeded to carry out his testamentary arrangements. In one particular these arrangements were not fulfilled to the letter. The estate at Chisledon did not go to the Old Minster. The clergy relinquished their claim to it for a consideration, and shortly afterwards Edward bestowed it on the New Minster then in

---

[1] The contrary mistake occurs in the Stoke charter, where "Æthelweard filius regis" has been written by mistake for "Æ. frater regis." Stenton considered CS 565 a forgery (*op. cit.*, p. 46). In the forty-two years between the publication of his early work on Abingdon and his *Latin Charters of the Anglo-Saxon Period* this great scholar's criticism of charters grew steadily more fruitful and conservative. It is most instructive to compare his abrupt dismissal of CS 282 in the former work (p. 29) with the much more favourable treatment in the latter (pp. 25–7).

[2] The grant is made to the clergy "intus ad refectorium" and confirmed "in sempiterno graphio." For gifts of land to a church's refectory, cf. R VII, a Peterborough charter dated 852, and R XVII, a bequest to Winchester, undated but probably *c.* 900; see also E. John, 'The Division of the Mensa in Early English monasteries', *Journal of Ecclesiastical History*, VI, 1955, pp. 143–55. The phrase "in sempiterno graphio" occurs in several charters of the early tenth century, and also in *Asser's Life of Alfred*, ed. W. H. Stevenson, 1904, p. 9; see Stevenson's note *ibid.*, pp. 191–3.

process of being established side by side with the Old.[1] How-
ever, two charters were now drawn up, the one conveying 50
hides at Hurstbourne, and the other 10 hides at Stoke by
Hurstbourne, to the elder church.[2] We have seen that in
Alfred's reign Hurstbourne was assessed at 60 hides; now there
are 50 there and 10 at Stoke. We may infer that the 10 hides at
Stoke were the separate property ("sundorfeoh") which
Alfred had added to his bequest when he directed that "Nether
Hurstbourne is to be given to Winchester on the conditions laid
down by my father, together with my *sundorfeoh* at Nether
Hurstbourne which I have entrusted to Ecgulf." In fulfilment
of this bequest Hurstbourne is now handed over, with a proviso that if at any time the clergy shall wish to sell or exchange
the property it shall be offered first to the royal family; and by
the companion charter Stoke also is transferred to the minster,
"with all the men who were there when King Alfred died,
and with all those who were then at Hurstbourne." And a
custumal is inserted, describing the services these peasants were
bound to perform for their masters' benefit. This is the document which Seebohm used to illustrate a manorial economy in
Wessex at the close of the ninth century.

In order to discredit Seebohm's thesis, Maitland sets himself
to undermine this important piece of evidence. "In a Winchester cartulary," he writes, "'a cartulary of the lowest
possible character,' there stands what purports to be a charter
whereby in the year 900 Edward the Elder gave to the church
of Winchester 10 *manentes* of land 'æt Stoce by Hysseburnan'. . .
At the end of the would-be charter stand the names of its

[1] CS 598. If Stoke by Hurstbourne, an estate of 10 hides, was all the Old
Minster received in exchange for the 50 hides of Chisledon, as CS 594
implies, it was a very unequal bargain; but no other consideration is mentioned. A peculiarity of the Stoke charter, and one which tells in its favour,
is that alone among the documents which deal with Chisledon it refers to
Sparsholt as an integral part of the estate. This detail is not likely to have
occurred to a forger after 901, when Chisledon was granted permanently
to another minster. The scribe of the Codex has fallen into the common
mistake of reading the OE 'p' as *wen*: he writes "illam terram æt Ceolsel-
dene aet [*sic*] æt Sweoresholte." Ekwall and *The Place-Names of Wilts.*, p. 36,
identify the place in question with Sparsholt near Winchester, more than
thirty miles from Chisledon, but much more probably it was Sparsholt
(now called Sparcells) in Lydiard Millicent.

[2] CS 592, 594.

witnesses. Then follows in English (but hardly the English of the year 900) a statement of the services which the ceorls shall do 'to Hysseburnan.' Then follow the boundaries. Then the eschatocol of the charter and the list of its witnesses is repeated. On the face of the copy are three suspicious traits: (1) the modernized language, (2) the repeated eschatocol, (3) the description of the services, for the like is found in no other charter. This is not all. Two other documents in the same cartulary bear on the same transaction. By the first Edward gave to the church of Winchester 50 *manentes* 'æt Hysseburnan' which he had obtained by an exchange for land 'æt Merchamme.'[1] By the second he gave to the church of Winchester 50 *manentes* 'ad Hursbourne' and other 10 'ad Stoke.' The more carefully these three documents are examined, the more difficult will the critic find it to acquit the Winchester monks of falsifying their 'books' and improving Edward's gift. Therefore this famous statement about the ceorls' services is not the least suspicious part of a highly suspicious document."

The description of the Codex Wintoniensis as "a cartulary of the lowest possible character" is borrowed from Stubbs. It means either that the monks who compiled the volume in the middle of the twelfth century deliberately invented non-existent charters and falsified those they found ready-made, or that they more or less innocently transcribed documents which had been fabricated or falsified before their time. What are the facts? The Codex gives us the text of one hundred and ninety charters and other documents, many of which survive in no other copy. Some are of doubtful authenticity; others have been condemned outright, not always justly, as will appear in the sequel; but others again — and they can be numbered in scores — have never been called in question. It is therefore a gross exaggeration to say, as Maitland does on another page, that the Codex is "full of lies."[2] In a volume of this mixed character each text has to be judged on its merits. A prosecutor is not allowed to recite the previous convictions of the man in the dock, and it is deplorable that Maitland, the classic historian of English law, should have opened his case in this fashion.

[1] This is a slip on Maitland's part. The text he is quoting represents not Edward but his great-grandfather Egbert as making the exchange.
[2] *Domesday Book and Beyond*, p. 332.

It is now known that most of the Winchester falsifications were perpetrated during the half-century following the *coup d'état* of 964. The arbitrary action of Bishop Ethelwold, supported by King Edgar, in thrusting monks from Abingdon into the place of the cathedral clergy naturally provoked strong resentment among the ejected canons and their influential friends. The Benedictine intruders for their part felt correspondingly insecure. To strengthen their hold on the cathedral endowments, they or their successors in the next generation went to work upon the charters. They claimed nothing to which the church was not legitimately entitled, but by interpolating existing texts and inventing one or two new ones they clothed with a spurious antiquity possessions and privileges which in fact rested on perfectly valid title-deeds. More than one genuine charter of Edward the Elder can be shown to have suffered in the process. The fruits of this misdirected ingenuity have been examined at length in another work.[1] At present we have to ask whether the Hurstbourne charters must be included in the catalogue of doctored texts.

It will have been noticed that while Maitland stigmatizes the custumal as "not the least suspicious part of a highly suspicious document," he refrains from declaring exactly what he suspects. It is insinuated that the Winchester monks were trying to "improve" Edward's gift by making the charter convey more than the king intended. Since we can hardly suppose that the king would hand the estate over to the church but keep for himself the labour services of its husbandmen if they owed any such, we must understand Maitland to imply one of two things: either that the churls owed none of these services in the year 900, or that they owed some but not all. Yet as far back as the reign of Ine (688–726) we hear of lords who demand service as well as rent, and of men, even free men, who incur penalties by working on Sunday without their lord's command.[2] The services of the peasants in Ine's Wessex may or may not have been as various and toilsome as those described in the Hurstbourne custumal, but, preconceptions apart, what warrant is there for denying that they were so by 900?

[1] H. P. R. Finberg, *The Early Charters of Wessex*, Leicester, 1964, Chapter VII.
[2] Laws of Ine, 3. 2; 67, in EHD I, pp. 364, 371.

If we choose to believe that at some date before the charter was transcribed into the Codex Wintoniensis — let us say, before 1150 — the lords of Hurstbourne wished to exact services other or greater than those which had been rendered in 900, the question arises how it would help them to have the services ostensibly set down in Edward's charter. Any notions concerning the ancient demesne of the crown and the writ *Monstraverunt* can be dismissed at once, for these are creations of a later day, later even than 1150. In cases of disputed land-ownership a royal charter might be produced in a court of law with decisive effect as to title; but questions of labour service would surely be decided, in the first instance at any rate, by the sworn testimony of neighbours who from inherited knowledge and their own observation could declare the custom of the country. A supposititious parchment might conceivably be used to confirm or contradict that testimony if the customs had been loosened by upheavals of one kind or another. Upheavals there had certainly been at Hurstbourne, caused, as we have seen, by frequent changes of ownership, but the last of them took place in this very reign of Edward the Elder, and for centuries thereafter the church of Winchester held the lordship of Hurstbourne in undisturbed possession. There were reasons, therefore, arising from the history of this particular estate, reasons better than at any subsequent period, for putting the customs into writing at the time of Edward's charter.

The English of the custumal, we are told, is hardly the English of the year 900. And it is true that in a parchment written at that date we should not find such verbal forms as *synd* and *hyra*. But when we come upon the very same forms in King Alfred's will, we do not begin to scent forgery: we merely reflect that the earliest extant copy was made a full century after Alfred's death, and we are not surprised that it has been innocently 'modernized' to some extent in the process of transmission. The Codex Wintoniensis was written two hundred and fifty years after the church took possession of Hurstbourne; small wonder, then, if the scribe half-consciously modernized the English as he went along. That his action was not fully conscious is proved by the fact that the older form *heora* occurs in the same line with *hyra*. The latter indeed occurs only once, as against *heora* twice and *hiora* four times. These are not the only indications of an older original. The scribe has twice fallen into the easy mistake of reading the Old English 's' as 'r': *gerawan* for *gesawan* and *bærer* for *bæres*. Here it is easy to recover the original; for the rest, we can only discern it through the mist of what may have been more than one process of copying. A large number of forms exhibit the ordinary inflections of classical West Saxon (*ceorlas, æceras, agenre, gebringan, healfne*), which could have been written by a forger as late as the twelfth century; some have late spellings (*thæ, gauol, wyda*) and late endings (*agenan, dagan*), which could equally well be the work of an innocent copyist. The text as we have it contains no forms which became obsolete soon after 900. Thus the linguistic evidence neither proves nor disproves the reputed date. All that can be said is that taken by itself it affords no reasonable ground for suspicion.[1]

Since we are considering possible anachronisms, it is pertinent to mention one point on which Maitland did not touch. The Stoke charter is dated "A.D. 900, in the third indiction, when King Alfred died and King Edward his son took up the kingship." In the south of England at this period the year was reckoned as beginning on the 24th of September; hence, as Alfred died on the 26th of October 899, the charter is correctly dated. In this respect it stands in marked contrast with the 'A' text of the Anglo-Saxon Chronicle, which was certainly written at the Old Minster from *c*. 950 onwards and may well have been there from the first. This version of the Chronicle puts Alfred's death erroneously in 901.[2] The contrast was pointed out by W. H. Stevenson, who while sharing Maitland's doubts concerning the Stoke charter, nevertheless admitted that its independence of the Chronicle and freedom from chronological error formed presumptive evidence in its favour.[3]

What of the other traits to which Maitland objected: the

[1] The form *emnihte* for earlier *efennihte* occurs also in CS 599, dated 902, and in CS 617, undated but 879 × 908. Both these charters are taken from the Codex Wintoniensis, but so far as I know, the authenticity of neither has been disputed. — In weighing the linguistic evidence, I have greatly profited by discussion with Professor D. Whitelock, Dr F. E. Harmer, and Dr C. A. Luttrell, to whom my best thanks are due for their help, but who must not be held responsible for my conclusions.

[2] EHD I, pp. 109, 189; for an explanation of the error see *ibid.*, p. 184, n. 7.

[3] EHR XIII, 1898, pp. 71–77, especially p. 73.

"repeated eschatocol" and the custumal, suspicious because "the like is found in no other charter"? It is difficult to perceive any ground for suspicion in either. If I were fabricating a charter in the name of Edward the Elder, granting X hides at Y to the holy community at Z, I should as a matter of course provide it with all the usual features: preamble, *verba dispositiva*, boundaries, anathema, date, and witnesses. If the preamble were sanctimonious enough, and the anathema sufficiently hair-raising; if I took care to consult Ekwall and the English Place-Name Society for early forms of the place-names, and other charters of the period for chronologically sound attestations, then I might reasonably expect the result to pass muster. The two things I should not do would be to write out the dating clause and the witness-list twice over, and to insert in the body of the text a paragraph the like of which is found in no other charter. These are not the tricks of a forger, however little he knows his business. Instead of condemning the charter because of their presence, we should rather enquire how they come to be there.

When Birch re-edited the charters, he hinted at the true explanation in a footnote. It is in all respects probable that the Hurstbourne charter (CS 592) and the Stoke charter (CS 594) were issued simultaneously. In that case the date and the witnesses would be the same for each. The twelfth-century copyist transcribed the main part of CS 592 into his Codex, then copied CS 594 in full, then returned to CS 592 and copied its dating clause and witness-list, thus producing an apparent duplication.[1] This may have been his way of rectifying a mere oversight, but it is much more probable that he perceived the two charters to be closely interdependent, and acted accordingly. CS 592 is a simple conveyance of the 50 hides at Hurstbourne, with a clause intended to discourage future alienation but reserving to the royal house the first refusal if such alienation should ever be proposed. CS 594 restores the original integrity of the estate by handing over Alfred's "sundorfeoh," the 10 hides at Stoke. It is much the more comprehensive document of the two, for it makes explicit reference to both properties. Its

---

[1] The duplication is not quite exact. The first list includes an "Ælfred dux" and an "Ælfred minister" who do not reappear in the second. "Orferd" becomes "Offerð" at his second appearance.

boundaries take in the united territory of Hurstbourne and Stoke in one survey.[1] It contains the vital clause exempting both from all secular burdens except the three common dues, bridge-work, fortress-work, and military service. Its custumal begins: "Here are written the dues which the churls must render at Hurstbourne," not, be it noted, at Stoke, for henceforth Stoke will again be part of the main estate. It was therefore not at all an irrational proceeding to insert the whole of this charter like a sandwich-filling in the midst of its companion: which, in effect, is what the copyist has done. The one would lose much of its force without the other.

As for the custumal, its presence requires no sinister explanation. The peasants of Hurstbourne, let us remember, had been tossed this way and that like shuttlecocks. From a king of Wessex the lordship had passed to an ealdorman, and from him to a church in Berkshire. After a while it had come back to the king, and it had remained in royal hands for the next half-century, though under promise from 858 onwards that it should finally come to the Old Minster. Under Alfred the minster had gained possession, but under stress of war and tribute the clergy had been obliged to borrow money from the king and to repay him by handing back the usufruct. At this time the 10 hides at Stoke become detached from the main body of the estate as a "sundorfeoh" which Alfred in his will says he has "entrusted to Ecgulf," a thegn, perhaps, or a royal reeve. Now Alfred is dead; Stoke and Hurstbourne are to be reunited; and at long last the minster is to take permanent possession. Amid the bustle and business of a new reign there has been a delay, perhaps, of several months in completing the transfer; it is even possible that the judgement of the *witan* has been invoked, for Edward speaks of the transaction as a "causidica res," a legally contentious matter, which has now been settled "elucubratim," not without dust and heat. However that may have been, such vicissitudes are apt to unsettle people's minds, and it is important that the economy of the

---

[1] The topography has been worked out in detail by G. B. Grundy, *Archaeological Journal*, LXXXIV, 1927, pp. 210–16. The scribe who rubricated the Codex inserted a heading "Haec sunt territoria utriusque terrae," but made the mistake of inserting it at the head of the custumal, i.e. a paragraph too soon.

demesne shall not be injured by subtraction of dues or clandestine withdrawals of man-power. The charter therefore betrays visible anxiety that both Hurstbourne and Stoke shall come to the minster with all the men who were there when the great Alfred went the way of all flesh; and to close any remaining loophole the obligations of these men are recorded in detail. The circumstances may not have been unique, but they did surely justify exceptional precautions.

Maitland's final objection to the Stoke charter is that it accords ill with CS 592 and 593, which he describes as "two other documents in the same cartulary." The description is incorrect: CS 592 does indeed come from the unpopular Codex Wintoniensis, but 593 is taken from Dugdale, who printed it from an unspecified source. It is merely an epitome of the Stoke and Hurstbourne charters, put together by somebody who meant to record the gist of both without the trouble of copying them in full. It is therefore no touchstone for the authenticity of the Stoke charter which Maitland is discussing. The latter, far from betraying any incompatibility with CS 592, is its inseparable companion and complement, as we have seen. In fact, these two, and the whole group of charters examined here, tell a consistent and credible tale.

Thus Maitland's criticisms, when examined closely, turn out to be unexpectedly superficial, mere weapons of controversy snatched up in haste. There may be other and more valid reasons for impugning the authenticity of the Stoke charter, but if so they have not yet come to light. Until they do, historians will be fully justified in accepting it as it stands and in citing the custumal to illustrate manorial arrangements in the Wessex of Alfred's day.

CHARLTONS AND CARLTONS

CHARLTON is a very common place-name. In the official Index compiled from the census of 1951 it takes up forty-eight entries, and there are also three Charletons. To these we may add, for reasons that will appear in the course of this study, two Chaltons, one Charlston, and seventeen Chorltons. The same Index has seventy-seven references to Carltons and Carletons. These figures must be abated somewhat, for when a place is both a civil and an ecclesiastical parish it is sometimes entered twice over. Allowing for such duplications, we are left with forty-eight different places named Charl(e)ton or one of its variants, seven Chorltons, and forty Carl(e)tons: ninety-five places in all, not confined to any one part of England. When plotted on a map, their distribution fully bears out the opinion of philologists that these names were originally one and the same, but that in regions historically exposed to Danish or Norse occupation the Scandinavian *karl* has superseded the Old English *ceorl* as the first element.[1]

What exactly does it mean?

From time to time in the Old English period Ceorl was used as a personal name or nickname. The Anglo-Saxon Chronicle, in its annal for 851, records a defeat of the Vikings by an ealdorman so named. When compounded to form a place-name, it naturally becomes the genitive singular *Ceorles*, as in *Ceorles wyrthe* (962), now Chelsworth. But the great majority of Charltons have as their first element the genitive plural *ceorla*; they must therefore have been places occupied by a group of *ceorls*. This word means, first of all, a husband, 'man' as correlative to 'wife'. Then, by extension, it comes to mean the head of a peasant household. This is its most usual sense in Anglo-Saxon texts. It corresponds to the Latin *rusticus*,[2] and the exact equiva-

[1] E. Ekwall, *The Concise Oxford Dictionary of English Place-Names*, 4th ed., 1960, p. 88; A. H. Smith, *English Place-Name Elements*, I, p. 90, II, p. 2.
[2] In translating the *Dialogues* of Gregory the Great, Bishop Wærfrith repeatedly uses *ceorl* for *rusticus*. — *Bibliothek des Angelsächsischen Prosa*, v,

lent in modern English is not 'churl', its lineal descendant, but 'husbandman'. Now since every village and hamlet in England must have been peopled by husbandmen of one sort or another, the problem arises: what special characteristic led the Charltons

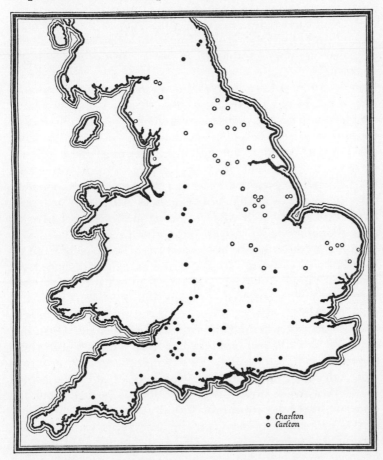

● *Charlton*
○ *Carlton*

and Carltons to be singled out for description as 'husbandmen's villages', and how did this mark them out from the rest?

To Professor Stenton, writing fifty years ago, the name Charlton implied unmistakably "an original settlement of free

ed. H. Hecht, Leipzig, 1900, p. 35, l. 2; p. 41, l. 32; p. 45, l. 24; p. 213, l. 13. The terms are also equated in the twelfth-century *Quadripartitus*. — *Die Gesetze der Angelsachsen*, ed. Liebermann, I, p. 127.

and independent *ceorls*."[1] Professor Ekwall is more cautious. According to him, "Old English *ceorl* means 'a freeman of the lowest rank, a free peasant'. But it is quite possible that already in OE times the word had come to be used also of a villein. Whether the name *Ceorlatun* means 'TUN of the free peasants' or 'TUN of the villeins', it suggests that manorialism had made a good deal of advance in OE times, for even 'TUN of the free peasants' presupposes that there were villages not held by freemen."[2]

In defining *ceorl* as a free peasant, all the lexicographers are at one. It is however important to note that 'free' in this context is a gloss with not the slightest etymological foundation. It must be supported, if it can be maintained at all, on other than philological grounds, for the root meaning 'husbandman' carries with it no connotation of either freedom or unfreedom. Further, there is good evidence that the word was used generically, to cover husbandmen of all degrees. Alfred the Great must have known very well what it meant, and for him the typical *ceorl*, though not a slave, was a peasant who had still some way to go before he could be accounted free. This is clear from his translation of Orosius. Orosius relates that the Volscians freed their slaves indiscriminately; then the former slaves, now freedmen (*libertini*), conspired to gain full freedom, and even mastery. Alfred writes: "They had freed some of their slaves, and also became too mild and forgiving to them all. Then their churls resented the fact that they had freed the slaves and would not free *them*" (i.e. the *ceorls*).[3] He has misunderstood the original here, not seeing that Orosius is speaking of only one group, the former slaves, now freedmen.[4] But the misunderstanding does not affect the conclusion we must draw from his use of *ceorl* as equivalent to *libertinus*. The decisive words are "and hi nolde." They prove that in Alfred's mind the *ceorl*, like the *libertinus* of his text, and like the villein of later centuries, was

---

[1] F. M. Stenton, *The Place-Names of Berkshire*, Reading, 1911, p. 25.

[2] Ekwall, *op. cit.*, p. 96.

[3] *King Alfred's Orosius*, ed. H. Sweet (Early Eng. Text Soc., 79), 1883, p. 162. "For þæm þe hie sume heora þeowas gefreodon, 7 eac him eallum wurdon to milde 7 to forgiefene. þa ofþuhte heora ceorlum þæt mon þa þeowas freode, 7 hi nolde."

[4] S. Potter, in *Anglia*, LXXI, 1952–3, p. 417.

usually a man still only half-free, one who needed a further act of emancipation before he could enjoy the full status of a free-man.

From Alfred's code of laws it appears that in the Wessex of his day some *ceorls* were prosperous enough to own slaves. These well-to-do peasants may have been fully free, but there is nothing in the code to suggest that if so they were typical of the majority. In Alfred's treaty with the Danish king Guthrum, some if not all of the English *ceorls* in East Anglia are equated with Danish freedmen, the half-free *liesengas*.[1]

There seems to be only one Old English document which refers explicitly to the condition of the peasants in a village named Charlton. It is a will, drawn up in 950 or thereabouts by a lady named Wynflæd, who possessed much property in Wessex. Of the estates named in the will, some belonged to her in her own right; but two appear to have been leaseholds, for neither at Chinnock nor at Charlton Horethorne does she make a bequest of land, and she expressly states that Chinnock will belong to the nuns of Shaftesbury after her death. She does however direct that two men and one woman at Charlton shall be set free; and she leaves the rest of the men, "except the freedmen," with the livestock, to her daughter. The implication is that she or her predecessor in the leasehold had stocked Charlton with husbandmen and oxen, and that men and beasts alike remained her property. The men are clearly of servile condition, and those who have not been freed may presently be sold off by her daughter, or removed to some other estate. The freedmen, however — that is, the three named in the will, and any others who may have been emancipated before the will was made — pass with the land, either to the next lease-holder or to the owner of the estate. In practice they have security of tenure, but the fact that they have it by express stipulation suggests that they are still very much at Wynflæd's disposal. It is at any rate clear that many of the husbandmen at Charlton Horethorne were not free, while those who were so were in no sense "independent."[2]

When we come to the Domesday period, we do find in the

---

[1] *Die Gesetze der Angelsachsen*, I, pp. 62, 126.

[2] *Wills* III; cf. T. H. Aston in *Trans. Royal Hist. Soc.*, 5th ser., VIII, 1958, p. 71.

Carltons of the eastern shires a good many peasants described as freemen (*liberi homines*), and side by side with them a more numerous category of sokemen. On many estates these two classes coexisted with the usual manorial population of villeins, cottagers, and slaves, but as a rule they are enumerated separately. It has been commonly supposed that they were descended from the rank and file of the Danish armies which conquered East Anglia in the ninth century; but after the searching criticism directed at this hypothesis by Mr R. H. C. Davis, no one is likely to propound it in future without qualms.[1] Whatever the conditions of their tenure, the freemen must be assumed to have been personally free. Beyond that, it has been found impossible, even after much discussion, to ascertain what distinguished them from the sokemen.[2] The latter, at any rate, are known to have been subject in varying degrees to seignorial control. They were justiciable in their lord's court; they were liable to agricultural service on his demesne, sometimes to the extent of one day in seven; they owed him substantial payments in money or in kind. As to their early history, we are still very much in the dark. Among historians who have discussed the subject, Professor Stenton is not alone in manifesting a wish "to maintain the original freedom of the normal sokeman."[3] Those who approach it without any desire to maintain either this or the opposite thesis may consider it equally probable that the peasants of eastern England before the Viking period were no freer than those of Wessex. The turmoil of the Danish invasions must have done much damage to the social structure, especially in those lordships which extended their authority over villages miles away from the administrative centre. It would not be surprising if numbers of peasants had taken advantage of the upheaval to emancipate themselves, by purchase or mere usurpation, from the demands of lordship, the degree of emancipation varying from manor to manor, and even between one sokeman and his neighbour. On this view, a process not essentially dissimilar

[1] R. H. C. Davis, 'East Anglia and the Danelaw', *ibid.*, v, 1955, pp. 23–39.
[2] cf. R. Lennard, *Rural England*, Oxford, 1956, pp. 225, 226.
[3] F. M. Stenton, *Types of Manorial Structure in the Northern Danelaw*, Oxford, 1910, p. 35; for the incidents of the sokeman's tenure, see *ibid.*, pp. 21–39.

from the decay of villeinage in the fourteenth and fifteenth centuries may have been set in motion by the Danish conquest, with results that were still being felt when the Normans came and reimposed seignorial control.[1]

The only habitative elements with which *ceorl* is combined are *-tun* and the relatively humble *-cot*. It is never associated with the more ancient and lordly *-ham*. With *-wudu*, denoting woodland in which peasants had the right — possibly an exclusive right — to cut timber, it occurs in Essex, Surrey, Sussex, Wilts, and Devon; and with *-graf* (grove) in Oxfordshire and Gloucestershire. An unidentified *ceorla den* is named in a charter of 939 (CS 741) as one of five woodland pastures belonging to Meopham, Kent.[2]

Neither Charlton nor Carlton belongs to the earliest stratum of English place-names. Carlton, as we have seen, is a product of Danish and Norse occupation; apart from a spurious Peterborough charter (CS 22) it is not found before the Viking period. Neither does Charlton occur in any fully authenticated text before the tenth century, for the Cropthorne charter (CS 235) is universally rejected, and the list of dependent vills, including Charlton, in Cædwalla's grant of Pagham (CS 50), dated 680, looks very much like a tenth-century interpolation.[3] The fifteen hides at Charlton, near Tetbury, given away by Ethelred of Mercia in 681, are not named in the charter (CS 58, 59); they are merely said to lie "near Tetta's minster."

The foregoing remarks illustrate the difficulty of interpreting *ceorl* in place-names, and they do not explain how certain villages came to be known and recognized as 'husbandmen's villages'. That is a problem which can be solved only by the detailed historical and topographical investigation to which we now turn. To include all the places thus named might be mis-

---

[1] Cf. also the process by which after the Conquest many villeins on the royal demesne acquired a position of qualified privilege as 'villein sokemen'. — R. S. Hoyt, *The Royal Demesne in English Constitutional History*, 1950, pp. 192–204. On the pre-Danish history of the sokemen, see *The Kalendar of Abbot Samson*, ed. R. H. C. Davis, Camden 3rd ser., LXXXIV, 1954, pp. xliii–xlvii, and P. H. Sawyer, *The Age of the Vikings*, 1962, pp. 164, 238.

[2] For the distribution of these and some other less frequent compounds see A. H. Smith, *op. cit.*, I, p. 90. To the list given there add *-brook* (D, Co).

[3] Mr Michael Roper points out that there is a similar list of dependent vills in CS 64, another (possibly inflated) charter ascribed to Cædwalla.

leading, for there is at least one Charlton which is known to be of different origin.[1] The notes which follow are therefore limited in the first instance to those places of which the derivation can be verified from Domesday Book or earlier texts. They are arranged in alphabetical order of counties.

CHALTON (in Moggerhanger, Beds.). *Cerlentone* 1086, *Cherleton* 1173.

Described in DB as a berewick or outlying dependency of the formerly royal manor of Potton, 5 miles away to the east. — VCH *Bedfordshire*, I, p. 260b.

CARLTON (Beds.). *Carlentone* 1086, *Carleton* 1198.

Six Domesday holdings are enumerated under this name. Half of them were held in 1066 by dependents of the king and queen. It looks as if the village had once been royal property. — *ibid.*, pp. 224a, 245a, 254b, 264a.

CHARLTON (in Wantage, Berks.). *Ceorlatun* 956, *Cerletone* 1086.

The charter of 956, a grant by King Eadwig, may or may not refer to this Charlton. Wantage belonged to the king from the time of Alfred the Great until after the Norman Conquest, and Charlton, less than a mile away in the same parish, was clearly an appendage of the royal manor. As late as the fifteenth century it was held under the lords of Wantage. — VCH *Berkshire*, IV, pp. 324b, 325b.

CHARLTON (in Hungerford, Berks.). *Cerletone* 1086.

This place is not marked on present-day maps, but it adjoined North Standen. With Hungerford it was probably carved out of Kintbury, an ancient royal manor. — *ibid.*, IV, pp. 185b, 193b; VCH *Wilts.*, II, p. 149a.

CARLTON (Cambs.). *Carletun* 975 × 1016, *Carletona c.* 1080, *Carlentone* 1086.

In 974 King Edgar granted 3 hides in the adjoining settlement of West Wratting to a thegn named Ælfhelm, who later made a will leaving Carlton to his wife. — CS 1306; *Wills* XIII.

CHORLTON (Cheshire). *Cerletune* 1086.

In the ecclesiastical parish of Wybunbury, a village which belonged in 1066 to the bishop of Lichfield. The dedication of Wybunbury church to St Chad suggests an early connection with the bishopric, and both villages may have formed part of its original endowment. — Chetham Soc., LXXV, pp. 91, 93 n., 152.

CHARLETON (Devon). *Cheletona* 1086, *Cherleton* 1242.

This place is 1½ m. s. of Kingsbridge, the name of which suggests an ancient royal possession. It may originally have lain in the hundred-manor of Chillington, which belonged in 1066 to K. Harold's mother. — PN *Devon*, p. 305; DS p. 304.

[1] Charlton near Sunbury-on-Thames, Middlesex, the DB *Cerdentone*, explained by Ekwall as 'the TUN of Ceolred's people'.

CHARTON (in Axmouth, Devon). *Cherletona, Cheletona* 1086.

Before the Norman Conquest Charton paid 15d a year to the ancient royal manor of Axminster. — VCH *Devon*, I, p. 404b.

CHERITON (in Payhembury, Devon). *Cherletona* 1086.

About halfway between Payhembury and Feniton. There are now two settlements, Higher and Lower C.

CHARLTON MARSHALL (Dorset). *Cerletone* 1086.

A royal manor 3 m. s. of Pimperne, with which it was associated in the king's ownership. — DB I, fo. 75b.

CHARLTON ABBOTS (Glos.). *Cerletone* 1086.

A village on the wolds 2½ m. s. of Winchcombe and belonging to Winchcombe Abbey, which was a royal foundation dating from 798.

CHARLTON (Herts.). *Cerletone* 1086.

A hamlet in the royal manor of Hitchin. According to DB, "the soke was always in Hitchin." — VCH *Herts.*, I, p. 303a.

CHARLTON (Kent). *Cerletone* 1086, *Cerlentune c.* 1100.

Now a ward in the metropolitan borough of Greenwich. In DB it appears as a manor which until the Norman Conquest had been held of the king. — VCH *Kent*, III, p. 224a.

CHARLTON by Dover (Kent). *Cerlentone* 1086, *Ceorletun c.* 1100.

Probably appendant to the royal borough of Dover, for in later centuries the manor of Dover Priory had claims over the greater part of it. — Hasted's *Kent*, 2nd ed., IX, p. 471.

CARLETON (Lancs.). *Carlentun* 1086.

Described in DB as 4 carucates belonging to Earl Tostig's manor of Preston-in-Amounderness. — VCH *Lancashire*, I, p. 288a.

CARLTON CURLIEU (Leics.). *Carletone, Carlintone* 1086.

A dependency of the royal manor of Great Bowden. — VCH *Leicestershire*, I, p. 308a.

CARLTON SCROPE (Lincs.). *Carletune* 1086, *Carlentona* 1115.

Described in DB as sokeland of Hough on the Hill. K. Harold had 5 ploughlands in Carlton, and Hough belonged to Ralf the Staller, an officer of high rank in the service of the Confessor. — DB I, fo. 347d.

NORTH CARLTON (Lincs.). *Nortcarletone* 1086.

3½ m. N. of Lincoln, close to the junction of Ermine Street and the Roman road connecting Doncaster with Lincoln, no. 28a in Margary's *Roman Roads in Britain*, II, p. 141.

SOUTH CARLTON (Lincs.). *Carlentone* 1086.

3 m. N. of Lincoln. In 1086 it belonged to the bishop of Bayeux, but Ernuin the priest declared that "it ought to be the king's." — DB I, fo. 342a. Both N. and S. Carlton may once have been appurtenant to Lincoln.

LITTLE CARLTON (Lincs.). *Carletone* 1086.

According to DB I, fo. 354*b*, half of this manor was sokeland. It may, like Manby, the adjoining settlement, have belonged to the royal soke of Gayton.

CARLTON LE MOORLAND (Lincs.). ?*Carlatune* 1066 × 1068, *Carletune* 1086.

It is uncertain whether this was the *Carlatune* which was left by will to Peterborough; in any case, the will did not take effect. — *Wills* XXXIX. Carlton le Moorland belonged in 1066, with the adjoining manor of Bassingham, to Earl Morcar. — DB I, fo. 338*a*, 360*c*.

EAST CARLETON (Norfolk). *Karltune* 1046, *Carletuna, Karletuna* 1086.

In 1046 a lady named Wulfgyth left her estates at Walsingham, East Carleton, and Harling to her sons Ulfketel and Ketel. — *Wills* XXXII. Twenty years later Ketel held Walsingham, and Godric, a freeman of Ketel, East Carleton. DB records that "the king and the earl have the soke." — VCH *Norfolk*, II, p. 177*a*. The manor was subsequently held by the service of carrying yearly to the king's residence twenty-four herring pies, the ancient fee-farm rent of the city of Norwich. — Blomefield's *Norfolk*, V, p. 102.

CARLETON FOREHOE (Norfolk). *Kasletuna, Carletuna* 1086.

1½ m. NE of Kimberley, with which most of it was held in 1066. DB enters it among the royal lands farmed by Godric. — VCH *Norfolk*, II, p. 50*a*. "Most of these, if not all, had at some time belonged to Earl Ralf, either as 'comital' manors or by inheritance . . . or by the grants made by K. William." — *ibid.*, p. 13.

CARLETON RODE (Norfolk). *Carletuna* 1086.

Five estates here are enumerated in DB. The principal one was held by the sheriff, Roger Bigod, with his manor of Forncett, 3 m. away to the east, and continued to be associated with Forncett until modern times. — VCH *Norfolk*, II, p. 112*a*; Blomefield's *Norfolk*, V, p. 128.

CARLETON ST PETER (Norfolk). *Karlentona* 1086.

This too was divided between five owners in 1086. The principal one had been held before the Conquest by a freeman under K. Edward. — VCH *Norfolk*, II, p. 158*a*.

CHARLTON (in Newbottle, Northants.). *Cerlintone* 1086.

There were two Domesday holdings here, one of which had been the freehold of four thegns in 1066. We are told that the soke lay in the royal manor of Kings Sutton, 2 m. away to the west. — VCH *Northants.*, I, pp. 309*a*, 324*b*.

EAST CARLTON (Northants.). *Carlintone* 1086.

One Domesday estate here was a freehold in 1066. Another estate in the same hundred, unnamed, but held of the king by R. Paynel, is thought to have been East Carlton, which is described in the survey drawn up some thirty years later as being of the king's soke. — VCH *Northants.*, I, pp. 322*b*, 336*a*, 386*a*.

CARLTON IN LINDRICK (Notts.). *Carentune, Carletone, Careltune* 1086.

There were six manors here in 1066, and two ploughlands described as belonging to the royal soke of Mansfield. — VCH *Notts.*, I, pp. 251*a*, 262*a*.

CARLTON ON TRENT (Notts.). *Carletone, Carletune, Carlentun* 1086.

½ m. N. of Willoughby, with which it was held in the royal soke of Grimston. — VCH *Notts.*, I, pp. 250*b*, 254*a*, 255*a*, 275*b*, 276*ab*.

CARLTON (Notts.). *Carentune* 1086.

Now a suburb of Nottingham. Held with Gedling in 1086 as sokeland of Stoke Bardolph. — VCH *Notts.*, I, p. 276*a*.

CHARLTON ON OTMOOR (Oxon.). *Cerlentone* 1086.

2 m. E. of Islip, the birthplace of Edward the Confessor. The hamlets of Fencott and Murcott in Charlton were later held by Westminster Abbey as part of the manor of Islip which the Confessor is said to have given to the abbey. — VCH *Oxfordshire*, VI, p. 82*b*.

CHARLTON (in Wrockwardine, Salop). *Cerlitone* 1086.

Wrockwardine was a royal manor before the Norman Conquest, and Charlton, 1½ m. to the west, was one of its berewicks. — Eyton, *Antiquities of Shropshire*, IX, pp. 19, 30.

CHARLTON (in Shepton Mallet, Somerset). *Cerletone* 1086.

1 m. W. of Doulting, and in DB part of the manor there which Glastonbury Abbey held by gift of K. Ine. — Adam of Domerham, ed. Hearne, pp. 53, 636.

CHARLTON ADAM (Somerset). *Cerletone, Ceorlatona* 1086.

CHARLTON MACKRELL (Somerset). *Cerletune, Ceorlatona* 1086.

These are adjacent villages, only ½ m. apart. Though separate manors by 1086, they were not yet distinguished by name, and the older inhabitants even today refer to them as East and West Charlton. Until the ecclesiastical parishes were united, there were constant disputes over tithes collected by one parish from the territory of the other. It seems clear that they were originally one settlement. Lying as they do between *Kings*don and *Keint*on Mandeville (*Chintune* DB, i.e. *cyne-tun*, royal manor) and about 2½ m. E. of Somerton, they would seem to have formed part of a large royal estate, with headquarters probably at Somerton, which, as we learn from the chronicler Æthelweard, was a royal manor in the eighth century. — VCH *Somerset*, I, pp. 479*a*, 495*b*; *Monumenta Historica Britannica*, p. 507.

CHARLTON HORETHORNE (Somerset). *Ceorlatune c.* 950.

3 m. N. of the royal manor of Milborne Port, and in the same hundred. The hundred-court used to meet on Horethorne Down. The tenant of Charlton *c.* 950 was a lady named Wynflæd, who left the stock and men

there to her daughter, subject to a gift of livestock to Milborne. — Anderson, *The English Hundred Names,* II, pp. 56, 57; *Wills* III.

CHARLTON MUSGROVE (Somerset). *Cerletone* 1086.
¾ m. NE of Wincanton.

CHAPEL CHORLTON (Staffs.). *Cerletone* 1086.
5 m. N. of Eccleshall. It figures in DB as one of eleven 'members' of Eccleshall, belonging with it to the bishop of Lichfield. — VCH *Staffordshire,* IV, p. 42a.

CARLTON (Suffolk). *Carletuna* 1086.
An outlying portion of the hundred of Hoxne, though situated ½ m. N. of Saxmundham in Plomesgate hundred. DB records that "the soke over the whole belongs to the abbot of Ely." The abbot held two manors in Hoxne hundred: 'Wineberga' (unidentified) and Soham, which is 10 m. W. of Carlton. — VCH *Suffolk,* I, p. 438ab. A second manor of *Carletuna* was in the soke of Kelsall, an adjoining settlement belonging to Roger Bigod. — *ibid.,* p. 450a.

CARLTON COLVILLE (Suffolk). *Carletuna, Karletuna* 1086.
1½ m. NE of Mutford, which was a royal manor in DB. "The king and the earl have the soke" over Carlton. — VCH *Suffolk,* I, pp. 443a, 544b.

CHARLTON (in West Dean, Sussex). *Cerletone* 1086.
In 1066 this manor was held by a tenant of K. Edward. — VCH *Sussex,* I, p. 411b.

CHARLTON (in Pagham, Sussex). *Ceorla tun* 680.
A lost tithing in Pagham; it lay near Aldwick coastguard station, but is now under the sea. — L. Fleming, *History of Pagham,* p. 135. The charter dated 680 (CS 50) is a grant by King Cædwalla to Bishop Wilfrid, giving him Pagham with Charlton and several other places in the neighbourhood. It survives in a handwriting of the late tenth century, but may represent a seventh-century original.

CHARLTON (Wilts.). *Ceorlatun c.* 970, *Cerletone* 1086.
2 m. NE of Malmesbury. Between 968 and 971 Ælfheah, ealdorman of Hampshire, left 20 hides *æt Ceorlatunæ* to Malmesbury Abbey, which is shown holding them in DB. — *Wills* IX, VCH *Wilts.,* II, p. 126.

CHARLTON (Worcs.). *Ceorletune* 780, *Ceorletune* 1086.
The charter of 780 (CS 235) purports to be a grant by Offa giving the royal manor of Cropthorne with its 'members', of which Charlton was one, to the church of Worcester. It is not authentic, but there is no reason to doubt the facts. Cropthorne certainly belonged to the church before 964 (CS 1135). It is about a mile from Charlton.

CARLTON (Yorks. ER). *Carlentun* 1086.
¾ m. W. of Aldbrough, in Holderness.

CARLTON (in Stanwick, Yorks. NR). *Cartun, Cartune* 1086.

½ m. NW of Aldbrough, and described as "inland" of Aldbrough in DB. There were also two ploughlands here which belonged to the soke of Gilling, Count Alan's in 1086, Earl Edwin's before the Conquest. — VCH *Yorkshire*, II, pp. 231*a*, 232*a*.

CARLTON in Coverdale (Yorks. NR). *Carleton* 1086.

1½ m. SW of Coverham. Waste in 1086. — VCH *Yorkshire*, II, p. 237*a*.

CARLTON HUSTHWAITE (Yorks. NR). *Carelton* 1086.

1½ m. N. of Husthwaite. A manor belonging to the archbishop of York, but waste in 1086. — VCH *Yorkshire*, II, p. 212*b*.

CARLTON MINIOTT (Yorks. NR). *Carletun, Carleton* 1086.

Held partly as a berewick of Bagby, ½ m. to the south, partly as a royal estate. — VCH *Yorkshire*, II, pp. 203*a*, 275*a*.

CARLTON (near Stokesley, Yorks. NR). *Carletun* 1086.

2½ m. S. of Seamer, and reckoned as sokeland of Seamer and Tanton, but waste in 1086. — VCH *Yorkshire*, II, p. 221*a*.

CARLTON (Yorks. NR). *Careltone, Careltun* 1086.

½ m. E. of Stockton on the Forest. An estate belonging to the archbishop of York. — VCH *Yorkshire*, II, pp. 212*b*, 313*a*.

CARLTON (in Guiseley, Yorks. WR). *Carletune* 1086.

Waste in 1086. About 1¼ m. from Otley and Guiseley, both of which belonged to the archbishop. — VCH *Yorkshire*, II, p. 275*b*.

CARLTON (Yorks. WR). *Carlentone* 1086.

½ m. SW of Rothwell, and in the same ownership. — VCH *Yorkshire*, II, p. 251*b*.

CARLTON (in Royston, Yorks. WR). *Carlentone, Carleton* 1086.

¾ m. S. of Royston, and in the same ownership. Some of its land was held with Shafton, which adjoins Carlton on the E. — VCH *Yorkshire*, II, p. 249*a*.

CARLETON (in Craven, Yorks. WR). *Carlentone* 1086.

1 m. SE of Skipton, which was a berewick of Bolton. Some of its land was held with Lothersdale. — VCH *Yorkshire*, II, p. 290*a*.

CARLTON (in Snaith, Yorks. WR). *Carletun* 1086.

1 m. N. of Snaith, on the other side of the R. Aire. Enumerated in DB as "land of the king's thegns." — VCH *Yorkshire*, II, p. 285*a*.

The fact that many of the places examined here ranked as manors by the time of the Domesday inquest tells us nothing about their earlier history. More significant is the character so many of them bear as satellites of other manors. This peculiarity has not escaped the notice of scholars like Ekwall and A. H. Smith. Professor Smith thinks it probably means that "a *ceorla-tun* was land on the outskirts of an estate, taken in for cultivation, fenced, and allocated to peasants."[1] Allocated, presumably, by the owner of the original estate, but for whose benefit: his own, or theirs? In a period when man-power was far from abundant, is he likely to have waived all further claim on their rents and services? The idea that the Charltons were marginal settlements finds little support from the topographical evidence. It is not on the outskirts of Wantage, Hitchin, Dover, and Wrockwardine that we find them established, but within a short walk of those royal seats: uncomfortably close, we may think, if they are really to be the homes of independent communities.

Bearing in mind these characteristics of manorial subordination and geographical proximity to more important centres, let us glance at a few more villages, the evidence for which, though later than Domesday Book, points to the same etymology.

CHARITON (in St Ive, Cornwall). *Cherlton* 1224, *Chirleton* 1306.

½ m. s. of Penharget, the Domesday *Pennehalgar*, in which manor it lay. In the fourteenth century *Churleton* superseded *Pennehalgar* as the name of the manor. — *Devon & Cornwall Notes & Queries*, XXIII, 1948, p. 202.

CHARLTON KINGS (Glos.). *Cherlinton* 1190, *Cherleton* 1236.

Part of the royal manor of Cheltenham, and included in it in DB. — C. S. Taylor, *Analysis of the Domesday Survey of Glos.*, pp. 143, 240.

CHARLTON (in Henbury, Glos.). *Cherltone c.* 1182, *Cherleton* 1204.

This hamlet, 1¼ m. NE of Henbury, was destroyed some years ago to make room for the Bristol Aeroplane Company. In the twelfth century it belonged, with a mainly villein population, to the manor of Henbury, which had been given to the bishopric of Worcester by K. Ethelred of Mercia in the seventh century. — CS 75; *Red Book of Worcester*, p. 407.

CHARLTON (in Tetbury, Glos.). *Chorlton* 1281.

½ m. w. of Tetbury, and described in the fourteenth century as a member of that manor. — Rudder's *Gloucestershire*, p. 731. In 681 Ethelred of Mercia gave 15 hides at a place unnamed "near Tetta's minster" to Aldhelm, abbot of Malmesbury (CS 58, 59), and in their cartulary the monks of that house identified the place with "Cherletone juxta Tetteburi" (BM Lansdowne MS. 417, fo. 2).

CHARLTON (Hants.). *Cherleton* 1192.

I m. NW of Andover, and a tithing in that parish. Andover was a Domesday manor, always in royal hands. — VCH *Hampshire*, IV, p. 346ab.

[1] A. H. Smith, *op. cit.*, I, p. 89.

CHARLTON (near Bellingham, Northumberland). *Carlton* 1195.

A member of the manor of Tarset, which seems to have belonged to Waltheof, earl of Northumberland. — *History of Northumberland*, xv, pp. 242, 251.

QUEEN CHARLTON (Somerset). *Cherleton* 1291.

1½ m. sw of Keynsham, which belonged to the Crown before and after the Norman Conquest. Charlton, with Whitchurch, was parcel of the royal manor. — Collinson's *Somerset*, II, p. 417.

CHARLTON (in Standlynch, Wilts.). *Cherleton* 1209.

A tithing in the hundred of Downton, which was an ancient possession of the bishops of Winchester. — Hoare's *Wiltshire*, III, Downton, p. 59.

CHARLTON (in Hartlebury, Worcs.). *Cherletona c.* 1182.

In the twelfth century this hamlet, with a mainly villein population, belonged to the manor of Hartlebury, which had been given to the see of Worcester by K. Burgred of Mercia. — *Red Book of Worcester*, p. 205.

CHORLTON-UPON-MEDLOCK (Lancs.). *Cherleton* 1177.

This township was comprised in Withington, a sub-manor of Manchester. Before the Norman Conquest Manchester and its dependencies belonged to the king's manor of Salford. — Tait, *Mediaeval Manchester*, 1904, pp. 6, 23.

Although the material summarized here scarcely lends itself to statistical analysis, it is noticeable how frequently the Charltons turn out to be appendages of royal manors, or of manors which at some distant time have been carved out of the royal domain in order to endow favoured subjects. This relationship links them with one of the cardinal facts of Anglo-Saxon history. "Far back in the Old English period," Professor Stenton tells us, "the *cyninges tun* or *regia villa*, which was the predecessor of the royal manor, had been a fundamental unit in the organization of justice and finance. It was at the *cyninges tun* that the peasants of the surrounding country had paid the food-rents by which they maintained the king, and in many cases the profits of justice in adjacent hundred courts had been rendered there."[1] We must think of places like Axminster, Wantage, and Mansfield as being not only the administrative centres of districts covering a hundred hides or more, but also as the head-quarters of agrarian units which may comprise any number of appendant villages and hamlets. But very early in the history of these great estates a process of erosion sets in. Provision has to

[1] *Anglo-Saxon England*, pp. 474, 475.

be made for the king's younger sons; great noblemen demand favours; old companions in arms expect their reward; and there are churches to be endowed. Piece by piece the royal domain is granted away. Whether or not this process impoverishes the Crown, it greatly enriches local nomenclature. Many of the component villages, hitherto undifferentiated by name, or differentiated only by reference to their geographical features, now have the names of their new owners permanently attached to them. The *tun* granted to Sibba becomes known as Sibton; Tyrdda's becomes Tredington; and so on. Presently all but one of the settlements on the original estate have acquired distinctive names of one kind or another. The one exception is the subordinate *tun* which the king has not granted out, but keeps in hand because without the food-rents and the agricultural services rendered by its husbandmen the economy of the central manor would break down. If the central estate has its home-farm, this will quite possibly be worked by slaves, but we may be sure that at busy seasons of the year the peasants of the subordinate village will be called in to lend a hand. This village, geographically distinct from the king's *tun*, and tenurially distinct from the alienated *tuns* which now pay dues to other lords, becomes known as Charlton because it is where the king's own husbandmen live, tilling the soil partly on their own account, but partly also, and perhaps chiefly, for the king.

To illustrate the development postulated here, we may glance at the early history of Cheltenham. It is a safe assumption that this royal estate served as the agrarian and administrative centre of at least the thirty hides which formed the Domesday hundred of that name. At some time before the close of the eighth century a minster was established within the area and endowed with a substantial extent of land. The bishop of Worcester, in whose diocese it lay, presently gave a lease of this property to the bishop of Hereford.[1] A century later the ecclesiastical estate was known as *Preosda-byrig*, the priests' manor (now Prestbury),[2] and by 1066 it was permanently annexed to the temporalities of Hereford. Meanwhile the swine-pasture, or Swindon, north-west of Cheltenham, and Leckhampton (*leac-*

[1] CS 309.　　[2] CS 560.

heantun), the steep ground where leeks grew at the base of the Cotswold scarp, had also passed into private hands. There remained to the king Cheltenham itself, and, a mile and a half to the south-east, Charlton Kings, where a cluster of peasants tilled their common fields and paid their dues to the king as lord of the manor. Not until the reign of Stephen did Charlton cease to be Crown land; but even in private ownership it was still accounted a 'member' of Cheltenham.[1]

Sometimes a royal manor developed urban characteristics, as at Dover, Milborne Port, and Winchcombe. These too had their Charltons, and here the name would usefully serve to distinguish the king's rustics from his burgess tenants.

The name Charlton, then, in the first instance, denotes a village on an estate which includes more than one unit of settlement. It is not the principal unit, being situated a mile or more away from the seat of lordship, but it is subject to the same lord, and the dues and services rendered by its husband-men are vital to the economy of the estate as a whole. In regions where the Anglo-Saxon pattern of settlement has been overlaid by Danish or Norse occupation the name assumes the scandinavianized form, Carlton.

The fact that the Charltons and Carltons appear so frequently on Crown land means no more than that the king is the greatest landowner in the realm. Where conditions are similar, the name and the thing may equally well occur on private estates. The Cornish Domesday supplies a possible example. In 1066 the small manor of Penharget belonged to the abbot of Tavistock; twenty years later it was held under the abbot by one of his Norman knights. The knight is recorded in Domesday Book as having enough arable land in demesne to employ one plough-team; he also has three cows, two swine, thirty sheep, and six goats. There are no slaves to drive his plough or tend his livestock. All the work of the demesne must be performed by members of the six villein households who make up the entire population of the manor. These households may have been established at Penharget itself: we cannot be sure that they were not; but it seems equally if not more probable that they formed a separate cluster at *Cherlton*, half a mile away, now

---

[1] BGAS LIV, 1932, pp. 145–49.

Chariton, which is known to have been the centre of population in the fourteenth century.[1]

The evidence examined here gives no support to the conception of a *ceorla-tun* as the home of an independent village community. On the contrary, it emphasizes the part such villages played in the economy of lordly estates. We catch a glimpse of this function in the Dorsetshire Domesday. There we read that the royal manor of Pimperne with its appendages, which included Charlton Marshall, owed the king an annual render equivalent to half of one night's provision.[2] It is true that the peasants on such estates as these acknowledged no superior but the king, but that is only because the king was also their landlord. Nor does this circumstance make them personally free. Some historians of repute have understood the designation *ceorl* as automatically excluding any trace of serfdom, inherited or acquired; but it has been shown that this interpretation lacks etymological warrant and is contradicted by at least one explicit text.[3] The typical peasant of the Charltons may well have been no freer than the bondmen of Charlton Horethorne whom the lady Wynflæd disposed of by will, or the serfs on the royal manor of Benson who were uprooted by the ealdorman Ethelred in 880 and transferred bodily, with their offspring, to an estate under new ownership five miles away.[4] There may still be room for argument here, but it can at least be said with assurance that there is nothing in the known history of the Charltons and Carltons to contradict the weighty judgement of Liebermann, that "from the earliest Anglo-Saxon times the peasant's obligation to pay rent, and therefore the village on the soil of a landlord, must have been the rule."[5]

[1] DB IV, fo. 181.   [2] DB I, fo. 75*b*.   [3] Above, p. 146.   [4] CS 547.
[5] *Die Gesetze der Angelsachsen*, II, p. 298 ('Bauer', 5).

THE MAKING OF A BOUNDARY

THE voyager from oversea who arrives in Plymouth
Sound may easily be misled by the implications of its
modern name. Ever since the thirteenth century, when
the fishing village on the shore began to develop into a great
sea-port, this majestic harbour has been known as Plymouth,
and its true, original name has been laid aside. But no ancient
geographer or annalist alludes to it by any other name than
Tamar-mouth; and if one sails upstream, past the ships of war
lying at anchor in the roadstead, past Saltash and its railway
bridge, past Warleigh Point and Landulph, one soon forgets
the tributary river Plym. For even up here the Tamar flows
rapidly down a broad and navigable channel. In the narrower
reaches above Calstock the wooded cliffs on the Devonshire
bank tower up like ramparts. And any one who sails up the
estuary, or explores on foot the upper reaches, watching the
salmon leap in the water while the dragonflies hover in the sun-
shot glades, will be visited sooner or later by the thought that
this noble and lovely stream is also a predestined boundary, the
natural western frontier of Devon.

At the close of the seventh century a contemporary of St
Aldhelm wrote some verses alluding to his travels through
"grim Devon and bare Cornwall." This is the earliest surviving
record of the division of the south-western peninsula into two
unequal halves.[1] It is likely enough that even then the Tamar
was the dividing line between them. For over a thousand years
now it has also been the administrative boundary between the
two shires. At the present day, however, it does not coincide
at all points with the county boundary. The county of Devon
includes 13,519 acres lying west of the Tamar, and distributed
among six parishes as follows.

North Petherwin	8209 acres	Pancrasweek	408
Werrington	3874	Luffincott	2
West Bridgerule	1015	Northcott	2
East Bridgerule	9		13,519 a.

[1] DA LXIV, 1932, p. 108.

Against this we may set 1058 acres lying east of the river which now belong to Cornwall. —

North Tamerton	1043 acres
Kilkhampton	$12\frac{1}{2}$
Launcells	$\frac{1}{2}$
Whitstone	2
	1058 a.

From these lists we may delete, as lacking in historical significance, West Bridgerule and North Tamerton, which were transferred to Devon and Cornwall respectively for parliamentary reasons under an Act of 1844.[1] On the other hand, we must take account of 1451 acres not mentioned in either list. This piece of territory lay in the parish of Maker, on the western shore of Plymouth Sound, and until transferred under the Act of 1844 it belonged to the county of Devon.[2]

It will be perceived that Devon is the shire which has profited most from these irregularities. The largest gain of all, approximately nineteen square miles in extent, consists of two adjoining parishes, North Petherwin and the greater part of Werrington, bounded on the south by a tributary of the upper Tamar called the Ottery or Attery, and on the north by a wavering line that rejoins the Tamar some three miles further upstream. This is an anomaly which has puzzled generations of antiquaries and map-makers. For the inhabitants of the two parishes it involves the practical inconvenience that, with Launceston only a mile or two away, they have to obtain their driving licences from Exeter, and cannot bury their dead until they have registered the decease at Holsworthy. According to their tale, the boundary was determined by officials who had been so royally entertained at Werrington that they mistook the Ottery for the Tamar, and when they discovered the mistake, made their way back by the erratic steps natural to men in their plight. Putting aside this pleasant fiction, can sober history explain such kinks in a boundary fore-ordained, as it would seem, by nature?

To answer this question, we must hark back to the time when the men of Wessex first invaded the Dumnonian peninsula.

[1] 7 & 8 Victoria, cap. 61.   [2] DA LXVI, 1934, pp. 280, 281.

The English conquest of Devon began early in the seventh century. Several laws enacted in the reign of Ine (688–726) point to a colonizing movement directed and controlled by the State. In this process of expansion the Church also took a hand. In 705 Ine founded an episcopal see at Sherborne and appointed his kinsman Aldhelm as its first bishop. Aldhelm had previously addressed a friendly letter to Geraint, the British king of Dumnonia, urging him to bring the ecclesiastical usages of his realm into conformity with those of the Roman Church. As bishop of Sherborne Aldhelm now assumed responsibility for the government of all the English churches west of Selwood. The records of his diocese, if only they had been preserved, would have cleared up many dark points in the early history of Devon. As it is, we have no means of knowing how far westward the diocese extended. We shall find the bishops of Sherborne in possession of a considerable estate lying between Plympton and the shore of the Tamar estuary, but it must remain a matter of surmise whether this had been acquired from Ine or some later benefactor. One very remarkable entry in the surviving register of Sherborne informs us that King Geraint endowed the see with "five hides of land at Macuir by the Tamar." Macuir is the West-Welsh name of the place now called Maker.[1] This gift, and Aldhelm's letter, were evidently moves in a diplomatic game which cannot now be followed in detail.

In 710 war broke out between Ine and Geraint. Ine was assisted by the king of Sussex, and although the chronicler does not say so, their victorious campaign probably completed the conquest of Devon. Charters dating from the reign of Cynewulf (757–86) are attested by seven *prefecti* or *principes*, who seem to have been governors of shires; and one of these, in all probability, was the ealdorman of Devon.[2] In 815 Egbert demanded that the Britons of Cornwall should recognize him as their overlord. Upon their refusal he invaded Cornwall and

---

[1] BM Cotton MS. Faust. A. ii, fo. 23. Dugdale misreads the name as Macnir (*Monasticon*, I, p. 337). Ekwall associates it with the Welsh *magwyr*, meaning wall or ruin (*Concise Oxford Dictionary of English Place Names*, p. 311). For the Glastonbury tradition which associates Ine with another grant of land by the Tamar, see p. 100.

[2] DA LIII, 1921, p. 175, and LXV, 1933, p. 140.

harried it from one end to the other. By this campaign he reduced the Cornish king to the status of a vassal. Ten years later the Britons rallied their strength and marched across the Tamar into Devon. Thereupon Egbert called out his troops, marched down through Crediton and Okehampton, and met the Cornishmen on Galford Down, near Lew Trenchard, where he again defeated them. The last round of the long-drawn struggle took place thirteen years later, in 838. This time the Cornishmen, in their despair, joined hands with a force of Scandinavian pirates who had been plundering the coast of Wessex. But Egbert was prepared, and met them before they could invade Devon. In a great battle fought on Hingston Down he wiped out the confederate host; and under this final blow Celtic sovereignty in the peninsula went down for ever.

One consequence of Egbert's victory was that the Cornish bishop acknowledged the archbishop of Canterbury as his canonical superior.[1] Another was that the king of Wessex acquired large demesnes in Cornwall, of which he gave a tenth to the Church. The conflict of jurisdiction between Sherborne and the native Cornish bishopric appears to have been soon resolved by the suppression of the latter. By Egbert's donation the bishop of Sherborne received three Cornish estates, "Polltun, Cællwic, and Landwithan."[2] Polltun, that is Pawton in St Breock, lay midway between Bodmin and Padstow, the two great centres of the cult of St Petroc, whose monks had until then dominated a vast territory on both sides of the Camel.[3] Cællwic, elsewhere called Cælling, should probably be identified with Kelly in Egloshayle.[4] Landwithan, now Lawhitton, included the future parishes of Dunheved, Lawhitton, Lezant, Trewen, and South Petherwin. Here too, as in the case of Pawton, the episcopal estate appears to have been deliberately carved out of properties belonging to the native Church. The unit broken up in this case was a district seemingly known as Petherwin. No such district is to be found on the map today, but a clue to its former existence is provided in the names of two villages. North and South Petherwin stand five miles

[1] *Councils and Ecclesiastical Documents*, ed. Haddan and Stubbs, I, p. 674.
[2] *Crawford Charters*, ed. Napier and Stevenson, p. 106.
[3] C. Henderson, in *The Cornish Church Guide*, Truro, 1925, p. 59.
[4] *Ibid.*, p. 87; *Devon & Cornwall Notes & Queries*, XXVII, 1956–8, p. 225.

apart, with the Ottery and the Kensey flowing between them. Without any natural feature in common, they share the name, and their churches are both dedicated to the Celtic saint Paternus, father of that Constantine, king of Dumnonia, against whom Gildas in his day let loose a characteristic torrent of invective. In the course of the English conquest North Petherwin was annexed to the royal demesne. Its incorporation into the crown-land of Wessex was the signal for an influx of English colonists, whose area of settlement is roughly defined by place-names, for if a line be drawn from the north-western extremity of the parish of North Petherwin through Pound-stock to the sea, it will be found that west of that line English names are few, while east of it Celtic names are rare or absent.[1]

North Petherwin, with its mother church of St Paternus, continued to be the ecclesiastical centre of a large district; but the principal English colony or *tun* was established some three miles nearer to the Tamar, and was called Wulfrædingtun, the modern Werrington. For secular purposes this *tun* from hence-forth gave its name to the whole area comprised in the modern parishes of North Petherwin and Werrington, and including part of St Giles-on-the-Heath. Some five square miles lay east of the Tamar; all the rest, including Werrington itself, lay on the Cornish side.[2]

In Cornwall the shadow of British royalty still lingered. We may picture the titular king as dispensing justice to subjects of his own race in accordance with their tribal code. Two high-reeves appointed by the king of Wessex administered that monarch's crown-lands and kept the English colonists in order. One of these officials made his headquarters at Stratton, about twelve miles north-west of Werrington. The proportion of English place-names in the Stratton district is nearly as high as that in north Devon. In other words, there was no linguistic

[1] PND pp. xxi, 158.

[2] St Giles-on-the-Heath, a parish of 3147 acres, includes part of the manor of Werrington and the whole of the ancient manor of Panson. The latter be-longed for some time after 981 to the abbey of Tavistock, but by 1066 it had passed into the hands of one Leuegar. After the Norman Conquest Ralph de Pomeroy conveyed it to Ruald Adobed in exchange for three other manors. At some date before 1103 Ruald became a monk at Exeter, and Panson was either given or sold to the abbot of Tavistock, of whom it was thenceforth held by knight service till the Dissolution. — DA lxxv, 1943, p. 249.

boundary along the upper Tamar; but south and west of the Ottery Celtic names have survived in much greater numbers.[1] The lesser density of settlement across the lower Tamar helps to explain why the king's reeve who administered this region did so from Lifton, a royal *tun* on the Devonshire side of the river.[2]

When Alfred the Great drew up his will, *c.* 888, he bequeathed Lifton "and the lands belonging thereto, namely all that I have among the West-Welsh except Triconshire," to Æthelweard, his younger son.[3] Stratton went to Edward the Elder, and with it, probably, its dependencies in Triconshire: that is, in the future hundreds of Trigg, Lesnewth, and Stratton.

Asser, a Welshman who had come by Alfred's invitation from St David's to the court of Wessex, relates that Alfred gave him two monasteries in Somerset, and subsequently "Exeter, with all the diocesan territory (*parochia*) belonging to it in Devon and Cornwall."[4] "Exeter" here probably means the ancient monastery in that city where St Boniface had received his early schooling; but in referring to its *parochia* Asser clearly implies that he exercised episcopal functions in Devon and Cornwall. If so, he must have been acting as an auxiliary to Bishop Wulfsige of Sherborne, and not as a bishop with a diocese of his own. It is necessary to dwell upon this point a little, for we shall find a similar arrangement preceding the establishment of a new diocese in Cornwall. In modern times the bishop who administers a missionary area as papal vicar or serves as auxiliary to the bishop of an established diocese takes his title from Philippopolis or some other extinct eastern see. This is a device which dates from the time of the crusades.

[1] DA LXXIII, 1941, p. 94.

[2] For Stratton, see below, p. 170, and H. Cam, *Liberties & Communities in Medieval England*, pp. 79, 86. The connection between Lifton and Cornwall persisted long after the Norman Conquest. Under Henry II the Pipe Rolls frequently refer to Cornish manors "which belong to the 'farm' of Devonshire" (*Great Rolls of the Pipe*, p. 46; Pipe Roll Soc., XXXIV, p. 156); and in 1275 a complaint against the steward of Cornwall is made by "all the men of the county of Cornwall who belong to the manor of Lifton" (*Rotuli Hundredorum*, I, p. 75).

[3] CS 553; DA LXX, 1938, p. 105.

[4] Asser, *Life of King Alfred*, ed. W. H. Stevenson, Oxford, 1904, pp. 68, 321.

The celebrated prior of Bodmin, Thomas Vivian, was one such prelate; he was appointed titular bishop of Megara in order that he might consecrate churches and ordain priests as deputy for Bishop Oldham of Exeter. It would seem that Asser, without a titular see, but with an income derived from the endowments of the Exeter monastery where he chiefly resided, occupied a similar post under Bishop Wulfsige, with particular responsibility for the western portion of the Sherborne diocese.

On the death of Wulfsige Asser succeeded to his bishopric. A few years later he surrendered the estate at Plympton to Edward the Elder, who gave him in exchange three manors in Somerset.[1] The territory of Plympton at that time extended to the shore of Cattewater, where the Plym flows into the Tamar estuary,[2] and behind Edward's exchange we may perhaps discern the policy of a king solicitous to defend his realm against Viking invaders. If so, the desire to command both sides of this great estuary might equally well prompt him to cast an acquisitive eye at Maker on the opposite shore. No document survives to inform us that he did so, but Maker did undoubtedly cease to be the property of Sherborne, and we have it on the authority of Domesday Book that at some date before 1066 it was incorporated into the crown-lordship of Walkhampton, afterwards known as the hundred of Roborough, in which Plympton also stood.[3] Thus was effected the earliest of those administrative annexations by which territory on the Cornish side of the Tamar was included in the county of Devon.

The time was clearly ripe now for the division of the Sherborne diocese. In 909 a new bishopric was established for Devon and Cornwall, with Crediton as its episcopal see. To Crediton the bishop of Sherborne ceded his three Cornish estates, Lawhitton, 'Cællwic', and Pawton.[4] Lawhitton, which included the site of the present borough of Launceston, a position of great natural strength, would have been a safer as well as more

---

[1] CS 610.

[2] It almost certainly included Plymstock, which in later centuries was recognized as a chapelry of Plympton (Dugdale, *op. cit.*, II, p. 500). R. N. Worth remarks that well within historic times the tidal waters of what is now known as the Laira flowed up to the walls of Plympton castle. — *History of Devonshire*, pp. 230, 231.

[3] DB IV, p. 79, Macretona.   [4] *Crawford Charters, loc. cit.*

central place of residence than Crediton for the bishop of Devon and Cornwall; but Crediton had its ancient minster and its memories of St Boniface, whereas Dunheved-Launceston was then a bare hill-top, and so it remained until the advent of the Norman earls.

No further changes are recorded until the reign of Athelstan (925–39). According to William of Malmesbury, Athelstan, after asserting his supremacy over the Welsh princes, turned against the Britons of Cornwall "and attacked them with great energy, compelling them to withdraw from Exeter, which until that time they had inhabited on a footing of legal equality with the English. He then fixed the left bank of the Tamar as the shire boundary, just as he had made the Wye the boundary for the north Britons.[1] Having cleansed the city of its defilement by wiping out that filthy race, he fortified it with towers and surrounded it with a wall of square-hewn stone."[2]

On the strength of this passage, and of confused popular tradition, many writers have represented Athelstan as the conqueror of Cornwall. Detailed accounts are given of pitched battles fought at various places between the Tamar and Land's End, and even in the isles of Scilly. There is no need to discuss this mythical campaign.[3] William of Malmesbury himself recognizes that Cornwall had been "subjugated" long before by Egbert. His account of Athelstan's proceedings must be interpreted in the light of what we have learnt from older and better sources. We have seen that by the close of the eighth century Devon was fully organized as one of the shires of

[1] Apart from the deviations already noticed, the whole of the Tamar is in Cornwall, down to Weir Head. The tidal water below Weir Head is divided equally between Cornwall and Devonshire.

[2] *Gesta Regum*, p. 148. See p. 123 *supra* for the original text.

[3] See J. J. Alexander on 'The Athelstan Myth', DA xLVIII, 1916, pp. 174–79, and LVI, 1924, p. 273. Those who wish to read how Athelstan won a great victory at Boleigh, near Lamorna; how boats were then collected at Sennen Cove to transport his army to the Scilly Isles; and how on the morning when they were due to sail Athelstan heard mass at St Buryan's and vowed to build a church there, may do so in *Devon & Cornwall Notes & Queries*, xxiii, 1949, pp. 337 sqq., where they will also find a number of corroborative details with which the old men of the vicinity have regaled visiting antiquarians: burial grounds, where however no bones have been found; armour disturbed by the plough and afterwards lost, and so forth.

Wessex. It is named as such in 851, when the Anglo-Saxon Chronicle refers to the ealdorman and men of "Defenascire." But every border county is exposed to certain hazards, especially when its population includes a 'fifth column' of the same race as the malcontents and cattle-thieves across the border. That a movement originating in some border foray, and magnified by racial animosities at Exeter, may have become serious enough to demand the king's personal intervention is not hard to believe. It is on record that Athelstan held councils at Exeter in 928 and at Lifton in 931.[1] For the rest, the chronicler appears to be giving a somewhat confused summary of the measures taken at this time for the supersession of West-Welsh tribal custom by the law of Wessex.[2] Ordgar, ealdorman of Dumnonia as Florence of Worcester styles him, administered Cornwall as well as Devon, on one occasion freeing a slave at St Petroc's altar in Bodmin. This and several other manumissions performed at the same altar by visiting monarchs, from Eadmund to Æthelred II, are recorded in the Bodmin Gospels.[3] At the end of Edgar's reign a Benedictine abbey was founded at Tavistock, in Devonshire but only three miles from the Tamar, to enshrine the Cornish saint Rumon and familiarize Cornish churchmen with the ideal of monastic life now prevalent on both sides of the English Channel. In the matter of diocesan organization the precedent of Sherborne and Crediton would seem to have been faithfully applied, the appointment of a local auxiliary to the bishop of the diocese being followed after an interval by the establishment of a new see. The first step was taken when Athelstan appointed a bishop with a British name, Conan, to take charge of Cornwall "as far as the Tamar flowed."[4] A line of Anglo-Cornish bishops followed Conan, with their headquarters at St Germans. It seems, however, that they did not at first enjoy the full status of regular diocesan bishops, but served as auxiliaries to Crediton, for although two at least of these prelates are known to have enjoyed the usufruct of Lawhitton and the other two episcopal manors, it was still an open question *circa* 985 whether the

---

[1] CS 663, 677.   [2] Cf. p. 123 above.
[3] BM Add. MS. 9381, printed in Oliver, *Monasticon Dioecesis Exoniensis,* 1846, pp. 431–36.
[4] *Crawford Charters, loc. cit.*

manors belonged of right to Crediton or St Germans.[1] Finally, in 994 Æthelred II gave Bishop Ealdred a charter authorizing him "to govern and rule his diocese [of Cornwall] as the other bishops of my realm do theirs." The charter appears to contemplate the removal of the see from St Germans to Bodmin: a natural enough precaution at a time when Danish raiders were particularly active on the south coast.[2] Lyfing, a former abbot of Tavistock, succeeded in getting himself appointed bishop of Cornwall at some date before 1035, according to one authority, or after 1042 according to another.[3] He was already bishop of Crediton, and he held both bishoprics until his death. He was followed by Leofric, who also held the two south-western bishoprics until 1050, when they were merged into a single diocese with a new see at Exeter.

By this time the old tribal divisions of Cornwall had been reorganized as hundreds on the English model. Triconshire, which included Werrington and North Petherwin, became the hundred of Stratton, taking its name from the royal manor which had long been the administrative centre. But the boundaries of the hundreds did not always coincide with those of manors: witness the case of Tavistock, of which the portion lying east of the Tavy has always been in a different hundred from the rest of the manor and parish. It is therefore possible that Werrington east of the Tamar belonged then, as now, to the Devonshire hundred of Black Torrington. The nineteen square miles on the Cornish side undoubtedly belonged to Stratton; and as the whole of the ancient parish of St Paternus was until recently included in the deanery of Trigg Major,

[1] *Ibid.* The editors date this instructive document "between 980, the date of (the Cornish) bishop Wulfsige's last signature, and 988, the date of the death of Dunstan." Wulfsige, however, attests the foundation charter of Tavistock in 981 (EHR LVIII, 1943, p. 200), and, as the editors remark, he may have lived a few years after this.

[2] K 686. Some writers put the case the other way round, alleging that the see was moved from Bodmin to St Germans in 981, when the Danes, according to the Anglo-Saxon Chronicle, ravaged "St Petroc's-stow." But Petrockstow here is not Bodmin; it is Padstow. People who fear piratical descents do not move nearer to the coast; they go further inland.

[3] William of Malmesbury attributes this appointment to Lyfing's favour with Cnut (*Gesta Pontificum*, p. 200); Florence of Worcester to that of Edward the Confessor (*Monumenta Historica Britannica*, p. 621).

which coincided with the eastern portion of Triconshire, it is at least equally probable that in the eleventh century Cornwall stretched across the river at this point and took in the remainder of the manor.

Werrington continued to form part of the royal demesne until about 1020, when it was settled on the Danish princess Gytha, who had become the wife of earl Godwin. Gytha was an intensely pious woman. On one occasion, sooner than eat the produce of land which Godwin had taken from a monastic house, she went on hunger-strike. The earl had to buy up a neighbouring lay property in order to assure a supply of food that she could eat with a clear conscience.[1] After his death she gave two Somersetshire manors to induce the monks of Winchester to pray for his soul.[2] Her sons followed in Godwin's footsteps, paying scant respect to consecrated persons and things. Swein, the eldest, distinguished himself by seducing a lady abbess. His next brother, Harold, the future king, enriched himself at the Church's expense. From the canons of Bodmin he took a hide of land, and from the bishop of Exeter the important manor of Topsham.[3] There is no direct record of his despoiling Tavistock Abbey, but an ancient and credible narrative, derived apparently from the foundation charter, asserts that the large manor of Stoke Climsland belonged at one time to that monastery. By 1066 it was in Harold's hands.[4]

After the battle of Hastings Gytha offered the Conqueror a large sum for Harold's corpse, and presently came down to Exeter. From what has been said about her disposition, it may be assumed that she was anxious to undo, so far as possible, the misdeeds of a son who had come to so disastrous an end in this world, and to secure prayers for his salvation in the next. It is an undoubted fact that at some date between October 1066 and the early spring of 1068, when she left England never to return, Gytha conveyed the whole manor of Werrington to Abbot Sihtric of Tavistock. The abbot must have been well aware that any traffic with a member of the fallen dynasty involved him in some measure of risk; but if, as has been sug-

[1] DB I, p. 164b.   [2] Freeman, *Norman Conquest*, II, p. 358.
[3] For these and other encroachments by Harold, see Freeman, *op. cit.*, II, p. 560.
[4] See p. 196 below; DB IV, p. 94.

gested here, he had a good claim for restitution of property taken from him by the dead king, he might feel reasonably safe in accepting such compensation as Gytha had it in her power to offer.

In point of fact, no one demurred to the transaction. Sihtric remained in undisputed possession of the manor till his death in 1082. He was succeeded by the Norman abbot Geoffrey. An entry in the Cornish geld-roll shows that on the eve of the Domesday inquest the abbot had one hide and one virgate (= 20 ferlings) of demesne land in the hundred of Stratton.[1] The only other manor he possessed in that hundred was Trewornan, which was assessed at half a hide, with only one ferling of demesne.[2] Since this is insufficient to account for the assessment recorded in the geld-roll, it is clear that Werrington, or the greater part of it, still lay within this Cornish hundred. But when the Domesday commissioners came down to the south-west, the blow fell. According to their instructions, no conveyance of property effected after the death of Edward the Confessor was to hold good unless the grantee could show King William's writ or prove that he had been put in possession by King William's sheriff. In vain would the abbot contend that before the capitulation of Exeter William's writ had scarcely run in Devon; or alternatively, that Werrington had been given as compensation for the loss of property which had since passed into King William's hands. Against him it could be argued that Gytha had no right to alienate crown land, being herself a mere life-tenant. A note in the Exon Domesday records the judgement of the commissioners. "The abbot of Tavistock was seised of the manor called Olwritona on the day King William sent his barons to enquire into the lands of England; and his predecessor had been seised of it before him. He was disseised of it by the king's barons because the English testified that it did not belong to the abbey on the day King Edward was alive and dead."[3]

A bald statement, if ever there was one! Yet Vinogradoff describes it as being "tinged by a certain prepossession," and without other evidence decides that the Exon Domesday must have been "written for the use of the abbey of Tavistock, or,

[1] DB IV, p. 66.   [2] Ibid., p. 167, Tregrenou.   [3] Ibid., p. 165.

at any rate, by scribes prejudiced in its favour."[1] Freeman, misled by a narrative which will be examined presently, surmised that notwithstanding the decision of the Domesday commissioners, Tavistock remained in actual possession.[2] But the record is precise: *desaisitus fuit*. Moreover, in the Exchequer Domesday Werrington is entered (as "Ulvredintone") under the heading "King's Land," with nothing to show that it had been in the abbot's hands for the past eighteen years.[3] But for the reference to "Olwritona" in the Exon Domesday we should never have known of Sihtric's acquisition.

After appearing as defendant in the case of Werrington, Abbot Geoffrey came forward as plaintiff against the Conqueror's half-brother Robert, count of Mortain, in respect of "Boieton" and three other Cornish manors which he declared that Sihtric had purchased before King Edward's death.[4] Whatever the merits of the case, the abbot failed to recover seisin. It would be interesting to know whether Sihtric had purchased "Boieton" before or after his transaction with Gytha. For Boyton adjoins Werrington on the north, and if it was originally a sub-manor or dependency of Werrington, the anomalous-looking dip in the northern boundary of Werrington becomes intelligible: it is the result of the count's usurpation. This hypothesis is confirmed by an entry in the list of Lands Usurped in Cornwall ("Terrae Occupatae in Cornu Gallia"), stating that half a hide of land, formerly valued at £4 and now at 40s., has been taken from the manor of Werrington ("Vluredinton") and is now held by the count of Mortain.[5]

The entry under "Terrae Occupatae" is the only reference to Werrington in the Cornish Domesday. All the other

[1] *English Society in the Eleventh Century*, p. 228.

[2] *Norman Conquest*, V, p. 747.

[3] DB I, p. 101*b*. It is entered at the end of Harold's manors, but with a symbol in the margin indicating that it ought to have been placed with Gytha's. The corresponding entry in the Exon Domesday occurs at the end of fo. 98 (IV, p. 90), closing the section "King's Demesne in Devonshire," and preceding "King's Demesne in Cornwall," which begins on fo. 99.

[4] DB IV, pp. 168, 471.

[5] *Ibid.*, p. 471. The valuation and assessment agree with those of Gurdaualan (Worthyvale in Minster), but this manor is much too far distant to have been a part of Werrington. The assessment and geographical position both point to Boyton.

references occur in the Domesday of Devon. Yet the geld-roll has shown us that until the eve of the great inquest the greater part if not the whole of the manor had belonged to Cornwall. It follows that its incorporation into Devon must have been brought about by the inquest itself. The commissioners had dispossessed the abbot and seized the manor into the king's hand; but why should this change of ownership have had the effect of removing it from one county into another?

Had Gytha left half a dozen Cornish manors to be taken over by King William, Werrington would probably have been farmed out with them to Baldwin, sheriff of Devon.[1] For it was Baldwin who administered the lands of the fallen dynasty in both counties, paying a fixed annual sum to the Exchequer for each group of estates, and making his profit out of the surplus revenue, if any. But, as it happened, Gytha had never held more than three manors in Cornwall, and the other two, Poundstock and St Gennys, had already been granted to a sub-tenant of the count of Mortain. There was therefore no 'Farm of Gytha's lands in Cornwall'. There was no compelling reason for associating Werrington with Harold's Cornish estates; and the only other administrative and financial category into which it could be readily absorbed was that of the king's demesne in Devonshire. This was of course in Baldwin's hands, and already included all that remained of Harold's and Gytha's property in Devon.[2]

Such an arrangement would suit Baldwin exceedingly well. His farm of the forfeited lands was fixed at £375 a year,[3] and until such time as the Exchequer woke up to the fact that a large manor had been newly absorbed into his county, he would go on paying £375. The balance in his favour, represented by the difference between that sum and the actual revenue from the king's manors, would meanwhile be swollen by £20 a year, the income from Werrington. In other words, the whole of the £20 would go into the sheriff's pocket, not the king's.

We cannot be sure that Baldwin did in fact bring off this master-stroke. But we may observe that motive and oppor-

---

[1] For Baldwin's administration of crown-land in Cornwall, see the geld roll, *ibid.*, pp. 65–67.

[2] DB IV, p. 84 (Tauetona, Bradestana, etc.).　　　　[3] *Ibid.*, p. 89.

tunity were both present; and it is, to say the least, suspicious that such information as we have is derived not from the official copy of Domesday Book, the one compiled for use at the Exchequer, for that contains no hint of any connection between Werrington and Tavistock, or between Werrington and Stratton, but from the unofficial volume which never left Exeter, where it remained under Baldwin's hand.

It is at any rate certain that Werrington was now abruptly, though very unobtrusively, severed from Cornwall. Henceforth it lay wholly in Devonshire, and in the hundred of Black Torrington. The local officials who revised the geld-roll in the light of the Domesday returns made an interlineation in the Black Torrington list, crediting the king with half a hide of tax-free demesne in "Oluritona." Hitherto Black Torrington had been assessed at thirty-four hides, ten of which had been tax-free. The addition of "Oluritona" brought the figures up to $34\frac{1}{2}$ and $10\frac{1}{2}$ respectively, and the interpolator altered the first accordingly, but forgot to alter the second.[1] This alteration accounted for only half the Werrington demesne, which was assessed at a whole hide; and as no alteration was made in the Stratton geld-list, we may perhaps infer that the annexation was carried out in two stages, the eastern portion of the manor, lying between the Tamar and the Carey, being first incorporated in Black Torrington, and the inhabitants of the western portion being instructed soon afterwards to cease attending the Stratton hundred-court and to go to Black Torrington instead.[2] This would be no hardship, if the Black Torrington court met in those days where it did in later centuries, at Clawton Bridge, appreciably nearer to their home than Stratton.[3] Suit to the

[1] Ibid., p. 59. There are other interlineations, but they have no bearing on the case. The abbot of Tavistock is credited with half a hide of demesne in Black Torrington hundred, doubtless in respect of Hatherleigh. O. J. Reichel demonstrated that the original assessment of this hundred did not include Werrington. From this circumstance he concluded that at the date of the geld-roll Werrington must have formed a distinct hundred (The Hundreds of Devon, p. 207). The idea of looking for it in a Cornish hundred did not occur to him.

[2] Netherbridge, between the Tamar and the Carey, is mentioned in a charter of c. 1176 as demesne-land of Werrington, and I see no reason to doubt that it had been so from the first.

[3] DA xxxviii, 1906, p. 304.

Devon shire-court would follow as a matter of course, and the entries in Domesday Book would clinch the annexation.

No one in Cornwall would be likely to object. The sheriff of that county, Thurstan, was a man of little weight, not even a tenant-in-chief.[1] Robert of Mortain, earl of Cornwall in fact if not in name, had no intention of relinquishing Boyton. Among his other depredations he had seized two manors, "Lanliner" and "Trebichen," which before the Conquest had been dependencies of Lifton: a relic, no doubt, of the arrangement mentioned in Alfred the Great's will.[2] He had also helped himself to Maker and annexed it to his own shire.[3] Thus, in the game of tampering with the county boundary, the first move had been his. Obviously his cue was to say nothing.

So it was done; but ten years later there came another turn of the wheel. The Conqueror was dead, and Baldwin had been succeeded as sheriff of Devon by his son William. His daughter was married to a certain William Fitz Wymund.[4] The new abbot of Tavistock was named Wymund, and as he is known to have had a brother William,[5] it is tempting to postulate a connection by marriage between the abbot's family and the sheriff's. How useful this might be will appear in the sequel.

In the spring of 1096 Duke Robert of Normandy borrowed ten thousand marks from his brother of England to pay his expenses in the first crusade. The loan was secured by a mortgage on the duchy. Extraordinary efforts were made by William's government to fulfil his share of the bargain. Throughout England, we are told, money was "part given, part extorted." The primate, Anselm, mortgaged his manor of Peckham for seven years to raise two hundred pounds; and some of the churches went so far as to melt down their altar vessels.[6] It seems that at this juncture Ralph Flambard, the king's efficient and therefore highly unpopular financial minis-

[1] Mr R. Welldon Finn thinks it possible that in 1086 a single shire-court served both Devon and Cornwall.

[2] DB IV, p. 84. Trebichen is Trebeigh in St Ive, one of the four manors claimed by the abbot of Tavistock. Lanliner has not been identified, but is, I believe, a scribe's error for Landiner (Landinner in Altarnun), which, like Lifton, had been held in 1066 by Queen Edith.

[3] DB IV, pp. 79, 236. [4] *Ibid.*, p. 272. [5] Dugdale, II, p. 496.

[6] Eadmer, *Historia Novorum*, p. 142.

ter, bethought himself of the adage: "Justice is a great emolument." The Domesday inquest had produced a crop of counter-claims and appeals. Few, if any, of these had been determined to the satisfaction of the appellants. Why not appoint a commission to go round and adjudicate, at the same time letting it be understood that it would be useless to approach the court empty-handed?

Before Lent was over, Flambard appeared at Exeter. With him were joined in commission Walchelin, bishop of Winchester, William Capra, sheriff of Somerset in 1095 and lord of many a Devon village, and Harding, son of Eadnoth the Staller, an Englishman with a great reputation for legal subtlety.[1] How far their ostensible errand may have been connected with that revision of the Domesday assessment which Orderic, alone among the chroniclers of the time, ascribes to Flambard, is a question which cannot be discussed here.[2] We may safely assume that their chief object was to raise money for the Norman loan.

In due course Abbot Wymund appeared before them, stated his claim to Werrington, and no doubt made his proffer. No opposition seems to have been made by the sheriff: which is not surprising if the whole affair had been pre-arranged in family council.[3] Flambard and his associates decided to take the king's instructions; and when Rufus heard their report, he forthwith approved the bargain. In token of renewed seisin he handed Wymund an ivory knife that he was holding at the time, and a memorandum was hastily drawn up, stating that he had given "Wlerintun" to God and St Mary of Tavistock. This was attested by Walchelin of Winchester, John, bishop of Bath, and Abbot Thurstan of Glastonbury. Later a more formal notification was addressed to Osbern, bishop of Exeter, and the sheriffs of Devon and Cornwall. This document was drawn up in the

---

[1] Freeman (*op. cit.*, IV, p. 755) has an interesting note on Harding. William of Malmesbury describes him as "potens ac causidicus."

[2] Cf. R. Southern, 'Ranulf Flambard and Early Anglo-Norman Administration', *Trans. R. Hist. S.,* Ser. IV, XVI, 1933, pp. 106 sqq.

[3] At some date before 1102 Wymund alienated two of the abbey manors, Roborough and Cudlipp, to create a knight's fee in favour of his brother William (Dugdale, II, p. 496). If the latter was indeed the sheriff's brother-in-law, this may have been the *quid pro quo*.

customary edifying style. Nothing is said of purchase-money; the king professes to be making a free gift of Werrington "for the souls of my father and mother, and for my own."[1]

The true story of this transaction has to be read between the lines of a narrative penned long afterwards by a monk of Tavistock who preserved only a confused tradition of the facts. He had probably never heard of Gytha, and there was no copy of Domesday Book at hand to inform him that the manor had been confiscated in 1086. Omitting all mention of these cardinal circumstances, he gives his readers to understand that Flambard and his associates found the abbot in full possession of "Wlurintune." At first they questioned his title, but yielding to the force of evidence they finally joined in urging Rufus to confirm the abbot's right.[2] Any one who did not know the antecedents of the case would be misled by this inconsequent tale. The construction put on it by Freeman is that Rufus did not really part with anything except his knife![3]

It may have been expected that Werrington would now revert to Cornwall. But, as it happened, the abbot no longer held any Cornish manor in demesne. All his other property in that shire, except some glebe-land and tithes, had been settled on the knight Ermenald, ancestor of the Daunays. With the loss of Werrington, therefore, the abbot had ceased to be represented in any Cornish hundred-court. Its restoration to Cornwall, now that he had got it back, would have involved him in suit to the court of Stratton as well as to the shire court at Launceston. Plainly the line of least resistance was to leave Werrington in the county of Devon.

The church of North Petherwin was impropriated to the abbey by John, bishop of Exeter; and Celestine III confirmed this appropriation in 1193.[4] The papal bull refers to "Wulryngton, with the mother church of St Paternus, and the chapels thereof." These were the chapels of St Martin and St Giles,

---

[1] Similarly in the next reign a concession to the bishop of Ely is expressed as being made "for the love of God, and for the souls of my father and mother, and for the redemption of my own sins;" but we know from the Pipe Roll that it had cost the bishop £240. — Round, *Feudal England*, pp. 268 sqq.

[2] Dugdale, II, p. 497.　　　　　　　　　[3] Freeman, *op. cit.*, II, p. 507.

[4] EHR LXII, 1947, p. 369; Dugdale, II, p. 498.

now the parish churches of Werrington and St Giles-on-the-Heath.[1] The appropriation was challenged, however, by the canons of St Stephen's, Launceston, a church which had been founded or refounded shortly before 1086. Fostered by the earls of Cornwall, and especially by earl Reginald (1141–75), St Stephen's flourished exceedingly, and in time became the wealthiest priory in Cornwall. From an early date this house began to encroach upon the immemorial rights of St Paternus in both his churches. A dispute over the tithes of South Pether-win aroused great bitterness until St Stephen himself appeared in vision to one of the parties and stated that he had no desire to be enriched at the expense of his good friend Paternus.[2] A prolonged controversy with the monks of Tavistock over the chapelries of North Petherwin was settled by the mediation of Bishop Henry Marshall (1194–1206). At his suggestion it was agreed that Tavistock should give the canons a perpetual lease of the two chapelries.[3] Much later, in the time of Bishop Redman (1496–1501), it was arranged that a canon of Launceston should officiate in each chapel on alternate Sundays.[4] The territory of the chapels and mother church continued in the deanery of Trigg Major and the archdeaconry of Cornwall; and since 1876 all three parishes have been included in the modern anglican diocese of Truro. Thus the ecclesiastical boundary has consistently preserved its original outline, ignoring the secular annexation of 1086.

We have seen that the land in Maker which had belonged to Devon before the Conquest passed into the hands of Count Robert. In the Domesday record it is entered as a Cornish manor held under the count by Reginald de Vautort. It continued in Reginald's descendants, but well before the close of the thirteenth century it had been restored to the hundred of Roborough and the county of Devon;[5] and so it remained until 1844.

In 1929, at the instance of the Cornish county council, a bill was introduced into parliament which provided, *inter alia*, that

[1] The Ordnance Survey erroneously gives both saints to Werrington.

[2] G. H. Doble, *St Patern*, 1940, pp. 45, 46, translating a narrative by the grandson of the tithe-payer.

[3] EHR LXII, 1947, p. 373.   [4] A. L. Rowse, *Tudor Cornwall*, p. 145.

[5] *Feudal Aids*, I, pp. 340, 354, 404, 439, 449.

the Tamar should become the boundary of Cornwall over its entire length. This, if carried, would have restored North Petherwin to Cornwall, and with it the part of Werrington that lies west of the river. But there was opposition by the Devon county council, and when the bill came before a committee of the house of lords, the boundary provisions were defeated by a narrow margin.[1] More recently, a boundary commission has come and gone without effect. Thus, far from effacing the imprint of Norman jobbery, the lapse of eight and a half centuries has merely conferred upon it the respectability of age.

[1] Information supplied by the clerk of the Cornwall county council, Mr L. P. New.

THE DOMESDAY PLOUGH-TEAM

IT HAS BEEN generally agreed by Domesday scholars that the Domesday *caruca* was composed of eight oxen. There is no need to rehearse at length the arguments which point to this conclusion. Over a large part of England land and fiscal obligations were measured in carucates, each of which contained eight bovates, or ox-gangs. As a statement of taxable capacity in Yorkshire, for instance, the *caruca* certainly implied eight oxen, and to suppose that it represents some other number in Sussex is to make nonsense of the survey as a whole. Moreover, we can point to numerous entries in which groups of four oxen, so described in the local text, become half-teams in the Exchequer version. At the same time, most scholars are agreed that the full team of eight oxen, though not unusual in practice, was employed by the surveyors as a notional or fiscal unit. On a particular manor there might in fact be two ploughs, each of four oxen; but the clerks of the Exchequer would write that manor down as possessing one *caruca*.

Mr Reginald Lennard, however, has questioned these conclusions.[1] He argues that in the south-western counties the word *caruca* was sometimes used to signify a team of six. He supports this thesis by a number of comparisons between the Exon Domesday and the Exchequer version, quoting parallel passages in which three oxen in the one become a half-team in the other. We naturally wonder why the Exchequer version should be regarded as nearer to the facts of tillage than the more detailed local version. Mr Lennard replies that "for all we know" the royal clerks may simply have transcribed statements prepared at some intermediate local headquarters and sent to them ready-made.[2]

Coming as they do from a writer whose contributions to the agrarian history of England have been numerous and highly

[1] EHR LX, 1945, pp. 217 sqq.
[2] *Ibid.*, p. 231. Cf. R. Welldon Finn, *The Domesday Inquest*, 1961, pp. 166–91.

valuable, these arguments are bound to command attention. The most satisfactory way to test them will be to take the largest of the three counties involved, namely, Devonshire, and to examine systematically all the entries in the Domesday of that county which have any bearing on the subject.[1]

In the first place then, the Exon Domesday names four Devonshire manors on which a single ox was to be found in addition to a stated number of teams or half-teams. In the Exchequer text the single ox invariably disappears.[2] The case of Tavistock, one of the four manors in question, deserves particular notice. Here the abbot's knights have six and a half ploughs in demesne; and their tenants' resources are enumerated as one plough, half a plough, seven oxen, one and a half ploughs, and two oxen: in all, three ploughs and nine oxen. In the Exchequer Domesday this becomes four ploughs. Thus the normal reckoning of eight oxen to the plough holds good, and the surplus ox, as usual, is ignored. To these instances we may add two manors on which there were neither teams nor half-teams, but only single beasts: in the one case an ox, in the other an unspecified plough-beast (*animal in car'*). Here again, the Exchequer Domesday passes over the single animal in silence.[3]

We may therefore take it as an established rule that single beasts are left out of the final text. What happens when there are two? In a couple of instances the odd pair is carried over as such from the Exon to the Exchequer text.[4] But such conscientiousness is rare. On ten manors the presence of an odd pair is ignored, and on one manor its absence is equally disregarded. This is at Surleia, where "two ploughs less two oxen" become simply "two ploughs."[5]

So far, the results are just what would be expected by any one

---

[1] In the notes which follow, A refers to the page number of the Exon Domesday as printed by the Record Commissioners in 1816, B to the page and column of the printed Exchequer text (I, 1783).

[2] Torna, A 112, B 103*b*; Tauestocha, A 163, B 103*c*; Rochebera, A 196, B 104*d*; Assileia, A 295, B 108*d*.

[3] Fernehella, A 311, B 110*a*; Colrige, A 308, B 109*d*.

[4] Radenda, A 387, B 111*b*; Alra, A 438, B 117*c*.

[5] Hela, A 119, B 102*d*; Spreuuea, A 124, B 103*a*; Celuertesberia, A 124, B 103*a*; Widefella, A 191, B 105*a*; Cicecota, A 265, B 105*d*; Wica, A 266, B 106*a*; Tetecota, A 297, B 108*d*; Louenetorna, A 299, B 109*a*; Porlamuta, A 301, B 109*f*; Surleia, A 302, B 109*b*; Goseuuella, A 389, B 111*c*.

familiar with that contempt for small fractions which is written large all over Domesday. It is when we come to the groups of three that signs of hesitancy become apparent.

Here again there are two cases in which a trio is carried over as such from one text to the other.[1] Mr Lennard has noticed two Cornish manors, and none outside Cornwall, where groups of three oxen are passed over in silence. There are, however, three manors in Devon where this occurs.[2] Then there are four Devonshire manors where three oxen in the local Domesday become half a plough in the Exchequer version.[3] Mr Lennard attaches great importance to these and similar entries which he cites from other counties. It will, however, be noticed that the Devonshire statistics provide four instances of the equation 3 oxen $= \frac{1}{2}$ plough, against five instances where three oxen are not thus equated.

Before discussing the figures it will be advisable to complete this survey of the fractional teams. Groups of four oxen present no variation at all. There are five manors where they occur, and in every case the Exchequer Domesday equates them with half a *caruca*.[4] There appears to be only one group of five. This is at Appledore; and here again they are equated with a half-team, the surplus ox being ignored as usual.[5] But when we come to groups of six, the same hesitation and inconsistency become apparent that we noticed in the treatment of threes. In one instance the group is carried over from one text to the other.[6] Then we come to a manor where one and a half ploughs and six oxen are equated with two ploughs.[7] Does this point to an exceptional twelve-ox team? On the whole, and Mr Lennard himself seems inclined to allow this, it seems more probable that once again a surplus pair of oxen is being disregarded. At Lochetona and Edetona there are six plough-beasts (*animalia in car'*) and at Blacheorda six oxen, which the Exchequer

---

[1] Oteri, A 376, B 110d; Mollanda, A 381, B 115c.

[2] Melefort, A 112, B 103b; Chiempabera, A 384, B 115a; Estatforda, A 352, B 116c.

[3] Tornelouua, A 296, B 108d; Oteri, A 319, B 114b; Estapeleia, A 437, B 117c; Betunia, A 451, B 118c.

[4] Harestana, A 201, B 104d; Niuuetona, A 198, B 105a; Bichecoma, A 392, B 113b; Galmentona, A 427, B 113d; Sigeforda, A 386, B 115b.

[5] Apledora, A 273, B 106c. [6] Cheneoltona, A 118, B 102c.

[7] Botreforda, A 305, B 109c.

scribes have reckoned as full teams.[1] But when we look more closely at the Exon text, we find that the lord of Blacheorda has six oxen on his demesne, and his tenants have two ploughs. If the six really constituted a full team, would it not have been more natural to say at the outset that the lord had one plough and the tenants two?

Only two groups of seven are to be found in Devonshire. In the one case, the Exchequer text ignores their existence;[2] in the other, it treats the seven as a full team, doubtless on the principle that the absence of a single ox can be as lightly disregarded as its presence.[3]

Lastly, there is a manor with six oxen on the demesne, and two belonging to the peasants. The Exchequer Domesday says merely: "On this manor there is one plough."[4]

Thus, on a close inspection, the Devonshire Domesday amply confirms the traditional reckoning of eight oxen to the full team. Wherever a group of four occurs, it is invariably set down as a half-team. At Wadestan we have the equation $6+2=1$ caruca; and at Tavistock $7+2$, which would have made a team and a half had six-ox teams been recognized, is in fact described as one team. It seems quite certain that full teams of eight and half teams of four were the two standard units recognized in the south-west and employed throughout the survey. One or two beasts more or less were not allowed to interfere with the standard reckoning. It was only the threes and sixes that gave any difficulty; and the surveyors were obviously in two minds about them. Most income-tax payers have made acquaintance at one time or another with the technique by which the agents of the Revenue assess a man's income somewhat above its maximum, and leave him to disprove the assessment if he can. Something of the same sort may be perceived in Domesday Book. If a man had three oxen, was that near enough to half a team to justify his being assessed at half? If six or seven, could he be safely charged with a whole team? The clerks of the Exchequer answered these questions sometimes affirmatively, sometimes negatively; and the really significant

[1] Lochetona, A 229, B 109a; Edetona, A 301, B 109b; Blacheorda, A 306, B 109c.
[2] Cridia, A 319, B 114c.   [3] Buchesurda, A 190, B 104c.
[4] Wadestan, A 278, B 107a.

fact in the whole business is their hesitation. They never hesitated when they had to deal with groups of four and eight.

Are we then to conclude that the six-ox team had no place in south-western agriculture? By no means. In Marshall's time "four aged oxen, or six growing steers" was the normal team throughout west Devon,[1] and similar teams may well have been common in 1086. But it is useless to interrogate the Domesday records on such a point. The great inquest was not undertaken in order to provide the officers of the Exchequer with a picture of life in the fields: what they wanted was a statement of land values. Hence the attempt to draw agricultural inferences from fiscal equations is doomed to failure, like the gallant but equally hopeless attempt to learn something about hides and acres from the infuriating fractions of the Geldroll.[2] It is likely enough that on one of those isolated farms which already abounded in the Devon of 1086 the arable was ploughed by a team of four oxen. Those oxen belonged to the farm, and seldom or perhaps never moved outside its ring-fence. Elsewhere in the same manor there might be a cluster of three poor husbandmen tilling a common field with another team of four, one man contributing a pair of oxen, and his neighbours one each. All that the Exon Domesday will tell us in such a case is that the peasants of this manor have one *caruca* between them. Sometimes we meet with the apparently descriptive statement: "they plough with two oxen." But, as Maitland pointed out, this may only mean that they contributed a pair of beasts to the full village team.[3] Lastly, there is the case of the husbandman who joins with a neighbour to provide a single ox. The record credits him with a *semibos*; but we are certainly not meant to conjure up the nightmare figure of a beast with one fore leg, one hind leg, and a single horn.

[1] Marshall, *Rural Economy of the West of England*, 1796, I, p. 116.
[2] Maitland, *Domesday Book and Beyond*, pp. 478–80.
[3] *Ibid.*, p. 142.

CHILDE'S TOMB

FAR out in one of the least inviting tracts of Dartmoor is a spot marked on the Ordnance map as Childe's Tomb. There, in the trackless marshy ground between the Swincombe valley and Fox Tor, stands a cross of hewn granite, which in its present form has no strong claim to be regarded as an authentic piece of antiquity, for it has been re-erected twice within the last hundred years. It is said, however, to occupy the site and to include some of the materials of a cross that was destroyed in 1812; and we have it on the authority of Risdon that in the seventeenth century there stood, here or elsewhere on the moor, some kind of sepulchral monument commemorating the death of Childe.[1] Westcote, another seventeenth-century topographer, gives the story of Childe's fate in what is probably its earliest written form. —

"There was one named Childe, of Plympstock, a man of fair possessions, who, having no issue, ordained by his testament that at what place soever he was interred, that church should inherit his land. It fortuned that riding forth a hunting in a cold season, in the forest, he casually strayed from his company, and having also lost his way, in long seeking of both he was so benumbed at length with the cold that he was forced to kill his horse and embowel him and creep into his belly, but that could not preserve him: frozen he was to death, and found dead by the men of Tavistock, who, with all convenient speed, carried him to be buried in the Abbey; which was not so privily done but the inhabitants of his own parish of Plympstock had intelligence thereof, and so mustered their best strength to prevent the other, and came with a great multitude to the passage of the river, which of necessity the Tavistock men must

---

[1] T. Risdon, *Survey of the County of Devon*, p. 198. For the destruction early in the nineteenth century, see the note in N. T. Carrington's *Dartmoor*, 1826, pp. 168, 169. The cross was re-erected in 1890 by E. Fearnley Tanner (Rowe, *Perambulation of Dartmoor*, 3rd edn, p. 189), and again some twenty years later by Lieut. L. Royle, R.N. (*ex inf.* Mr C. D. P. Nicholson).

pass, or nowhere, as they thought, and there waited; but they were deceived by a feat of guile, for the Tavistock inhabitants builded presently a slight bridge over the river and so without trouble buried the corpse and had the land; and in remembrance of this guile, the bridge, even to this age, is called Guile Bridge."[1]

It is hardly necessary to point out that the story as told by Westcote is improbable and indeed self-contradictory. The body is carried off "with all convenient speed," yet there is time for a party to come up from Plymstock. There are also time and materials to build a bridge over the river, while the men of Plymstock obligingly stand waiting at a distance. All this, too, on a winter day. No document that has come to light so far refers to a "Guile Bridge" in or near Tavistock, but in 1651 the Tavistock Guildhall is called "Guilehall."[2] If there was a Guile Bridge, therefore, it was probably so called because constructed or maintained by a parish guild.

For these reasons most of the local antiquaries have been inclined to reject the tale of Childe as mythical. A tradition, perpetuated with zealous care by some organized body, may be good evidence of happenings not otherwise recorded; but this tale is not traditional in that sense. It is pure folk-lore, a legend handed down orally by the scattered dwellers of a wild moorland region, and probably embroidered in the process. On the other hand, since disbelief can be as misleading as credulity, it will perhaps be worth while to re-examine the mysterious tale, and see if criticism, based on documentary research, can discover in it an element of truth.

A document signed and sealed in 1287 provides the first clue. In that year Robert Champeaux, abbot of Tavistock, assigned the tithes of Woodley in Lamerton to the almoner of his monastery for the purpose of endowing certain obits. Out of the income thus settled on him the almoner was to purchase bread for distribution to the poor on each anniversary of the four personages whom the convent revered as its chief benefactors. Their names are recited in the preamble to the deed.[3] Lyfing, abbot of Tavistock until 1027, and thereafter bishop of

---

[1] T. Westcote, *View of Devonshire in 1630*, Exeter, 1845, p. 386.

[2] R. N. Worth, *Calendar of the Tavistock Parish Records*, 1887, p. 99.

[3] Woburn Abbey Muniment Room, Devonshire MSS., G Bdle 5, no. 23.

Crediton, naturally has a place among them, for his benefactions to the abbey, as described by William of Malmesbury, were "many and conspicuous." His name is followed by that of a contemporary, "the lord Edwyn, brother of St Edward, king and confessor." More accurately, this prince's name was Eadwig, and he was the Confessor's half-brother, being a son of Æthelred II by his first wife. After the death of his elder brother, Edmund Ironside, in 1016, he was excluded from the succession in favour of Cnut the Dane. The reason why Eadwig was regarded as a benefactor is disclosed in an account drawn up by the almoner for the year ending Michaelmas 1396. He is there described as "Edwynus de Plymstoke." The manor of Plymstock, formerly included in the crown-lordship of Plympton, had evidently been detached to form part of Eadwig's personal estate, and he had given or bequeathed it to the abbey. Its pre-eminently fertile soil was highly valued by the monks. At an early date they recognized its aptitude for corn-growing, and from the twelfth century until the Dissolution they depended on it for their main supply of wheat.

The chroniclers are not at one in their accounts of Eadwig. All agree that he met his end in Cnut's reign, but the further he recedes into the past, the more elaborate become the tales of secret conversations and treacherous murder plots. These narratives have been subjected by Freeman to a destructive analysis,[1] and in the light of the Tavistock records they appear less plausible than ever. William of Malmesbury gives an altogether different and less sensational account. He says: "Edwy, a young man of excellent character, left the kingdom by Cnut's order, an order prompted by the traitor Edric. After long wandering by sea and land, he returned stealthily to England; but, as often happens, sickness of mind brought on bodily ill-health, and he ended his days while lying concealed among his fellow-countrymen. He was buried at Tavistock."[2] This fact of the prince's burial in the abbey which regarded him as one of its chief benefactors has never been disputed. William of Malmesbury collected the traditions of the abbey at first hand, and it was at Tavistock that the true story was most likely to be known.

[1] *Norman Conquest*, I, p. 700.
[2] *Gesta Regum*, ed. Stubbs, Rolls ser. 90, p. 217.

What light, if any, does it throw on Childe of Plymstock? There is nothing inherently improbable in the supposition that the unfortunate prince may have lost his way among the mists and mires of Dartmoor, and perished of exposure, like many since his day. But the best authenticated narrative, we have seen, ascribes his death to bodily sickness brought on by grief and exile. If we accept this as giving the truth, the explanation of the Dartmoor legend must be sought elsewhere.

On further examination the deed of 1287 yields another and a more promising clue. The first of the four benefactors named in the preamble is that Ordulf who is elsewhere described as the original founder of the abbey. It will be convenient to refer to him as Ordulf I. With his name is coupled that of his wife, hitherto known only from a rather carelessly written passage in the register of Bishop Stapeldon, where it appears in the impossible form "Abina."[1] In our document she is described as "the lord Ordulf's consort, the most excellent dame Aluina" — clearly a Latinized form of the Old English Ælfwynn. To appreciate the significance of this name we must recall, first, that there is a village and parish in north-west Devon called, in the Exon Domesday, Alwinetona, now Alwington. The authors of *The Place-Names of Devon* (p. 84) remark upon "the absence of medial *s*" in this place-name, and hold that it "favours the OE feminine name Ælfwynn rather than the masculine Ælfwine." This argument is now strikingly confirmed. For Alwington is the parish immediately adjoining Abbotsham; and according to a very early tradition, which will be considered presently, Abbotsham, with several other properties in the neighbourhood, was presented to the abbey by Ordulf's wife. We turn to Domesday Book in order to learn what had become of Alwington by 1066, and we find that it then belonged to a great landowner named Ordulf: we may call him Ordulf II. The identity of his name, and the fact that he was lord of Lamerton and Bere Ferrers, two manors which adjoin Tavistock on the north and south respectively, strongly suggest that he was descended from the original founder. Geography and written record now combine with philology to make it virtually certain that he inherited his name from the first Ordulf and his manor

[1] *Reg. Stapeldon*, ed. F. C. Hingeston-Randolph, p. 403.

of Alwington, or Ælfwynn's *tun*, from the first Ordulf's wife.

We are thus confronted with a pedigree spanning the last hundred years before the coming of the Normans. The family was allied by marriage with the royal house, and since it was also directly associated with the fortunes of Tavistock Abbey, we may pertinently ask what information about its members can be gleaned from other sources. A word should be said here about the methods by which family connections were indicated at this period. Two of the commonest devices were variation and repetition of name-themes. Variation consists of giving to the child a name of which one element is the same as an element in the father's name and the other is different. "Variation could be either of the first element (e.g. *Eadmund* son of *Alkmund*) or of the second element (e.g. *Eadgar* son of *Eadmund*). In England end-variation was rather the commoner." The other device, repetition, was usually practised in alternate generations, a child being named after his grandfather.[1]

The first member of the family who can be described as such with any certainty was named Ordgar. He must have been born *circa* 915. The twelfth-century chronicler Gaimar states that he was the son of a "count" — that is, an ealdorman — and that he was a rich man who owned every village between Exeter and Frome.[2] But as Gaimar credits him with only one child, a daughter Ælfthryth, whereas Ordgar I is known to have had at least two sons, his account cannot be wholly trusted. The late J. J. Alexander conjectured that Ordgar was perhaps a son of the ealdorman Wulfgar who attests charters from 931 to 948; and the name-sequence Wulfgar, Ordgar, Ord(w)ulf, certainly tallies with the custom of the period. However this may have been, Ordgar makes his first recorded appearance in 958 as one of the *ministri* in attendance on King Eadwig and witnessing his charters. His name is to be found in royal charters of every year from 958 to 970 inclusive.[3] About the year 960 his daughter Ælfthryth married Æthelwold, ealdorman of East Anglia, who died some two years

[1] E. G. Withycombe, *Oxford Dictionary of English Christian Names*, 1945, p. xix.

[2] Gaimar, *Lestorie des Engles*, Rolls ser. 91, ll. 3606–8, 3629–30.

[3] A list of his attestations is given in DA LXXVIII, 1946, p. 279.

later; and in 964 the young widow became Edgar's queen. Ordgar's promotion followed speedily upon his daughter's marriage; before the end of the year he was appointed ealdorman of Devon and Cornwall. Of his public acts during his term of office nothing is known except that on one occasion he liberated a female slave named Wencenethel "for the good of his soul." The manumission took place at St Petroc's altar in Bodmin.[1] Ordgar I died in 971, and Florence of Worcester informs us that he was buried at Exeter.[2]

William of Malmesbury, in a passage that will be considered presently, states that Tavistock Abbey was founded, or at least planned ("surgendi exordium accepit") by Ordgar. The statement is not borne out by any earlier writer. It is at variance alike with the foundation charter and with the constant tradition of the abbey. Moreover the Anglo-Saxon Chronicle distinctly refers to the house as "Ordulf's minster."[3] In the course of this enquiry it will appear that William of Malmesbury has confused two distinct personages and sadly muddled his chronology. Other writers have followed suit. His remark about Ordgar was transcribed verbatim by a Worcester annalist of c. 1135, who proceeded to adorn it with a rubric of his own devising: "Thavestoca construitur A.D. 961."[4] Apparently he arrived at this by the simple process of subtracting twenty years from the date of the foundation charter, and ten from that of Ordgar's death. He was followed by Matthew Paris, from whose *Chronica Majora* the erroneous date was handed down, via 'Matthew of Westminster', to mislead several modern writers.

The name of Ordgar's wife is unknown. She is said to have been of royal birth, but here again we have only Gaimar's word for it. She, and a son of Ordgar's, also unnamed, were buried at Tavistock before 981. The only other children of the marriage, so far as is known, were Ælfthryth and her brother Ordulf. From a narrative composed during Ælfthryth's lifetime we catch a glimpse of her at Edgar's coronation banquet, robed in fine linen and bedecked with jewels, presiding from a dais

[1] K 981 (IV, p. 310), from BM Add. MS. 9381.
[2] *Monumenta Historica Britannica*, p. 577.   [3] *Anno* 997.
[4] *Ungedruckte Anglo-Normannische Geschichtsquellen*, ed. Liebermann, p. 20.

over the table set apart for abbots and abbesses, while the bishops and ealdormen dined at another table with the king.[1] There is little or no justification for the legends which have depicted Ælfthryth as a beautiful ogress plotting the death of her stepson. Her story, however, belongs to the general history of the period, and cannot be discussed here.

Ordulf I may be supposed to have been born *circa* 945. He attests his first charter as a *minister* in 975, just before Edgar's death, and is then lost to view until 980. It is natural enough that he and his family should have played no leading part during the reign of Edward, the so-called Martyr (975–79). At this period he must have been actively engaged in supervising the foundation of Tavistock Abbey. According to a Tavistock tradition, he had previously built a small chapel there, a little east of the abbey site, and dedicated it to the Four Evangelists. Ramsey, the first considerable new foundation of the monastic revival, was consecrated and enfranchised in 974, having taken five years to build.[2] If we allow five years for Tavistock, and reckon backwards from the date of its charter, we arrive at 976 as the latest possible date for the beginnings of the abbey. In all probability this date should be put back a little, for the monks believed their abbey to have been founded in Edgar's reign, and the anti-monastic demonstrations which broke out after that king's death may well have put a brake on Ordulf's proceedings. We shall not be far out, therefore, if we decide that he began to build his minster *circa* 974. By 981 it was ready for its charter. In this document Ordulf is naturally mentioned in the most laudatory terms. Like other founders at this period, he exercised the privilege of nominating the first abbot, and the charter records his intention of providing the new monastery with a generous endowment.[3]

Ordulf I receives especial mention as a supporter of monastic interests in two other charters of Æthelred's reign.[4] As the boy-king's uncle, he must have been an influential personage during Æthelred's minority, and even later; but he was never promoted to his father's rank. Florence of Worcester styles him

---

[1] *Historians of the Church of York*, Rolls ser. 71, I, p. 438.
[2] Dugdale, *Monasticon*, II, p. 554.
[3] H. P. R. Finberg, *Tavistock Abbey*, Cambridge, 1951, p. 280.
[4] K 1312 and 684*.

"Domnaniae primas." It is generally understood that "primas" means *hēah-gerēfa*, that is, high-reeve;[1] but if so, the chronicler's phrase must not be taken as implying that Ordulf administered all Devon and Cornwall, for the Anglo-Saxon Chronicle shows that there might be two or more high-reeves in one shire: indeed, a certain Kola is named as a "king's high-reeve" in Devonshire during Ordulf's lifetime.[2] In point of fact, his recorded activities in the south-west are limited to Cornwall and the western part of Devon. The Bodmin Gospels show him freeing a serf at St Petroc's altar "for the soul of Ælfsige," Ælfsige being perhaps the brother who lay buried at Tavistock.[3] In the Life of St Rumon, the patron saint of Tavistock, it is related that the saint's relics were enshrined at Ruan Lanihorne in Cornwall "until the time of Ordulf, earl of Cornwall and the neighbouring part of Devon" (*comes Cornubie et Deuonie adiacentis*).[4] Reasons have been given elsewhere for believing that in the ninth century the king's lands in Triconshire were administered from Stratton, and his other Cornish estates from Lifton.[5] By Ordulf's day both of these manors had become hundredal centres. The hundred of Lifton comprised the district between Okehampton and Tavistock. All of it lay in west Devon, but the officer in charge retained his jurisdiction over a number of royal manors in Cornwall. This is the post which may with most probability be assigned to Ordulf I. No doubt his patrimony included land in more than one shire, but as the king's high-reeve of "Lifton and the lands belonging thereto" he was in the best position to superintend the foundation of Tavistock Abbey and to assign portions of the area for its maintenance.

For information concerning his benefactions we turn to the *Fundationis Historia*, a narrative printed by Dugdale from the great register of the abbey commonly called the Maynard Cartulary. This cartulary is now lost, but White Kennett, who studied it towards the end of the seventeenth century, states

---

[1] *Monumenta Historica Britannica*, p. 582; *Crawford Charters*, ed. Napier and Stevenson, Oxford, 1895, p. 122; *Two Saxon Chronicles*, ed. Plummer, II, p. 180.
[2] *Two Saxon Chronicles*, I, p. 132.   [3] K 981 (IV, p. 309).
[4] *Ex inf.* the late Canon G. H. Doble; see his *St Rumon and St Ronan*, p. 13.
[5] Above, p. 166.

that it was written about the time of Henry IV (1399–1413).[1] The opening narrative, however, bears evident signs of having been compiled from much older materials. It gives a list of endowments which appears to have been transcribed directly from the charter of 981. Translated, the passage reads as follows.[2] "The estates which were granted . . . by Ordulf, or by his wife, or by his relatives or friends, are these. Tavistock, Milton, Hatherleigh, Burrington, Leigh, Downeckney, *Chuvelin*, Linkinhorn: these by the husband. By the wife these: Abbotsham, Worthygate, Orleigh, Annery, Rame, Sheviock, Panson, Thornbury, *Colbrok*, *Lege*, *Wlsithetun*, Stoke Climsland."[3]

It is noticeable that while Ordulf is said to have given eight manors, and his wife twelve, no particular gifts are ascribed to those "relatives or friends" who are mentioned with them. Evidently the second list is composite. It begins with Ælfwynn's donations, and passes on without pause to those of other benefactors. The four properties which head the list, Abbotsham, Worthygate, Orleigh, and Annery, may well have been Ælfwynn's own gift, for they are all in the immediate neighbourhood of Alwington, the village which bears her name. When, looking somewhat ahead, we find a later Ordulf in possession of Alwington, and also of Wear Giffard, Alverdiscott, Monkleigh, and Frithelstock, Ælfwynn begins to stand out very clearly as the possessor in her own right of a vast estate on both sides of the Torridge.[4]

[1] MS. note in W. K.'s copy of Dugdale's *Monasticon*, now in the Bodleian Library. It was almost certainly the cartulary which, according to BM Egerton MS. 3671, fo. 21, Abbot John Mey (1402–22) caused to be written by his clerk John Ludegard.

[2] Dugdale, *op. cit.*, II, p. 494.

[3] On the identification of the place-names see H. P. R. Finberg, *op. cit.*, p. 280.

[4] Was Ælfwynn a daughter of Athelstan, the 'half-king' of East Anglia? The half-king's patrimony lay in Devon, according to his sons (*Liber Eliensis*, ed. E. O. Blake, Camden third ser., XCII, p. 80), and his wife, according to a Ramsey chronicle, was named "Ælfwen." His eldest son Æthelwold was married to Ordulf's sister Ælfthryth, and it is well known that Æthelwold's untimely death gave rise to sinister, though baseless, rumours when King Edgar shortly afterwards married the young widow. A double marriage alliance between the half-king's family and the house of Ordgar would explain much in the politics of Edgar's reign and that of his successor.

From 982 to 1005 Ordulf I constantly witnesses Æthelred II's charters.[1] He must have been living when Ælfwold, bishop of Crediton, drew up his will *c.* 1008, for the bishop left him two books, a martyrology and a work by Rhabanus Maurus.[2] We may suppose that he died *c.* 1010; and the calendar of the Leofric Missal gives the 16th of December as the day of his obit.

The next member of the family who comes into view is another Ordgar. Tempting as it is to make him a son of Ordulf and grandson of the ealdorman, most genealogists would consider it necessary to postulate an intermediate life, ranging in date from *circa* 970 to 1035. This will hardly do for Ordgar II, who attests charters as a *minister* from 1018 to 1050. In 1042, within the first six months of his reign, Edward the Confessor granted him half a hide of land at Littleham, near Exmouth.[3] In the following year Ordgar witnessed earl Leofric's charter to Coventry, being there styled "Ordgarus Deuonensis," no doubt in order to distinguish him from his contemporary and namesake the sheriff of Cambridgeshire.[4] An undated document of *c.* 1045, drawn up at Exeter, is witnessed by Sihtric, abbot of Tavistock, Ordgar, and Ordgar's two brothers, Ælfgar and Escbern.[5] His name occurs for the last time in the record of some manumissions entered on a page of the Leofric Missal,[6] which may be translated as follows. —

"These are the names of the men who were freed for Ordgar at Bradan stane [Bradstone] where he lay sick: that is, Cynsie from Liwtune [Lifton], and Godcild of Lamburnan [Lamerton], and Leofric of Swuran tune [Sourton], Dolawine's son, and Eadsige of Cyric forda [? Churchford in Meavy], and Ælfgyth of Boc lande [Buckland ?Monachorum], and Smala of Ocmund tune [Okehampton], and Wifman of Brada stane, and Byrhflæd of Tref meu tune [Trematon], and Ælflæd of Clymes tune [Stoke Climsland], in witness of Wynstan the mass-priest, and Wulfsie at Lamburnan, and of all the minster-priests there.

"And Ælfgyth of Swuran tune; and thereto is witness Cynsie the priest, and Goda the priest, and Ælfric the priest who wrote

---

[1] DA LXXVIII, 1946, p. 279. [2] *Crawford Charters*, p. 23.
[3] DA *loc. cit.*, p. 280; K 1332.
[4] K 939; for the date, see *Crawford Charters*, p. 112, n. 2. [5] K 1334.
[6] Bodleian Library, MS. Bodl. 579, fo. 8*b*.

this writing. This was done at Borslea [Boasley in Bratton Clovelly] for Ordgar.

"... Eadgyfu freed Leofrune at Curri tune [Coryton] for Ordgar, in witness of Brown the mass-priest and of all the minster-priests there."

The late Canon Warren, who edited the Leofric Missal for publication by the Clarendon Press, identified this Ordgar with Ordgar I, and stated that the entries are made "in an earlier and more faded handwriting" than others in the volume.[1] But no one who examines the page at all carefully will fail to notice that they are in more than one handwriting. The manumissions have been entered at different times, possibly by different hands, and probably soon after the event. Mr R. W. Hunt, Keeper of Western MSS. in the Bodleian Library, and Dr Neil R. Ker, who have kindly re-examined the page at my request, agree with this account of it. They also agree that the script is too late for c. 970, the date suggested by Warren, and that it properly belongs to the middle of the eleventh century. Much that has been written about Devonshire in the tenth and eleventh centuries by O. J. Reichel, J. J. Alexander, Mrs Rose-Troup, and the authors of The Place-Names of Devon, is vitiated by their unqualified acceptance of the earlier date.

Eleven places are named in connection with these manumissions. Two of them, Cyricforda and Boclande, cannot be identified with absolute certainty. Of the remainder, seven are situated in the hundred of Lifton, and the other two (Stoke Climsland and Trematon) in that part of Cornwall over which the high-reeve of Lifton exercised a measure of control. Lifton itself was a royal manor, and remained so until the reign of John. Stoke Climsland, once the property of Tavistock Abbey, had clearly passed, by the middle of the eleventh century, into other hands, presumably the king's, for in Domesday Book it appears as a crown-lordship. In freeing slaves from these manors, therefore, Ordgar cannot have been acting in his own right. It seems probable that he too was the king's high-reeve, and that Ordulf's bailiwick of Lifton with its Cornish appurtenances, obeying a common tendency at this period, had become hereditary.

[1] The Leofric Missal, ed. F. E. Warren, Oxford, 1883, p. lx.

The Eadgyfu who acted as Ordgar's deputy at Coryton may have been his wife.[1] The manumissions must be dated somewhere between 1030 and 1050, and Ordgar II probably died in 1051 or soon after. He was buried, according to William of Malmesbury, at Tavistock. William, who wrote before 1125, gives a description of Tavistock Abbey and its surroundings too vivid and exact to have been composed at second hand. After enumerating its amenities, he devotes a few lines to St Rumon, surmising that if there had ever been a written life of the saint it probably disappeared in 997, when the abbey was burnt down by Danish raiders. Then he continues:

"In the same monastery is to be seen the tomb of Ordgar. The sepulchre of Ordgar's son is reckoned one of the sights of the place because of its abnormal size. He was called Edulfus: a man of gigantic stature and prodigious strength. A brief instance of this will not be out of place. He was travelling to Exeter in company with King Edward, his kinsman. On dismounting from their horses at the city gate, they found the door doubly bolted and barred against them. The porter, as it happened, being unaware of their arrival — for they had ridden at a leisurely pace — was some distance away. Thereupon Edulfus seized the bolts with both hands, and with very little apparent effort broke them to pieces, tearing down part of the wall as he did so. Then, warming to the work and gnashing his teeth, he gave a second proof of strength. Loosening the gate with a kick, he forced open the hinges on either side with such violence as to shiver the door-posts. The rest of the company applauded, but the king pretended to make light of it, saying that he must be possessed of the devil's own strength.

"He gave another remarkable display of prowess in a wood near Horton, in Dorset, where there is a monastery, now destroyed, which thanks to his generosity ranked in those days as an abbey. To this place he used to resort in his moments of leisure. There, down a ravine which abounds in game, a stream flows ten feet wide. Edulfus used to bestride this, and with a small knife, using slight and almost nugatory strokes,

[1] Similarly Æthelflæd, wife of the ealdorman Æthelwerd, freed a slave at Liskeard for "her soul, and the soul of her lord," and the ealdorman subsequently confirmed this by repeating the ceremony at St Petroc's altar (K 981).

would strike off the heads of the beasts of chase that were driven towards him, so that they fell into the water.

"For all his size and strength, he died in the prime of life ("adhuc aetatis calore praefervidus"), leaving instructions that he was to be buried at Horton. But as he had directed certain legacies to be given to the church with his body ("secum"), his wishes were frustrated by the violence of Abbot Sihtric, who carried off both gifts and giver to his own monastery. Later on, under King William, Sihtric turned pirate, to the disgrace of his order and the discredit of his church."[1]

The account of Tavistock which precedes this remarkable tale ascribes the foundation of the abbey, erroneously, to Ordgar I. Most readers, therefore, naturally identify the Ordgar whose tomb William of Malmesbury saw at Tavistock with the ealdorman of Edgar's reign, and suppose that Edulfus, his gigantic son, was Ordulf I. Westcote and Risdon both understood the passage in this sense, and most later writers have fallen into the same trap. It is evident that Malmesbury himself was in some confusion between the two Ordgars and two Ordulfs. But the ealdorman was buried at Exeter, not Tavistock, and there is no early tradition or other evidence that Ordulf I was of exceptional stature. Since his active career extended from 975 to 1005, he cannot have ridden to Exeter in company with Edward the Confessor (1042–66), nor can his funeral have been arranged or disturbed by an abbot who survived into the Conqueror's reign. Clearly the tombs Malmesbury saw were those of Ordgar II and of his son, the second Ordulf.

About the latter there is information from several other sources. He attests a few charters as *minister* and *nobilis* between 1044 and 1059. In 1049 he witnessed a grant of Cornish land by the Confessor, in company with Ordgar II and Abbot Sihtric of Tavistock; and in the following year the same three persons were at Exeter together for the solemn installation of Bishop Leofric.[2] Ordulf II was still living in 1066, at which date he appears in Domesday Book as lord of nineteen manors in Devon, two in Cornwall, and one in Somerset.[3] In various

---

[1] *Gesta Pontificum*, ed. Hamilton, Rolls ser. 52, p. 203.

[2] See the list of charters attested by him, DA *loc. cit.*, p. 280.

[3] Brushford in Somerset; in Cornwall, Tehidy and Moresk. His Devonshire manors were: (in Shebbear hundred) Alwington, Monkleigh, Frithel-

parts of Devon there were landholders who had engaged themselves to him under the semi-feudal tie of 'commendation'.
Thus near Bratton Fleming there were three thegns, two of
whom were Ordulf's men while the third was not; and a certain Wado held one hide at Modbury "with which he could go
to any lord," and one virgate, which he held from Ordulf "and
could not separate himself from Ordulf with that virgate."[1]
This aggregate of manors and commendations is more than
once called "Ordulf's Honour." By 1086 the whole honour
had fallen into the king's hand, and had been granted to the
count of Mortain, with the exceptions of Lamerton and Wear
Giffard, which were given to Ruald Adobatus; Broad Clyst,
which was held in farm under the crown by one Reginald,
probably Reginald de Vautort; and Woodhuish, which had
passed to Richard Fitz Torulf.

The half-hide at Littleham which had been granted in 1042
to Ordgar II belonged in 1066 to Horton Abbey. We may infer
that it had been given either by the giant or by his father.
Horton was a small monastery in the east of Dorset, founded
some time between 1033 and 1061.[2] Ordulf's wish to be
buried there, rather than with his ancestors at Tavistock, is not
explained. The legacy that was to accompany his burial was,
however, in line with established custom. Such gifts are not
always easily distinguishable from the 'soul-scot', which was a
church due, regulated by law, and payable to the minster which
had a right to it. If a testator desired to be buried elsewhere,
he contracted with that other church by promising a gift in

stock, and Wear Giffard; (in the adjoining hundred of Fremington) Alverdiscott; (in Braunton hundred) Bratton Fleming, Haxton, and Croyde,
where a sister of his, unnamed, held a virgate of land under him; (in Haytor
hundred) Little Hempston, St Marychurch, and Woodhuish; (in Ermington
hundred) Bigbury and Harford; (in Budleigh hundred) Shobrooke, West
Raddon, and Wyke; (in Cliston hundred) Broad Clyst; (in the immediate
neighbourhood of Tavistock) Lamerton and Bere Ferrers. Woodhuish is
entered in the Exchequer copy (fo. 133b), but omitted from the Exon
Domesday.

[1] DB IV, pp. 192, 201.

[2] The 'caput abbatiae' consisted of seven hides at Horton which Cnut had
granted in 1033 to the thegn Boui (K 1318). Edward the Confessor's charter
enfranchising the abbey is dated 1061 (K 1341). The foundation must therefore have taken place between those two dates. Cf. Stenton, *Anglo-Saxon
England*, p. 408.

return for burial.[1] Such dispositions might well give rise to litigation; and if so, the church in actual possession of the body would have a strong case, all the more so if it could prove an antecedent claim to soul-scot. Of the litigation that followed Ordulf's burial at Tavistock there is a distinct trace in the Exon Domesday, where the description of Antony in Cornwall is followed by a note: "The abbot of Horton lays claim to this manor."[2] At the date of the great inquest Tavistock had six properties in Cornwall. All of these had belonged to the abbey in 1066 except Antony. The previous owner's name is not recorded in Domesday Book, and it is clear that the manor was a recent acquisition. It was an eminently desirable one, as adjoining Sheviock and Rame, which had belonged to the abbey since 981. As it continued in the 'honour of Tavistock', the abbot of Horton evidently lost his case.

In the early eighteenth century, when the foundations were being made for what is now the Bedford Hotel, Tavistock, on the south side of the former cloisters, the workmen dug up a stone coffin which contained two thigh-bones of great antiquity and of exceptional length. One of them was 21 inches long, and $5\frac{1}{2}$ inches in circumference; the other $19\frac{1}{2}$ inches long, and $4\frac{1}{2}$ inches in circumference.[3] An expert in osteology, who examined them in 1914, pronounced them to be those of two men, and reported that the longer of the two was much eroded. "The man of whose frame it formed part must have been of extraordinary strength and stature. He was very old at the time of his death, but in his prime must have stood nearly seven feet high."[4] As Ordulf II died in the prime of life, the longer of the two bones cannot have been his, but the smaller may perhaps be assigned to him, and the larger to one of his kinsmen. We may recall here that Ordgar II had a brother named Ælfgar. It is tempting to identify him with a certain "Ælfgar the Tall" who in 1066 held Bradford and Lashbrook near Thornbury, a village belonging to the abbey by gift of Ælfwynn or some other member of the family.

The tale of the giant Ordulf, misnamed Edulfus by the

[1] Cf. *Anglo-Saxon Wills*, ed. Whitelock, pp. xxvi, n. 2, and 109.
[2] DB iv, p. 167.
[3] A. E. Bray, *Traditions of Devonshire etc.*, 1838, ii, p. 113.
[4] DA xlvi, 1914, p. 152.

chronicler, is thus corroborated at several points. Indeed, if the evidence of the thigh-bones is admitted, even that part of the story which looks most like a folk-tale may be founded on fact. Browne Willis reports that a broken effigy of Ordulf lay formerly under one of the cloister arches; and Mrs Bray, writing in 1832, adds the significant information that this arch, which may still be seen in the churchyard, "is generally denominated Childe's tomb."[1]

If we now compare Malmesbury's narrative with the legend of Childe as handed down by the inhabitants of Dartmoor, it becomes apparent that they are two versions of one and the same tale. The resemblances between them are too striking to be overlooked, and too numerous to be dismissed as mere coincidences. In each case, a rich landowner, fond of hunting, is overtaken by a premature death. In each case he leaves a manor to the church where his body is to lie. In each case there are rival claimants, and in each case it is Tavistock Abbey that receives the body and acquires the land. There is evidence enough to warrant us in believing that this series of events did occur once, but the chances are a million to one against its occurring twice.

How then does the name Childe come into the story? The answer will be found, not in any biographical collection, but in the dictionary. According to the *Introduction to the Survey of English Place-Names*, "the OE word *cild*, the ancestor of *child*, enters into a good many place-names as the first element . . . It is found in most of the Chiltons and Chilcotes . . . Its exact sense is uncertain. The singular is used as a title of honour in late OE times and this is found also throughout the Middle Ages, as in 'Childe Roland'. Of the social status of the 'children' who gave their name to certain places we know nothing definite. They were not children in the modern sense of the term."[2] Nor, we may add, are titles of honour usually bestowed on persons of uncertain standing.

Viewed in the light of this interpretation, the legend of Childe becomes quite credible. Each tale complements the other. From Malmesbury we learn that Ordulf perished "in the

[1] Browne Willis, *History of the Mitred Parliamentary Abbies*, 1718, I, p. 171; Bray, *op. cit.*, II, p. 53.
[2] *Chief Elements used in English Place-Names*, 1930, p. 16.

heat of his prime," and the phrase acquires new poignancy when we recollect that the Childe was frozen to death. All the essentials fall into place, while the accretions of error gathered during five hundred years of oral transmission drop away. Childe Ordulf meets his end too near Tavistock for there to be any thought of carrying his remains to a monastery far off in Dorset, whatever inclination he may have expressed while living. The spot is marked by a commemorative cross, a perennial reminder to the moor-men of the Childe's fate. On the northern slope of Fox Tor, near the spot where his body was found, are the remains of a barrow and stone cist. To this relic of the Bronze Age the name Childe's Tomb is presently attached, incongruously enough, since all accounts agree that he was buried at Tavistock. The moor-men remember also that there was a dispute over his soul-scot or burial fee, and that the dispute was resolved in favour of Tavistock Abbey; but as Antony is in Cornwall and was settled before 1086 on one of the abbot's knights, they forget it and transfer the manor in question to their own side of the Tamar, prompted no doubt by the fact that Plymstock is a demesne manor, always kept in hand, and also by the circumstance that Fox Tor is very near the source of the river Plym. Some centuries later a folk-etymology is thrown in to explain Guile Bridge. Next, an indifferent couplet is made up:

"They fyrste that fyndes and bringes mee to my grave,
"The priorie of Plimstoke they shall have."

There never was a priory at Plymstock, but there was one at Plympton, the canons of which had certain rights over the chapelry of Plymstock, rights which occasionally brought them into conflict with the monks of Tavistock.[1] Risdon (c. 1630) assures his readers that "these verses were once to be read" on the Childe's monument. Fuller (1662) has a different version:

"He that finds and brings me to my tomb,
"The land of Plimstock shall be his doom."

— and says that Childe wrote this with his horse's blood. Both rhymes are given in Prince's *Worthies of Devon* (1701), but Risdon's now has an improved second line:

[1] Dugdale, *op. cit.*, II, p. 500.

"My lands, which are at Plymstock, they shall have."

Fuller, again, says: "The exact date of this *Child's* death I cannot attain;" but Prince is better informed: "He is supposed to have lived in Ed. 3's reign."[1] Both of these authors are agreed that Childe's christian name is unknown, and Prince adds: "nor can it be at this day recovered;" but one modern writer calls him Amyas and another John. In conclusion, Fuller observes: "They must rise early, yea not sleep at all, who over-reach monks in matter of profit." Such was the moral drawn in the seventeenth century. The one we draw today is in a rather different vein. For us the story is not just one more instance of the wiliness of monks, but a challenge to historical criticism, and, in the upshot, an almost perfect specimen of folk-lore based on fact.

[1] Risdon, *op. cit.,* p. 223; T. Fuller, *Worthies of England,* 1840, I, p. 426; J. Prince, *Worthies of Devon,* 1810, p. 144.

UFFCULME

IT IS NOT the business of the local historian to re-write the history of England. On the other hand, since places otherwise obscure have had their moments of historical importance, it may happen that new information will emerge from detailed local studies, and the data thus brought to light will modify our conception of well-known events. Uffculme, a Devonshire village lying under the Blackdown Hills, near the Somersetshire border, is a case in point. One episode in its otherwise uneventful story not only provides a useful footnote to the Domesday record, but throws a wholly new searchlight on the tempestuous reign of Stephen.

The central document in the case, first published nearly a century ago by Thorpe in his *Diplomatarium*, has lately been reprinted by the Somerset Record Society. To an already long list of goodly publications the Society has now added the great cartulary of Glastonbury, edited appropriately enough by a Benedictine scholar, Dom Aelred Watkin. The register of so ancient and famous an abbey is naturally a source-book of the greatest value alike for local and general history; and among the contents of the first volume is a record concerning Uffculme which enables us to piece together a sequence of remarkable events.

Between Glastonbury and the Dumnonian peninsula there were contacts dating from the eighth century, possibly from an even more remote antiquity. King Ine is known to have given twenty hides of land at Linig by the Tamar to Berwald, or Beornwald, third abbot of Glastonbury after the English conquest (705–712).[1] In 802 Egbert gave the abbey five hides by the river Torridge. His successor Æthelwulf (839–55) gave twenty-four hides at "Offaculum," the modern Uffculme, and in the reign of Athelstan (925–39) the ealdorman of that name gave six hides at "Lim."[2] Lim, now known as Uplyme, appears in

---

[1] AD pp. 52, 97.   [2] AD pp. 68, 69, 71, 98, 99.

Domesday Book as a manor assessed at six hides, and from 1066 until the Dissolution it continued to be held by Glastonbury, though not without vicissitudes as we shall see. Uffculme, on the other hand, was assessed in 1066 at only fourteen hides.[1] It remains uncertain, therefore, whether the estate itself, or merely its assessment, had been reduced since Æthelwulf's time. Possibly the attribution of twenty-four hides is just a slip of the pen. What is hardly open to doubt is that by the eleventh century the abbey held this manor with plenary jurisdiction, for in the *Inquisitio Geldi* "Offecolum" figures as a hundred *per se*.[2]

The second quarter of the eleventh century was a time of great financial stress for Glastonbury. A series of crushing Danegelds brought the abbey to the verge of ruin. Abbot Æthelward (1027–53) found himself obliged to sell many properties and to mortgage others. It is said that all the Wiltshire manors would have been lost had they not been redeemed by the bishop of Ramsbury, Brihtwold, a former monk of the house.[3] This background of financial embarrassment explains why the abbot took the risky step of granting a life-lease of Uffculme in return for money down. The annual value of the manor was approximately ten pounds.[4] For the lease he asked seven marks of gold.

The dangers of such leases were notorious. They had been strikingly exemplified only three or four years previously, when the shire court at Exeter had witnessed an attempt by Sherborne Abbey to recover Holcombe [Rogus], a manor four miles from Uffculme as the crow flies, of which they had sold a life-lease to Edmund Ironside as long ago as 1012. Edmund had wished to buy the property outright, but the king his father had insisted that Sherborne should grant it only for a term of years, and in the end it had been agreed that Edmund should pay the abbey twenty pounds and have it for his life-time. Edmund died in 1016, and under his Danish successor Holcombe, instead of reverting to the abbey, passed into the hands of a Dane named Toki. It was still occupied by his sons Care and Ulf in 1045, when Sherborne brought its claim before the shire court. On this occasion the abbey was obliged to agree

---

[1] DB I, pp. 103 (3), 111. [2] *Ibid.*, IV, p. 62.
[3] AD pp. 90, 95, 96. [4] DB IV, p. 325.

that Ulf should retain possession for his lifetime; but we learn from Domesday Book that Ulf was in fact succeeded by one Seward, and he in turn by the Norman sheriff Baldwin. Plainly a monastic house which gave life-leases would find it no easy matter to get its property back again.[1]

It is therefore not surprising to learn that the abbot of Glastonbury, before handing Uffculme over to a lessee, took all and more than the usual precautions. Our knowledge of the affair is derived from a narrative entitled *Memoriale terre alienate de Offeculum*.[2] From this we discover that the lessee was a certain Edith, or Eadgytha, widow of Hemming. The king was asked to license the transaction, and the queen to witness it.[3] Besides paying seven marks of gold down for the lease, Edith undertook to leave the abbey two golden reliquaries (*feretra*) at her death, when the land would revert to Glastonbury. Her son and heir took an oath before the whole shire court at Exeter that Our Lady of Glastonbury should not be kept out of her own. At the same time Edith provided no fewer than sixteen sureties, including Leofric, bishop of Exeter, and the great earl of Wessex, Godwin. The bishop uttered a solemn anathema against any one who should break the agreement. Finally, a charter recording these terms was drawn up in triplicate, one copy being handed to the bishop, another to the abbot, and the third to Edith.

The date of this transaction is not recorded, but it must have fallen between Leofric's consecration in 1046 and September 1051, when Godwin was exiled, or else between Godwin's return in September 1052 and his death in the following April. As the king and queen are said to have been present, the most

---

[1] R pp. 146, 200, 392; and for the identification with Holcombe Rogus' *ibid.*, p. 448. The late Mrs F. Rose-Troup contributed to the *Transactions of the Devonshire Association* (LXII, 1930, pp. 261 sqq.) a characteristically muddled account of this affair. She identifies the Sherborne "Holancumbe" with Holcombe by Dawlish, which on one and the same page she describes as a "desirable residence commanding the estuary of the Exe" and "an insignificant strip of coast" not worthy of Edmund's notice, except on a series of far-fetched hypotheses which she proceeds to supply.

[2] *The Great Chartulary of Glastonbury*, I, p. 126, no. 172.

[3] So at least I would interpret the expression used in the *Memoriale*: "Edwardi regis Anglorum ac Eadgythe regine licencia testimonioque." There was no need of a licence from the queen.

likely date is 1050, when Leofric removed his episcopal see from Crediton to Exeter and the whole court assisted at his installation.[1]

Abbot Æthelward had certainly done his best to safeguard the rights of Glastonbury, but he had not reckoned with the Norman Conquest. The *Inquisitio Geldi* informs us that before 1086 the hundred of Offecolum had passed into the hands of a Fleming (Flandrensis) named Walter.[2] From Domesday Book we can identify this Walter with Walscin *alias* Walter of Douai, a soldier of fortune who had raised a contingent for the service of the Conqueror and had later been rewarded with over sixty manors in Somerset, Wilts, Devon, Kent, and Essex, on which he and his followers had settled. He was possibly the same "Walterus Flandrensis" who appears in Domesday Book as lord of some thirty manors in Northamptonshire and the adjoining counties. His Devonshire lands had at first included Ermington and Blackawton, but these had subsequently been exchanged for the royal hundred-manor of Bampton,[3] and his Devonshire barony accordingly became known as the Honour of Bampton.

The entry concerning Uffculme in the Exon Domesday begins as follows. "Walscin has a manor called Offecoma, which Etdeua [*in the Exchequer version* Eddeua] held on the day King Edward was alive and dead."[4] In Domesday terminology the verb *tenere* carries more than one sense. Where the king is both king and landlord, he is said to "hold" land in demesne. A baron whose tenure is subject to the performance of feudal service "holds" of the king in chief. A baron's knight who has been endowed with land on condition of performing some of his lord's feudal service "holds" as an undertenant. And then a mere lessee "holds" land in farm. In all these cases the word "hold" may be used without any distinguishing addition.[5] Now whenever the Domesday record says that X "held" a manor in King Edward's time, it is generally taken to mean

---

[1] Dugdale, *Monasticon*, II, p. 526.   [2] DB IV, p. 62.   [3] *Ibid.*, p. 78.

[4] *Ibid.*, p. 325. The Domesday forms betray a confusion, of which other examples have been noted, between the vernacular names Eadgyth and Eadgifu.

[5] In the first two cases the Exon Domesday as a rule prefers to say *habet*. The Exchequer version uses *tenet* of all four.

that X had no other holder behind or above him except perhaps the king. All the generalizations current in our textbooks regarding the transfer of property from English to Norman owners are based on this assumption, that the person named in Domesday Book as having "held" an estate in 1066 held what we should now call the fee-simple. But the *Memoriale* leaves us in no doubt as to the nature of Edith's tenure: she held Uffculme as a tenant for life. The real owner, St Mary of Glastonbury, is not mentioned at all. Even one such instance is enough to confirm the suspicion long since entertained by some Domesday scholars, that in speaking of King Edward's time the jurors now and again contented themselves with registering the name of a sitting tenant. And if that is so, its picture of land-ownership in 1066 requires to be accepted with some caution.

Another assumption commonly made is that the Norman entry upon English lands was in most cases a matter of legalized usurpation. Thus Reichel, in his chapter on the feudal baronage of Devon, refers to Edith as one of several English landholders who had been "dispossessed" in Walter's favour.[1] The *Memoriale* puts the matter in a somewhat different light. The truth is that Walter had married the widow. As her son by Hemming must have been at least twelve years old when he took an oath before the shire-court in earl Godwin's time, Edith cannot have been much less than fifty by the time Walter appeared on the scene, and she may well have been older still. To the question: what inducement was there for a brisk knight from Flanders to marry an English widow past her prime, Domesday Book supplies no answer. Only one other manor is recorded as having come to Walter from "Editda," namely, Hurtesberia, identified by most authorities with Berrynarbor in the hundred of Braunton. Here again, one suspects that some of Walter's other native predecessors, registered as such in Domesday Book, had been her tenants: that, in other words, her property was more extensive than appears on the surface of the record. It is clear that she and her first husband were people of some wealth and standing. As for their son, we are not told whether he died a natural death in the interval, or turned monk, or perished in the siege of Exeter (1068), or lived to be dispossessed

[1] VCH *Devon*, I, p. 563.

of his inheritance, which in any case did not include Uffculme. He makes no further appearance in the story.[1]

In the Devonshire Domesday Glastonbury figures only once. It had managed to retain possession of Uplyme, though even there its rights had been invaded, for "Lim" is one of the estates which the Conqueror, by a charter given at some date between 1081 and 1087, restored to the abbey.[2] This restoration either failed to take effect, or lost its efficacy very soon, for Abbot Herlewin (1101–20) found Uplyme and Mells in the hands of that influential personage Harding, son of Eadnoth the Staller, and had some trouble in getting them back again.[3] As for Uffculme, it makes no appearance in the list of *Terrae Occupatae*, or claims lodged in the course of the Domesday inquest and reserved for later adjudication. From this circumstance we may conclude, though with some hesitation, that Edith was still alive in 1086. So long as she remained on the scene the monks could make no move, beyond extracting from her lord a verbal acknowledgement of their reversionary title. This Walter gave before a number of witnesses. But when she did die he refused to surrender the manor. In the words of the *Memoriale*: "non prece nec precio nec vi illam ab eo abstrahere potuimus." It is most unlikely that he would have been able to take possession of it in the first instance without some sort of authorization from the Conqueror, such as a writ announcing that the king had awarded him the hand of Edith, and with her certain estates, including Uffculme. The existence of some such

[1] If it were not for this son's oath in the shire-court we could reduce the widow's age by several years and tentatively identify her first husband with Hemming, grandson of Thorkell the Tall, and son of earl Harold by Cnut's niece Gunnhild. After the earl's death in 1042 Gunnhild and her two sons came to England, where they stayed for two years, and then retired to Flanders (Florence of Worcester, *Chronicon*, in *Monumenta Historica Britannica*, p. 602 A; cf. *Encomium Emmae Reginae*, pp. 84, 85). If Hemming, the elder son, married Edith some time after 1042, their child would be still a minor at the date of the Exeter transaction; but Professor D. Whitelock suggests that some or all of the sixteen sureties may have taken the oath in the child's name, just as godparents utter the baptismal vows on behalf of an infant godchild.

[2] DB IV, p. 148; AD p. 111. Cf. *ibid.*, p. 325, and Davis, *Regesta Regum Anglo-Normannorum*, p. 71, no. 273. Davis regards the existing text as a clumsy attempt to reconstruct a lost charter.

[3] AD p. 117. For Harding, see Freeman, *Norman Conquest*, IV, p. 755.

document is implied when the cartulary scribe refers to the bestowal (*collacio*) of the manor by King William, and in two later charters which throw the blame for its alienation on that king.[1] Under the land-law of the Conquest such a writ might be held to create a permanently valid title, and it appears to have been so construed by Walter's heirs; but the indications are that Walter himself claimed only a life-interest, relying perhaps on what was later known as the custom of England, under which a widower could hold on to his wife's property for the term of his own life.

He now took to himself a second wife, whose name, Emma, suggests that she came from his own side of the Channel. She bore him a son, Robert, the future lord of Bampton. After a while sickness overtook him. He was in Somerset at the time, perhaps at his manor of Badgworth, twelve miles from Glastonbury as the crow flies. Believing his end near, he set out for the abbey, with the evident intention of at last restoring Uffculme, for he took with him the two golden reliquaries that were due to the abbey with the reversion. He was accompanied by his wife Emma, his brother Rainier, his chaplain Hubert, two of his knights, Ludo de Utreto and Ralph de Contivilla, Wluric his *dapifer* or steward, and other attendants.[2] The party reached Glastonbury on the 8th of September, feast of Our Lady's Birthday, when the place, as usual, was full of visitors, and they took up their lodging outside but near the abbey. As the sickness had now reached its crisis, Walter immediately sent his people to the abbey church with instructions to lay his glove on the altar in token of restitution. When they had done so they

[1] Stephen's charter and the brief of Innocent II: see below. The editor of the Great Cartulary was at first inclined to hold that the scribe had misunderstood or contradicted his documents at this point (*op. cit.*, p. 126); but he authorizes me to state that he is now in full accord with the construction I have put upon them.

[2] Rainier, Ludo, Ralph, and Wluric are all named in Domesday Book as subtenants of Walter; hence the date of this episode cannot be much later than 1086. On the other hand, the writer of the *Memoriale* says that Walter "had *long* detained the land to which he had no right."

On the possibility that Ralph de Contivilla may have been a half-brother of Robert, count of Mortain, see *The Domesday Monachorum of Christ Church, Canterbury*, pp. 28, 33, 34. The whole subject of the Douai fees and their descent would repay expert investigation.

forthwith despatched one of the monks to Uffculme so that he might take possession for the abbey. His brother asked Walter if he approved their action, and when he assented, said: "Take this glove, then, and place it in the prior's hands." This he did, at the same time handing over the two reliquaries. The next night he sent three times to beg that he might be clothed in the monastic habit: a very common request in such cases, for if granted it secured for the petitioner skilled medical attention in the infirmary while he lived and remembrance in the prayers of the brethren after his death. At last the monks went to the sick man's lodging. "But before we would clothe him with the habit we asked him if he wished to be made a monk, telling him, if he could not answer, at least to move his lips and close his fist as a sign. He did so, and then tried to pull the cowl to-wards him. We then asked all those present, his wife included, if they were willing that their lord should be made a monk, and they wept and begged us not to delay, 'for see,' they said, 'he is already dying.' Meanwhile one of those present approached with a knife and cut the shirt he was wearing down the middle, and we at length clothed him with the full habit and cut his hair and made him a tonsure; and should it be necessary we can still show the hair we then shaved from his head. After that we returned to the monastery, leaving two of the brethren to look after him until he could be taken by daylight to our infirmary, for he was too weak to be moved that night." However, before dawn came he began to mend; and seeing this, his brother asked him if he liked the monastic habit. He answered that he liked it in every way, and thanked God for allowing him to receive it. "But seeing him getting well, they were afraid that if they lost him they would never find so good a master again; and so, to cut the story short, they threw our monks out and dressed him again in his own clothes."

It is a pity that the writer breaks off his *Memoriale* at this point, for only a pen as graphic as his could do justice to the recriminations which no doubt ensued. We may take it that Walter and the brethren were thenceforth not on speaking terms; and it comes as no surprise to learn that when he died some years later he was buried not at Glastonbury but in St Peter's, Bath. To that church he bequeathed for soul-scot the church of Bampton, with its glebe-land and tithes. His widow and her son Robert, who appears to have been still a minor at this date, gave, "by the advice of their barons," the church of Bridgwater and half the tithes of Castle Cary; and on the same occasion Gerard, who had succeeded Wluric as the dead man's steward, gave the church of Bratton Seymour.[1] William Warelwast, who in 1107 was consecrated bishop of Exeter, subsequently stated that he had been present, as archdeacon, when these grants were made.[2]

Robert of Bampton, who now inherited his father's estates, is described in the *Gesta Stephani* as a hard drinker and a glutton ("vorax vini et escarum consumptor"). Another side of his character is brought out in the account given by his great-grandson of a dispute between Robert and the abbot of Ghent concerning the manors of Greenwich and Lewisham. The abbot lodged a claim to this property, and Robert lost the case by default. Henry I then issued a charter confirming the abbot in possession; but Robert and his friends "murmured" against both king and abbot, and their "murmurs" became so disagreeable that the abbot thought it well to grant the manors back to Robert in fee-farm at a yearly rent of twenty-five pounds. The document recording this grant was deposited for safe keeping in the manor-house at Uffculme.[3] It is clear that Uffculme had passed from father to son, and that Robert was not the man to relax his grip on anything that he regarded as his own.

In 1126 the great Henry of Blois became abbot of Glastonbury. Finding the house grievously impoverished, he set himself to recover its lost possessions; and an interesting memorandum which he drew up with his own hand relates his activities in detail. Concerning Uffculme he admits that he was in two minds. He saw that after the lapse of three-quarters of a century the rights of the abbey could not be re-established without a

---

[1] *Two Chartularies of the Priory of St Peter at Bath*, part I, p. 38. The widow also gave 60 shillings and a missal. Like so many of these mortuary gifts, that of Bratton church remained inoperative (*ibid.*, p. 81).

[2] *Ibid.*, p. 39. Neither Oliver, in his *Lives of the Bishops of Exeter*, nor the *Dictionary of National Biography* mentions that William had been archdeacon before his elevation to the see. The exact words are "tempore archidiaconatus nostri," but as he is writing to the chapter and faithful of that diocese we may presume that Exeter is meant.

[3] *Curia Regis Rolls*, VIII, p. 43.

struggle. If challenged, Robert of Bampton could point to the Domesday record, and probably also to King William's writ. Against these title-deeds the charter of 1050 and the remains of Walter's hair-cut would make but a poor showing. Henry therefore decided to bide his time.[1]

In 1129 he was appointed bishop of Winchester, but he continued to administer the abbey, and his opportunity came in 1136, just after his brother Stephen had ascended the throne. As Henry himself had done his utmost to secure the crown for Stephen, he was in the best possible position to exert pressure on that hard-pressed king. Within four months of his coronation Stephen was induced to issue a charter restoring to the church of Glastonbury "the manor of Offeculum, with its churches and chapels and all that belongs to it . . . which my grandfather King William took away from the aforesaid church."[2] Had Robert of Bampton been given any chance to defend his title? In the light of after-events we may take leave to doubt it.

The names of the witnesses, and the dating clause (Westminster, 1136) prove that Stephen's charter was issued at the first great council of his reign, held on the occasion of the Easter festival (March 22–29). The council then adjourned to Oxford, where, early in April, Stephen issued his more celebrated charter "on the liberties of the English church and realm."[3] This document has often been discussed, but the clause which deserves most attention has received the least. It confirmed the churches of England in possession of all the lands which had been theirs on the day of William the Conqueror's death, and reserved for adjudication by Stephen himself any claims to property of which they had been deprived since that date. Adjudication is perhaps too formal a term. The actual wording of the clause ("indulgentiae et dispensationi meae, vel restituendum vel discutiendum, reservo") implies that Stephen was assuming full power to dispense with legal process and to settle claims of this nature at his discretion, as he appears to have done already in the case of Uffculme.

The door now stood wide open for innumerable claims. Half

---

[1] AD p. 310.   [2] *Ibid.*, p. 327; *The Great Chartulary*, I, p. 126, no. 171.
[3] Stubbs, *Select Charters*, 9th ed., 1913, p. 143.

a century of peaceful tenure might be abruptly ended by the king's arbitrary fiat. No wonder the barons took alarm. Robert of Bampton in particular had reason to feel aggrieved. He had presumably joined with his fellow magnates, ecclesiastical and lay, in swearing allegiance to the empress Matilda at the bidding of the late king. It is certain that like them he had since done homage and sworn fealty to Stephen.[1] To him it must have seemed that the churchmen were reaping the fruits of perjury at his expense. He could, and apparently did, lodge a counterclaim; and *pendente lite* he refused to surrender Uffculme. Gathering a band of knights and archers into his castle at Bampton, he prepared to resist any transfer of seisin until judgement could be given by his peers. By rights, of course, the duty of maintaining the *status quo* pending appeal should have been undertaken by the sheriff. Unfortunately the hereditary sheriff of Devon, Richard Fitz Baldwin, lord of the great Honour of Okehampton, chose this very moment to disengage himself altogether from worldly cares. A sick and childless man, far more intent on supervising the foundation of a new Cistercian monastery near Okehampton than on keeping the king's peace, he died within the year, leaving his sister Adeliza to inherit the shrievalty. For the rest of her life Adeliza was known as the *vice-comitissa*, or sheriff-ess.[2] In these circumstances a man placed like Robert of Bampton had some excuse for resorting to self-help.

Only two of Robert's contemporaries give any details of the case. One is Henry, bishop of Winchester and administrator of Glastonbury; the other is the anonymous author of the *Gesta Stephani*, who was unquestionably a partisan of Bishop Henry.[3]

---

[1] AD *loc. cit.; Gesta Stephani Regis Anglorum*, ed. Howlett, Rolls ser. 82, p. 19. Howlett erroneously identifies "Batthentona" with Bathampton.

[2] Rose-Troup, 'The Hereditary Sheriffs of Devon', DA LXIV, 1932, pp. 402, 403. Richard began to build his monastery in 1133. He was alive on 3 May 1136, when a colony of monks arrived from Waverley to take possession (Oliver, *Monasticon Dioecesis Exoniensis*, p. 342). Robert of Torigny states that he died in the course of the same year (*Chronicles*, IV, p. 131). The monk who long afterwards compiled the *Fundationis Historia* does not give the date of his death, but says that he was buried 25 June 1137 (Oliver, *loc. cit.*).

[3] *Gesta Stephani*, pp. viii sqq. Mr R. H. C. Davis, who has recently propounded an ingenious theory attributing the authorship of the *Gesta* to Robert of Lewes, bishop of Bath, agrees that the author, whoever he was, belonged to the party of Bishop Henry. — EHR LXXVII, 1962, p. 222.

These are obviously biased witnesses; to arrive at the truth we must read between the lines. At the end of April the king fell ill, and Hugh Bigod, on a false rumour of Stephen's death, occupied Norwich castle, but was induced to give it up when Stephen himself appeared at Norwich. The king stayed in East Anglia till Pentecost (May 10). It was probably towards the end of May that his court sat to decide the case of Uffculme. Of this first hearing Bishop Henry says nothing at all. The author of the Gesta refers very briefly to Robert's "causa," meaning presumably his plea that the Conqueror's writ gave him a valid title, valid above the limit of date fixed by the April charter, and that Stephen's mandate in favour of the rival claimant had therefore been wrongfully procured. The countercharges that Robert was called upon to answer are reported more explicitly. In the first place, he was accused of rebellion. By holding on to Uffculme he had set the king's authority at naught. Secondly, more than one ("plures") of his neighbours accused him of depredation and damage to their property. The chronicler states that Robert's appeal failed ("causa ejus invalida") and that his answer to the countercharges was deemed insufficient ("responsio inefficax"). By the judgement of the court he was ordered to admit a royal garrison into Bampton castle; and all his possessions were declared to be at the king's mercy.[1] This was clearly not a sentence of forfeiture. It probably foreshadowed a fine, but we are not told that any fine was inflicted; and since litigants in those days habitually painted their opponents in the most lurid colours, the charge of rapine may well be exaggerated. No doubt Robert had sent the bishop's emissaries packing. Probably he had also taken steps to remove the livestock from Uffculme to Bampton, and if one or two of the neighbours' beasts were driven off at the same time, there would be nothing wonderful in that. The court exacted no penalty, but merely required him to hand over Bampton castle as security for his future good behaviour.

The lord of Bampton was a convivial spirit, but he was also tenacious of what he conceived to be his rights. For the moment he dissembled his intentions, and set out with a party of the king's knights to whom he professed himself ready to

[1] Gesta, p. 19.

hand over the castle. On the way down they paused at one of
Robert's manors, where he gave them a sumptuous entertainment; then, while they were all fast asleep, he mounted his
horse and rode off at top speed to warn the garrison. As soon
as Stephen heard of this he sped down to Devonshire and laid
siege to Bampton. It was not long before a poor wretch
attempting to leave the castle under cover of darkness was
captured by the royal sentries and hanged. Intimidated by his
fate, the garrison then promptly surrendered. It was either now
or soon after that Uffculme was laid waste and its manor-house
burnt down.[1]

It seems that Robert was not present at the siege of Bampton.
The chronicler describes him as going into hiding and afterwards taking the field with Stephen's enemies.[2] We can scarcely
doubt that he had ridden off to lay his grievance before the
other Devon magnates, and that he was directly implicated in
the revolt of Baldwin de Redvers, which broke out immediately afterwards and led to the prolonged siege of Exeter.

The only contemporary writer who offers any explanation
of this, the first serious rebellion of Stephen's reign, is Richard
of Hexham. He says that Baldwin rebelled "because he could
not have a certain honour he had sought from the king."[3]
This probably means the earldom of Devon, which the empress
conferred on Baldwin five years later. But if Baldwin had
really applied for it in 1136, is it likely that Stephen, notorious
as he was for his inability to say no, would have missed the
opportunity of conciliating the head of a powerful family,
barons of Plympton and lords of the Isle of Wight, a family
moreover which had been wholly trusted by the late king? On
this point the northern chronicler may well be retailing popular
guesswork, a surmise rendered plausible by after-events. But
even if there be a grain of truth in the story, as an explanation
of Baldwin's revolt it is patently inadequate. The siege of

[1] Robert's great-grandson is our authority for this devastation, which
according to him took place in the civil war of Henry II's reign; but this is
obviously an anachronism, for he makes it clear that the incident occurred
in Robert's lifetime. — *Curia Regis Rolls, loc. cit.*

[2] *Gesta Stephani,* p. 19.

[3] *Chronicles of the Reigns of Stephen, Henry II, and Richard I,* Rolls ser. 82,
III, p. 146.

Exeter lasted nearly three months, and cost Stephen fifteen thousand marks.[1] It was protracted until both the castle wells had run dry and the besieged had suffered agonies of thirst. To endure such hardships men require some motive stronger than pique. If we believe that Baldwin himself was actuated only by mortified ambition, we have still to ask why he was joined by the *élite* of the whole baronage.[2] It was not personal friendship alone that moved Alfred of Totnes to throw himself into Exeter castle under the very eyes of Stephen's troops. And what of those barons who, though ostensibly loyal and taking part in the siege under the royal banner, were all the while in touch with Baldwin, having themselves urged him to revolt?[3] It was their insistence which compelled Stephen, when the besieged at length capitulated, to let Baldwin and his followers go scotfree.[4]

Some modern writers have conjectured that these men were acting in Matilda's interest. But there is no indication that any correspondence had yet taken place between the empress and the disaffected party, and as another three years elapsed before she even set foot in England it is doubtful whether anybody was prepared to take up arms on her behalf so early as this. Other historians give up the search for causes, and are content to assume that a twelfth-century baron needed no incentive to revolt, being ready at any moment to risk his all from sheer love of mischief. In history, as in everyday life, there is always a label at hand if we choose to spare ourselves the trouble of divining other people's thoughts and feelings; and of all historical labels that of the lawless baron, or feudal anarch, is one of the most labour-saving. Yet all competent writers on the period are agreed that the barons as a class gave little or no trouble unless their interests were seriously threatened.[5] As a class they were consistently loyal to the first three Norman kings, and they had accepted Stephen without a murmur. Why then did they turn against him six months after his coronation?

---

[1] *Gesta Stephani*, p. 25.

[2] "... totius duntaxat Angliae florem," *ibid.*, p. 22.

[3] "... consultis illis ... quorum impulsu Balduinus se contra regem armaverat, qui et tunc cum rege dolose militabant," *ibid.*, p. 26.

[4] *Ibid.*, pp. 27, 28.

[5] Cf. F. M. Stenton, *First Century of English Feudalism*, 1932, pp. 222–25, on the conservative attitude of the barons under Stephen.

It will help us to enter into their state of mind if we recall Stephen's April charter, and especially that clause in it, so strangely overlooked by our historians, whereby Stephen took it upon himself to redress the wrongs of the churches. We shall never know the full extent of those wrongs, but there is no doubt that encroachments on church property had taken place on a considerable scale. Few indeed were the bishoprics and abbeys which had not had some of their land extorted from them on one pretext or another. By the terms of that fatal charter any ecclesiastic who could state a plausible case, not necessarily so well founded as that of Glastonbury, might secure a favourable decision from a king who owed everything to the Church. It is true that a limit had been set, and that claims antecedent to the death of William I were barred. But William had been dead nearly fifty years, and the case of Uffculme showed that even this limitation would not always be respected. Here a transfer of property which had taken place in the Conqueror's time, and which the Domesday commissioners had recognized, was being abruptly reversed. And if this could be done with Uffculme, why not with other manors too? All over the country monastic houses on the eve of the Conquest had granted some of their land out on leases for one or more lives, and had lost it when their English tenants, through death, forfeiture, or intermarriage, made way for Normans.[1] Injustice had certainly been done, but it was too late to reverse it now with any show of equity. Nor was there even a pretence of equity when churchmen were encouraged to reclaim their property while the layman with perhaps as good a case might seek redress in vain. So one-sided a concession was bound to provoke resentment, and may well have added fuel to the anti-clerical spirit that blazed up during the civil war.[2] Already at the siege of Exeter the rift between clergy and laity was manifest, with the bishop of Winchester on one side urging the king to insist on unconditional surrender, and the lay barons on the other insisting still more vehemently that no punishment should be meted out to the rebels.[3] Baldwin de Redvers and his peers, representatives of the class which had most to lose, knew what had befallen

[1] On this see Round, in VCH *Herts*, I, p. 291.
[2] Cf. *Gesta Stephani*, pp. 46, 47, 100.
[3] "Balduini dissensionis conscii et cooperatores," *ibid.*, p. 27.

Robert of Bampton, and in his ruin they beheld the firstfruits of a rash concession which not only threatened their own property but at many points undermined the whole established order. With some justification they might stand forth as the champions of settled right and law.

The fact that Baldwin retired to his island fortress of Carisbrooke, and after an ineffectual stand there went into exile, should not blind us to the gravity of his revolt. Stephen was able to maintain his supremacy for some time longer, but his throne was badly shaken. After the siege of Exeter he left Bishop Henry in charge of the castle and of the whole county of Devon.[1] The bishop was undoubtedly a more forcible character than the *vicecomitissa*, but from most of the peninsula Reginald of Cornwall and Stephen de Mandeville contrived to exclude even the shadow of Stephen's power. When the empress at last made her bid for the crown it was Baldwin de Redvers who led the main army of invasion.[2]

The bishop of Winchester was now at leisure to take seisin of Uffculme. His own not entirely candid account of the affair is that Robert of Bampton after his rebellion was condemned to forfeiture and exile; that he, the bishop, then publicly advanced his claim to Uffculme; and that with the consent of the entire *curia regis* Stephen then restored the manor to Glastonbury.[3] All this is doubtless true; but the bishop says nothing of the charter of restitution he had wrung from Stephen before ever the revolt broke out. The tell-tale word here is *palam*: he now claimed openly by legal process what he had privately sought to recover by a stretch of the royal power. In his zeal to secure justice for Glastonbury he had imperilled his brother's throne.[4] However, for the moment he had gained his object. On the 8th of April 1137 Pope Innocent II wrote to him about the affairs of Glastonbury, referring in particular to the pains Henry had taken to bring about the restitution of "the manor of Hoffecolum, with all its appurtenances, and with its church and chapel."[5] Four years later the bishop abandoned Stephen and

---

[1] *Ibid.*, p. 28.   [2] *Gesta Stephani*, pp. xxiii, l.   [3] AD *loc. cit.*

[4] An anecdote recounted by John of Salisbury makes it clear that the bishop of Winchester was regarded at the papal court as the bane of his country. — EHD II, p. 684.

[5] *The Great Chartulary*, I, p. 125, no. 170.

went over to the empress, from whom he secured a charter confirming Glastonbury in possession of all its lands, "and especially the manor of Uffculme." Round assigns this charter to May or June 1141.[1] At Christmas in the same year Stephen included in a grant to Geoffrey de Mandeville, earl of Essex, forfeited lands to the value of £100, and among them "all the land which Robert of Bampton held in Essex:" that is, the two manors of Rainham on the Thames and Great Holland near Clacton-on-Sea. Less than six months later Geoffrey was bargaining with the empress and securing, among other concessions, her confirmation of Stephen's grant.[2] Thus Robert, if he still lived, received small comfort even from Matilda's faction. After the siege of Bampton the kinsmen who had fought with him fled to Scotland, and the chronicler relates that Robert himself ended his life disastrously in exile.[3]

Uffculme is named among the temporalities of Glastonbury by Pope Lucius II in 1144,[4] but the bishop's changes of front were not conducive to a settled tenure, and he lived to see the manor revert to the heirs of Walter of Douai. Robert of Bampton left a daughter Juliana, who was married first to William Paganel, or Paynell, and afterwards to Warin de la Haule. The latter was holding Bampton and Uffculme in 1176.[5] Four years later Fulk Paynell, son of Juliana by her first husband, succeeded to the Honour of Bampton.[6] He gave the church of Uffculme to Bath Abbey.[7] The manor descended to his son and grandson, both named William.[8] "Uffecolm," says Pole, "in some records is a hundred; but always reputed a parcell of the hundred of

[1] AD p. 321; Round, *Geoffrey de Mandeville*, p. 83.

[2] Round, *op. cit.*, pp. 140, 167.

[3] *Gesta Stephani*, pp. 19, 20. Among those who took refuge in Scotland was a son of Robert whose name is not reported (*ibid.*, p. 35). The barony of Odell *alias* Woodhill *alias* Wahull in Bedfordshire, which had belonged to "Walter Flandrensis" in 1086, passed to a family named de Wahull, who claimed to be the direct male descendants of Walter (VCH *Herts*, III, p. 70; cf. Baker, *Northamptonshire*, I, p. 711). The relationship, if any, between these Wahulls and Robert of Bampton has yet to be worked out.

[4] AD p. 323.

[5] Dugdale, *Monasticon*, v, p. 204; Pipe Roll Soc., xxv, p. 150.

[6] *Ibid.*, xxix, p. 94.

[7] *Two Chartularies of the Priory of St Peter at Bath*, part II, p. 160.

[8] *Curia Regis Rolls, loc. cit.; Calendar of Inquisitions post Mortem*, 1st series, I, p. 33.

Baunton; & the lords of Baunton have contynually enjoyed the same."[1] Thus the bishop's well-meant but impolitic manœuvre, so baleful in its consequences to the king and kingdom, had gained nothing for Glastonbury but the ephemeral possession of a blackened waste.

[1] Sir W. Pole, *Collections towards a Description of the County of Devon*, 1791, p. 205. Uffculme retained enough of its hundredal status to be represented at the eyre by six jurors of its own. — PRO Assize Rolls, J.I. 1, 174, m. 24*b*.

INDEX

PRINTED IN GREAT BRITAIN BY ROBERT MACLEHOSE AND CO. LTD
THE UNIVERSITY PRESS, GLASGOW